Trial of Thomas Neill Cream.

Thomas Neill Cream

Trial of Thomas Neill Cream.
Cream, Thomas Neill
collection ID CTRG98-B3031
Reproduction from Yale Law School Library
Trial at the Central Criminal Court, Old Bailey, London in October, 1892, for the murder of Matilda Clover.
London : W. Hodge, [1923].
x, 207 p., [9] leaves of plates : port., facsims. ; 22 cm

The Making of Modern Law collection of legal archives constitutes a genuine revolution in historical legal research because it opens up a wealth of rare and previously inaccessible sources in legal, constitutional, administrative, political, cultural, intellectual, and social history. This unique collection consists of three extensive archives that provide insight into more than 300 years of American and British history. These collections include:

Legal Treatises, 1800-1926: over 20,000 legal treatises provide a comprehensive collection in legal history, business and economics, politics and government.

Trials, 1600-1926: nearly 10,000 titles reveal the drama of famous, infamous, and obscure courtroom cases in America and the British Empire across three centuries.

Primary Sources, 1620-1926: includes reports, statutes and regulations in American history, including early state codes, municipal ordinances, constitutional conventions and compilations, and law dictionaries.

These archives provide a unique research tool for tracking the development of our modern legal system and how it has affected our culture, government, business – nearly every aspect of our everyday life. For the first time, these high-quality digital scans of original works are available via print-on-demand, making them readily accessible to libraries, students, independent scholars, and readers of all ages.

The BiblioLife Network

This project was made possible in part by the BiblioLife Network (BLN), a project aimed at addressing some of the huge challenges facing book preservationists around the world. The BLN includes libraries, library networks, archives, subject matter experts, online communities and library service providers. We believe every book ever published should be available as a high-quality print reproduction; printed on-demand anywhere in the world. This insures the ongoing accessibility of the content and helps generate sustainable revenue for the libraries and organizations that work to preserve these important materials.

The following book is in the "public domain" and represents an authentic reproduction of the text as printed by the original publisher. While we have attempted to accurately maintain the integrity of the original work, there are sometimes problems with the original work or the micro-film from which the books were digitized. This can result in minor errors in reproduction. Possible imperfections include missing and blurred pages, poor pictures, markings and other reproduction issues beyond our control. Because this work is culturally important, we have made it available as part of our commitment to protecting, preserving, and promoting the world's literature.

GUIDE TO FOLD-OUTS MAPS and OVERSIZED IMAGES

The book you are reading was digitized from microfilm captured over the past thirty to forty years. Years after the creation of the original microfilm, the book was converted to digital files and made available in an online database.

In an online database, page images do not need to conform to the size restrictions found in a printed book. When converting these images back into a printed bound book, the page sizes are standardized in ways that maintain the detail of the original. For large images, such as fold-out maps, the original page image is split into two or more pages

Guidelines used to determine how to split the page image follows:

• Some images are split vertically; large images require vertical and horizontal splits.
• For horizontal splits, the content is split left to right.
• For vertical splits, the content is split from top to bottom.
• For both vertical and horizontal splits, the image is processed from top left to bottom right.

NOTABLE BRITISH TRIALS SERIES.

Madeleine Smith. Edited by A Duncan Smith
Dr. Pritchard. Edited by William Roughead
The Stauntons. Edited by J B. Atlay.
Franz Muller. Edited by H B Irving
The Annesley Case. Edited by Andrew Lang
Lord Lovat. Edited by David N Mackay
Captain Porteous Edited by William Roughead
William Palmer. Edited by Geo H Knott
Mrs. Maybrick. Edited by H B Irving
Dr. Lamson. Edited by H L Adam
Mary Blandy. Edited by William Roughead
City of Glasgow Bank Directors. Edited by William Wallace
Deacon Brodie Edited by William Roughead
James Stewart. Edited by David N Mackay
A. J Monson. Edited by J W More
Oscar Slater. Edited by William Roughead
E. M. Chantrelle. Edited by A Duncan Smith.
The Douglas Cause. Edited by A. Francis Steuart.
Mrs. M'Lachlan Edited by William Roughead.
Eugene Aram. Edited by Eric R Watson.
J. A. Dickman. Edited by S O Rowan-Hamilton
The Seddons. Edited by Filson Young
Sir Roger Casement. Edited by Geo H Knott
H. H. Crippen. Edited by Filson Young
The Wainwrights. Edited by H B Irving
Thurtell and Hunt. Edited by Eric R Watson
Burke and Hare. Edited by William Roughead
Steinie Morrison. Edited by H Fletcher Moulton
George Joseph Smith. Edited by Eric R Watson.
Mary Queen of Scots. Edited by A Francis Steuart
Neill Cream Edited by W Teignmouth Shore.

IN PREPARATION

Bywaters and Thomson Edited by Filson Young
Dr. Philip Cross. Edited by P J O Hara
Henry Fauntleroy. Edited by Horace Bleackley.
H. R. Armstrong Edited by Filson Young.
S. H. Dougal. Edited by Gilbert Hair
Catherine Webster Edited by Elliot O Donnell
Adolf Beck. Edited by Eric R Watson
Ronald True. Edited by Donald Carswell.

Particulars may be had from the Publishers

Wm. Hodge & Co., Ltd., Edinburgh and London

Trial of Thomas Neill Cream

EDITED BY

W. Teignmouth Shore

LONDON AND EDINBURGH
WILLIAM HODGE & COMPANY, LIMITED

MADE AND PRINTED IN GREAT BRITAIN
BY
WILLIAM HODGE AND COMPANY, LTD
GLASGOW AND EDINBURGH
1923

Thomas Neill Cream
From a photograph by W. Armstead

TO

H H

GOOD FELLOW AND GOOD FRIEND

PREFACE

I TENDER hearty thanks to the many who have generously helped me, and without whose assistance the preparation of this volume would have been impossible, among others, Mr H L Adam, Dr John R Harper, Dr W J Harper, Mr Gilbert Hair, Mr Evan Johnson (Chicago), Mr W S Lennartson (Chicago), Mr E S Lovelock (Montreal), Mr George P Mann (Montreal), Mr Elliott O Donnell, Dr William Robertson (Edinburgh) Dr Hamblin Smith, Mrs George R Sims, Mr Eric R Watson, Mr George Perceval Wyatt, and to the authorities at Scotland Yard, in particular Superintendent Arthur F Neil, Superintendent A E Lawrence, and Inspector Frank C Page

Especial thanks are due to Sir William H Willcox, K C I E, C.B, C M G, M D, F R C P, Consulting Medical Adviser to the Home Office, for the loan of Sir Thomas Stevenson's original notes of the Cream case These are reprinted in full by the kind permission of Sir Thomas Stevenson's Executors, and will be of very great interest to medical readers and, indeed, to all students of toxicology

The report of the trial is a very careful compilation from many sources, and every care has been exercised to secure fullness and accuracy.

Whether my work is good or bad is for the kindly reader to judge

W TEIGNMOUTH SHORE

LONDON, *July, 1923.*

CONTENTS.

	PAGE
Introduction,	1
Leading Dates in the Cream Case	41

The Trial—

FIRST DAY—MONDAY, 17TH OCTOBER, 1892

Opening Speech for the Crown, ... 45

Evidence for the Prosecution

Edward Levy,	59	Elizabeth Masters,	60
Mary Burden,	59	Elizabeth May,	63
James Aitchison,	59	Dr William Henry Broadbent,	65

SECOND DAY—TUESDAY, 18TH OCTOBER, 1892

William Nixon Reece,	67	Dr Thomas Stevenson	84
John George Kirby,	67	John Wilson M'Culloch,	92
Lucy Rose,	69	George Percival Wyatt,	96
Emma Vowles,	73	Alfred Dyke Acland,	96
Francis Coppin,	75	Dr Joseph Harper,	97
Dr Robert Graham,	77	Dr Walter Joseph Harper,	98
John Measures,	79	Henry John Clark,	98
Elijah George Steers,	79	Fanny Taylor,	98
John Hare,	79	John Haynes,	98
Emily Sleaper,	79		

THIRD DAY—WEDNESDAY, 19TH OCTOBER, 1892

John Haynes (recalled),	101	Louisa Harris,	120
Patrick M'Intyre,	104	Charles Harvey,	123
George Harvey,	108	Charlotte Vogt,	124
Alfred Ward,	110	George Cumley,	125
John Bennett Tunbridge,	110	William Eversfield,	127
Frederick Smith Jarvis,	117	Dr Cuthbert Wyman,	127
Laura Sabbatini,	117	George Hackett,	128
Walter de Grey Birch,	118		

FOURTH DAY—THURSDAY, 20TH OCTOBER, 1892

Dr Stevenson (recalled),	129	Laura Sabbatini (recalled),	134
Alfred Ward (recalled),	131	W. de Grey Birch (recalled),	135, 137
Margaret Armstead,	132	John B. Tunbridge (recalled),	136
John M. Johnson,	133	George Rendall,	136
Dr Thomas Herbert Kelloch,	133	George Harvey (recalled)	136
John Haynes (recalled),	134		

CONTENTS

FOURTH DAY—Continued

	PAGE
Mr Geoghegan's Speech for the Defence,	137
The Attorney General's Closing Speech for the Crown,	148

FIFTH DAY—FRIDAY, 21ST OCTOBER, 1892

Mr Justice Hawkins's Charge to the Jury,	153
The Verdict	164
The Sentence,	165

APPENDICES

I	The Police and the Broadbent Letter,	169
II	The Scurrilous Postal Cards in Chicago,	170
III	The Murder of Daniel Scott,	172
IV	Cream's Handwriting	177
V	Coroner's Inquest on Matilda Clover,	178
VI	Sir Thomas Stevenson's Notes on the Cases of Marsh, Shrivell and Clover	192

LIST OF ILLUSTRATIONS

Thomas Neill Cream,		*Frontispiece*
The Metropole Circular,	*facing page*	17
Death Certificate of Ellen Donworth,	,,	20
Death Certificate of Matilda Clover,	,,	21
Thomas Neill Cream,	,,	41
Cream's Sample Case of Medicines,	,,	86
The Attorney General (Sir Charles Russell),	,,	148
Sir Henry Hawkins,	,,	153
Cream's Handwriting,	,,	177

THOMAS NEILL CREAM.
INTRODUCTION.

I

Thomas Neill Cream and his career afford much material of interest to the criminologist, to the alienist, and to the student of human nature. As must be the case, sufficient only of his doings to secure his conviction was brought forward at his trial, but glimpses of his terrible career of debauchery and crime illuminated the dark background as with flashes from a searchlight. In order that the reader should understand the man and follow intelligently the course of his trial, it is necessary to give his biography in as full detail as is possible. It will be a somewhat bald, but it is hoped, not unconvincing narrative. The bare facts are sufficiently hideous, they need no embroidery. The sinister figure of Cream stands clear cut against the occasional obscurity.

II

Thomas Neill Cream was born at 61 Wellington Lane, Glasgow, on 27th May 1850, being the eldest son and the first child of William Cream, clerk, and his wife Mary Elder. There were four other sons and three daughters.

Unfortunately, as is too often the case when writing the life of a saint or of a sinner, the records of his childhood are very meagre. There is no evidence procurable as to the surroundings amid which he opened his eyes upon life or of the circumstances which moulded his early years. Of his mother, what she was, there is no obtainable record; his father seems to have been an able, persevering, prosperous man, held in esteem and goodwill by those who knew him.

William Cream, with his wife and young children, emigrated to Canada in the year 1854 or 1855, and became manager to a thriving shipbuilding and lumber firm in Quebec. His son Thomas was apprenticed to the shipbuilding trade, but not with the same firm as that with which his father was connected. Later on the boy worked with his father, when the latter started business for

Thomas Neill Cream.

himself as a wholesale lumber merchant. Trade, however, did not appeal strongly enough to Thomas, and on 1st October, 1872, he entered M'Gill College, Montreal, signing the Register on 12th November of the same year.* Only the very barest facts are known of his student days, but it is on record that he earned the reputation of being fast and extravagant, maintaining a stylish carriage and pair, and being addicted to ostentatious clothes and superabundant jewellery. He took interest in sports and was a good musician. He is said to have possessed a pleasing voice and ingratiating manner. He was well supplied with money by his father. A cynical light is cast on the character of this fast young man by the fact that he varied his occupations by teaching in a Sunday School. A photograph taken of Cream with the graduation class to which he belonged shows him with short bristling hair and long side whiskers.

He studied medicine at the M'Gill College until 1876, graduating with merit and receiving his diploma of M.D. on 31st March. The address delivered to the graduates by the Dean of the Faculty had for subject, "The Evils of Malpractice in the Medical Profession." Strange enough! Also, it is stated, perhaps with truth, that Cream gained some distinction during his student days for an essay on chloroform.

Going back, on 15th September, 1875, Neill effected a fire insurance on his personal goods, wearing apparel and so forth, in his lodgings at 106 Mansfield Street, Montreal, for the sum of $1000 with the Commercial Union Insurance Company of Montreal. On 18th April 1876, shortly after the close of his college career, a fire occurred in his rooms, and, although little damage was done, he sent in a detailed claim for $978.40. Strongly suspecting incendiarism, the company refused to pay; but, after the matter had been referred to arbitration they compromised for $350.00. Possibly this was the first of the many occasions upon which Cream committed a crime without being called upon to pay proper penalty.

Early in the same year Cream met with Flora Eliza Brooks, daughter of the proprietor of the principal hotel at Waterloo, some seventy miles from Quebec she being on a visit to Montreal. The acquaintance quickly ripened into friendship, and they were

---

* When Cream was convicted at Chicago in 1881 his name was removed from the Register.

Introduction.

counted as an engaged couple. During the night of 6th September the girl became very ill, and the family physician informed her father that she had been *enceinte* and that abortion had been procured. Brooks went off to Montreal, sought out Cream at the Ottawa Hotel and, threatening to shoot him, demanded that he should marry his daughter at once. Cream returned with him to Waterloo, and the pair were made one on the evening of the 11th. Next day Cream left the house, saying that he was about to go to England to complete his medical training. The unfortunate girl died of consumption on 12th August, 1877, and upon hearing of her decease the widower claimed under the marriage contract the sum of $1000.00, but was pleased to accept $200.00! Was this the first tragedy in which Cream played the part of villain? Perhaps not.

III

The exact date of Cream's first visit to London is not known, but some time in October, 1876, he seems to have paid his fee to attend a course of lectures and to receive other instruction at St. Thomas's Hospital. He informed the hospital authorities of his Canadian medical degree, and was known as Dr. Cream. He probably lodged in Lambeth Palace Road, a locality afterwards notoriously connected with his name. He was what is known as a post-graduate student, and studied at the hospital until some time in the year 1878, during part of his time acting as a temporary obstetric clerk. On 16th April, 1877, Cream was examined at the Royal College of Surgeons in anatomy and physiology at the primary examination for membership but failed to pass; he gave as his schools Toronto and St. Thomas's Hospital. In the following year, on 13th April, Thomas Neil (*sic*) Cream obtained, after examination, what was designated as the double qualification of the Royal Colleges of Physicians and of Surgeons at Edinburgh. So that Cream embarked upon his career of murder and medical malpractices with a quite adequate knowledge of medicine and surgery.

IV

About a month after gaining his honours at Edinburgh, Cream

Thomas Neill Cream.

was back in Canada, starting practice in London, Ontario, at Hiscock's Building, Dundas Street.* During his residence there the mysterious death of a young woman named Kate Hutchinson Gardener, a chambermaid in a hotel, created considerable stir. The body of the girl, a bottle of chloroform by her side, was found in a privy behind the premises occupied by Cream. At the adjourned inquest it came out that the girl had been frequenting Cream's office in order to get abortion procured. Cream said that she accused a prominent dry goods merchant in the city with being the cause of her trouble, but that gentleman brought strong proof of a foiled attempt at blackmail. Other evidence pointed plainly to murder instead of suicide, several doctors swearing to the impossibility of the girl chloroforming herself as she was found. Her face was fearfully excoriated from the application of some irritant. The verdict was returned that "The deceased died from chloroform, administered by some person unknown." Suspicion against Cream was so strong that his practice was ruined, and shortly afterwards he left for the United States.

V

At Chicago Cream soon earned a very unsavoury reputation, starting a surgery at 434 West Madison Street and being more than suspected of practising as an abortionist.

On 23rd August, 1880, he was arrested, the charge being that of the murder of a Canadian girl named Julia Faulkner, an illegal operation being alleged as the cause of death. She had been under Cream's treatment at the house of a 'coloured' woman, and died as the result of an operation for procuring abortion. The body was discovered by the police. Cream and the woman were arrested, but the evidence against him was not considered to be conclusive of guilt, and he again escaped.

In December a Miss Stack died after taking medicine prescribed by Cream, and in the early part of the following year (1881) he sent blackmailing letters to Mr Frank Pyatt, a chemist, who had made up for Miss Stack a prescription of Cream's. This

---

* He did not, as was asserted at the time of his trial in London, England, ever reside at Hamilton or Kingston, Ontario.

Introduction.

persecution was put an end to by the Stott trial. Cream was advertising a nostrum which, it was claimed, was a specific for epilepsy. A station agent on the North-Western Railway named Daniel Stott, who lived at Grand Prairie, Boone County, Illinois, a sufferer from epilepsy, sent his pretty young wife to visit Cream at Chicago to procure the famed cure for him. Stott was a man of sixty-one, his wife aged only thirty-three. Julia Stott became Cream's mistress, paying frequent visits to Chicago with the excuse of obtaining fresh supplies of medicine for her husband. On 11th June 1881 Mrs Stott was given a prescription by Cream and took it to a druggist to be made up. Subsequently, at the trial, when she was admitted as State's evidence, Mrs Stott asserted that after the medicine was ready she was with Cream in his office, and that she there saw him put a white powder into the medicine and into some rhubarb pills which she also took home. On 14th June Stott took the medicine and died within twenty minutes. In the meantime Cream had been endeavouring to insure the unfortunate man's life!

The sudden death did not arouse any suspicion, being credited to an epileptic seizure, and but for Cream's amazing hardihood the crime might have escaped detection. But Cream calmly communicated with the coroner of Boone County, asserting that Stott's death had been due to a blunder on the part of the chemists who had made up the prescription, they having put in too large a quantity of strychnine. He demanded that the body should be exhumed. At the same time Cream persuaded Mrs Stott to give him a power of attorney to sue the chemists for heavy damages. As the coroner did not take any notice of Cream's communication, he addressed himself to the District Attorney, who did act, the body was exhumed, and, on analysis, four grains of strychnine were found in the stomach.

At this time Cream was out on bail on a charge of having violated the mails by sending scurrilous matter through them,* he fled to Canada but was arrested near Windsor, Ontario, was brought back to Chicago and he and Mrs Stott were indicted for murder. He was found guilty of murder in the second degree, and after some of the law's delays was sentenced to imprisonment for life. The woman got off without punishment. Cream was

* See Appendix II

Thomas Neill Cream.

incarcerated on 1st November in the Illinois State Penitentiary at Joliet (where he was known as Thomas N. Cream, No. 4374).

About this time Cream was officially described as of stout, solid build, 5 feet 9 inches in stature, colour of hair brown, eyes light grey, full face and forehead, hair quite thin on top and front of head, jaws and chin massive.

In December, 1890, Cream wrote from prison to Mr. Frank Murray, of Pinkerton's National Detective Agency, asking that some one should be sent to see him. He requested that Mrs. Stott should be traced, in the hope that she could be persuaded to swear an affidavit in his favour, and so enable him to secure his release. But the woman was never found.*

Cream's father had died on 12th May, 1887, at Dansville, New York, aged sixty-four,† and an agitation was then commenced to obtain the remittance of the remainder of Cream's sentence. On 12th June, 1891, the life sentence was commuted by Governor Fife to one of seventeen years, and an allowance of time for good conduct while in prison brought this reduced term to a conclusion on 31st July, 1891. Cream then returned to Canada, and in September was supplied by his father's executors with funds to enable him to visit England for the benefit of his health. Apparently it was at this time that there began to be a suspicion among his relations and intimates that Cream was insane.

VI.

On 1st October, 1891, this sinister man landed at Liverpool, having crossed from America on the "Teutonic."

On 5th October he arrived in London, and put up at Anderton's Hotel, in Fleet Street, signing the register as Dr. Neill. He remained there two days, and on the 7th removed to lodgings at 103 Lambeth Palace Road, hard by St. Thomas's Hospital. To the somewhat sordid and very depressing portion of South London that lies in the triangle bounded by Blackfriars Road, Lambeth Road and the Thames, Cream practically confined his activities,

---

* For fuller account of the trial see Appendix III.

† Leaving Cream a fortune of some $16,000.00 in The Merchants Bank of Canada Stock.

Introduction.

finding there the victims whose slaughter brought him to the scaffold. He commenced operations at once. On the evening after his arrival in town, Tuesday, 6th October—a wet and dismal night—he met a woman of the streets, Elizabeth Masters, at Ludgate Circus. He gave her some wine at a near-by public-house, and then went with her to her rooms in 9 Orient Buildings, Hercules Road, a turning off Lambeth Road. Thence they went to Gatti's Music Hall in Westminster Bridge Road. Cream told the woman that he had come to England to claim some property, and that in his younger days he had been a student at St. Thomas's Hospital. He was fond of exhibiting photographs. On this occasion he showed those of his mother and himself. While so doing the girl noted a peculiar look in his eyes and what she termed a squint.

From various sources a fairly complete picture of the man can be put together: rather heavily built, with fairly square shoulders, brown hair, the front half of the top of the head entirely bald, scalp showing clearly through the hair at the back; moustache a dark ginger colour, thick, but not long; deep-set eyes turning in towards the nose, the left one more so than the right, gold-rimmed spectacles. On this evening it is said that he wore a dark-coloured mackintosh and a square (that is to say, flat) topped hard felt hat.

At the bar of the music hall another girl joined them, one Elizabeth May, who occupied the room adjoining that of Masters. After a drink or so they went in a cab back to the public-house, the King Lud in Ludgate Circus. Cream promised Masters that he would see her again and would write making an appointment when he had settled into lodgings. Then the party broke up.

Earlier in the day Cream had called at 103 Lambeth Palace Road, where he saw Miss Sleaper, the daughter of the landlady, and arranged to move in on the next day, Wednesday, 7th October, engaging a front room on the second floor. Here also he dubbed himself Dr. Neill, and said that he had come to England on account of his health. He was wearing a brown mackintosh and a flat topped hard felt hat.

Friday, 9th October, was eventful. Cream paid a visit to Mr. James Aitchison, an optician at 47 Fleet Street, who examined his eyes, finding that he was suffering from hypermyopia, which was of lifelong duration, the left eye being very much more defective

Thomas Neill Cream.

than the right, it turned inwards towards the nose, giving him a decided squint. He ordered two pairs of spectacles which were delivered to him on 17th October.

On the morning of this Friday Masters received a letter from Cream saying that he would call upon her in the afternoon between three and five o'clock, and that she was not to be so cross as she had been when he first met her. Also, and this is important, he asked her not to destroy the letter, but to keep it till he called. The postmark was "Lambeth." Masters showed the letter to her friend May, and at the appointed time the two sat at the window, watching for the visitor. They saw, coming along on the same side of the street, a girl named Matilda Clover, a prostitute whom they knew by name only. She was turning round and smiling at their expected visitor, who was following her. On this occasion he wore a tall silk hat and dark clothes. The two watchers put on their hats and followed the pair to the corner of Hercules Road and Lambeth Road. They saw Clover at the door of No. 27 Lambeth Road, saw her joined by Cream, saw them go into the house together. They loitered there for some half-hour, but did not see either Clover or Cream come out.

On or about this date—at any rate, before 12th October—Cream paid a visit to the shop of Mr. Priest, chemist at 22 Parliament Street. He told the assistant, John George Kirkby, that he was attending a course of lectures at St. Thomas's Hospital. He desired to make a purchase of nux vomica, and as this was a scheduled poison, he was asked for his name and address. He then wrote out an order, signing it "Thomas Neill, M.D., 103 Lambeth Palace Road." A day or two later he called again and said he wished to purchase some gelatine capsules, these, not being in stock, had to be procured for him. On the 13th, another noteworthy date as will be seen, Cream called for these, and said that those procured for him were too large. A day or two later he was provided with a box of No. 5 capsules, probably those known as Planter's capsules. On various other occasions Cream bought supplies of nux vomica.* Now, on Tuesday, 13th October, a woman named Donworth was poisoned by a fluid, and on 20th October Matilda Clover was done to death by poison administered in capsules.

---

* The seeds of *Strychnos Nux vomica* contain two alkaloids, brucine and strychnine. See Dr. Stevenson's evidence, pages 84 ff. See also Appendix VI.

Introduction.

VII

It was frankly and properly admitted by the prosecution that there was not direct evidence sufficient to bring home to Cream the murder of Ellen Donworth. She was "one more unfortunate," aged only nineteen, living at 8 Duke Street off Westminster Bridge Road. Her death, as a witness at the trial said,* "caused a fearful sensation in South Lambeth, and was known as 'The Lambeth Mystery.'" In consequence of a letter she received, she went out on the evening of 13th October, between six and seven o'clock, to keep an appointment. It was stated that she met a man at the York Hotel, in Waterloo Road. At about a quarter to eight a man named James Styles was standing outside the Wellington public-house, in Waterloo Road, when he saw Donworth, who had been leaning against the wall opposite, fall upon her face. He ran to her aid, assisted her to rise, got from her the address at which she lived, and helped her to go home. She staggered, trembled very much and her face twitched. To her landlady, who thought at first the girl had been drinking, she said in an interval of her torture "A tall gentleman with cross eyes, a silk hat and bushy whiskers gave me a drink twice out of a bottle with white stuff in it." The poor woman's convulsions were so fearful that it took several people to hold her down.

An assistant of Dr. Lowe, medical officer of the South Lambeth Medical Institute, was called in and found Donworth suffering from tetanic convulsions such as would be caused by an overdose of strychnine. He considered that she was in a dying condition and ordered her immediate removal to the hospital. To him also she stated that she had accepted a drink in the street from a tall dark cross-eyed man. She was dead when the hospital was reached and the house physician, Dr. Kelloch, could find nothing external to account for death, nor did a post-mortem examination reveal any cause. But the secret was revealed by an analysis of the contents of the stomach —strychnine.

Just prior to her death Donworth told Inspector Harvey that she had received two letters, the second on the morning of 13th

---

* George Harvey, page 109.

Thomas Neill Cream.

October, from a tall, dark, cross-eyed man, to whom at his desire she had returned them both on meeting him by appointment in the evening.

An inquest was opened at St. Thomas's Hospital upon the body of Donworth on 15th October, and on the 19th Cream wrote an extraordinary letter to the deputy coroner for East Surrey, Mr George Percival Wyatt.* In it he asserted that he was in a position to produce evidence that would lead to the conviction of the murderer of Ellen Donworth, "alias Ellen Linnell," "provided your Government is willing to pay me £300,000 for my services." This amazing epistle was signed "A. O'Brien, detective."

The inquest closed on 22nd October, the jury bringing in a verdict of death by poisoning with strychnine and morphia by a person unknown.

Then, on 6th November, a letter was received at the offices of Messrs W. H. Smith & Son, 186 Strand, addressed to Mr F. W. D. Smith, signed "H. Bayne." It was in Cream's handwriting, as also was an enclosure. The writer declared that he held proof that Mr Smith was Donworth's murderer, in substantiation of which claim he enclosed a copy of a letter which he stated had been received by the girl on the morning of 13th October. He added that he was a barrister, and, if retained by Mr Smith at once would be able to save him. He suggested that a paper should, on the following Tuesday, be pasted upon one of the windows of the Strand offices of the firm, with a request for Mr Bayne to call.

The copy of the letter enclosed read thus—

Miss Ellen Linnell,

I wrote and warned you once before that Frederick Smith of W. H. Smith & Son, was going to poison you, and I am writing now to say that if you take any of the medicine he gave you for the purpose of bringing on your courses you will die. I saw Frederick Smith prepare the medicine he gave you, and I saw him put enough strychnine in the medicine he gave you for to kill a horse. If you take any of it you will die.

(Signed)   H M B

At the desire of the police, a paper, as requested, was stuck upon one of the office windows on 12th November, and strict watch kept, but "H. Bayne" did not show up.

---
* See page 96.

Introduction.

VIII

So far there is grave suspicion, small proof

It will be remembered that on 9th October Masters and May saw Cream go with Matilda Clover into the house in which she dwelt. Eleven days later, during the night of the 20th, Clover was murdered. Cream was accused of the crime, tried, convicted, executed. There is no doubt that this "unfortunate" woman was murdered. There is no doubt that Cream was the murderer.

Matilda Clover, a pleasant-looking young woman, brown-eyed, with somewhat prominent teeth, lived at 27 Lambeth Road, occupying the front room on the second floor. Her age was twenty-seven. She had had a child, at this time two years old, by a man known as "Fred," with whom she had quarrelled—or he quarrelled with her—and parted some month or so before her death. By strange coincidence Cream was known as "Fred" to some of the "unfortunates" who were unfortunate enough to know him. The landlady of the house was a Mrs. Phillips, more usually known as Mrs. Vowles, and on the day of the murder the household consisted of herself, Mr. Vowles, who drove a cab, a servant named Lucy Rose, aged twenty-one, Matilda Clover and her baby, and a grandson of the landlady named Edgar.

As is the case with so many of her class, Clover was over-fond of drink. She was a patient of a Dr. Graham, whom she first consulted some twelve days or so before her death. He saw her several times, and judged her to be suffering from alcoholism. The last time he saw her alive was upon 19th October. Dr. Graham prescribed bromide of potassium. Under cross-examination he stated it as his opinion that if a person were undergoing a course of sedative medicine and then drank brandy, "it would have a marked effect upon her." When asked what would happen if such a person took an excessive amount of spirit, he answered, "The two things acting on one another in the body of a person in a weak state of health would produce a kind of fit if the person took an excessive amount of spirit." Upon this and some supplementary statements the defence based the plea that Clover had poisoned herself with alcohol. But they could not disprove that strychnine had been found in the body.

On the day previous to Clover's death Lucy Rose was in the

Thomas Neill Cream.

former's room, and noticed a letter lying open upon the table. The envelope was there, and had come through the post, but the girl did not notice the postmark. She read the letter, and being, apparently of singularly retentive memory, was able some considerable time later to give its contents in considerable detail. It was signed "Fred," and Rose said that it ran to the following effect:—"Miss Clover, meet me outside the Canterbury at 7.30 if you can come clean and sober. Do you remember the night I bought you your boots? You were so drunk that you could not speak to me. Please bring this paper and envelope with you.—Yours, Fred." This statement of the contents of the letter the Attorney-General was not able to produce at the trial. The letter vanished, presumably taken away by "Fred." After Clover's death it was searched for, but not found.

On the evening of 20th October Clover went out, and on returning some time between seven and ten o'clock, was admitted by Lucy Rose. At the inquest Rose said that "there was an oil lamp in the hall which did not give a very good light," but she saw the man by whom Clover was accompanied distinctly enough to describe him as tall and broad, with a heavy moustache, and aged apparently about forty. Wearing a large coat with a cape, and a tall silk hat. But—*she did not recognise Cream as the man she had seen that night.* Shortly afterwards—according to Rose's evidence—Clover went out to get some beer, leaving the man alone in her rooms. After that the man departed, Clover seeing him out and saying "Good-night Fred." About an hour later Clover left the house asking Rose to look after her child. Rose went to bed about ten o'clock, after Clover had gone out. She slept on the first floor, underneath Clover's bedroom. The landlady said, "I went to bed at all hours because I used to sit up for my husband," and stated that Clover was in her room about 10.30, when actually in bed no one knew. About three o'clock in the morning both Mrs. Vowles and Lucy Rose were awakened by screams of agony from Clover's rooms.

Three people stood by the deathbed of Matilda Clover, and the evidence given by them is important. First, Lucy Rose,* roused by the screaming, called Mrs. Vowles, and going into Clover's

---

* The following is a mosaic of Lucy Rose's various statements.

Introduction.

bedroom found her lying on her back undressed across the foot of the bed with her head fixed between the bedstead and the wall. She was evidently in great agony, screaming terribly. She said to Rose—"I am glad you have come, I have been calling a long time," and later—"That man Fred has poisoned me." When asked how, she answered "He gave me some pills." There were times of relief, then again the fits when she was "all of a twitch." She was given a cup of tea, medicine (see later) and some soda and milk which she could not retain. She "complained of her throat, said she seemed as if she had something sticking in her throat. If she could get it up she thought she would be better."

Second, Mrs Vowles, who when she saw the state in which Clover was, went to fetch Doctor Graham who was unable to come. About seven o'clock Mr Coppin came (see later). She stated in her evidence that Clover was very sick, but she did not notice any trembling or spasms; she told Dr Graham later that Clover was "all in a mass of perspiration, trembling and very sick." She was not present at the moment of death.

Third, Mr Francis Coppin, unqualified assistant to Dr M'Carthy of Westminster Bridge Road, but a man of considerable experience and knowledge. He found Clover's pulse quick, she was bathed in perspiration and trembling. While he was with her she had a convulsion with twitching of the body. He was informed that she had been vomiting, and prescribed some medicine to allay that trouble. He concluded that she was suffering from fits due to alcoholic poisoning, in short from delirium tremens. This conclusion was doubtless assisted by his being told by Mrs Vowles that the girl had been drinking very heavily, mornings and evenings, and that almost every night she was brought home drunk. As we have seen, Dr Graham diagnosed alcoholic poisoning some days before the murder. As to whether or not the taking of pills was mentioned to Mr Coppin there is conflict of evidence.

Dr Graham gave a death certificate—in circumstances that gave rise to considered comment—to the effect that "to the best of my knowledge and belief the cause of her death was, primarily, delirium tremens, secondly syncope." The body was buried by the parish on 27th October at Tooting Cemetery.

With the grave would have closed the story of Matilda Clover,

Thomas Neill Cream.

but for Cream's extraordinary conduct. He seemed bent upon his own undoing.

On a date not definitely fixed, but said by Miss Sleaper to have been shortly after his going to lodge at Lambeth Palace Road, he asked her to take a letter round for him to a house in Lambeth Road; he said he had known a young woman there, he thought she had been poisoned and wanted to know if she were dead or not. Miss Sleaper refused to go, and at a later date Cream said it was just as well she had not gone.

IX

Except the administration of the poison, no one yet had any suspicion that Clover had been murdered.

But in September the Countess Russell, who was staying at the Savoy Hotel, London, received a letter in which her husband was accused of the murder, by poison, of a woman named Clover, who lived at 27 Lambeth Road.* Cream had said to Miss Sleaper that a young woman had been murdered in Lambeth Road by Lord Russell! There is little doubt, if any, that the anonymous letter was written by Cream. How came it that he knew that Clover had been done to death by poison?

Stranger still, on 30th November 1891, Dr William Henry Broadbent, one of the most distinguished physicians of the day, received through the post a letter dated 28th November and signed "M. Malone." The first paragraph was startling— "Miss Clover, who, until a short time ago lived at 27 Lambeth Road S.1, died at the above address on 20th October (last month) through being poisoned with strychnine."

Again, how was it that Cream, the acknowledged writer of this letter, knew at this time that Clover had been done to death by strychnine? His counsel at the trial was hard put to it to find an explanation.† The writer declared that he held complete proof of Dr Broadbent's culpability in the matter, and said that he was willing to sell the evidence either to the doctor or to the police for the sum of £2500. If the doctor would put a "personal" in the *Daily*

---

* Statement by Countess Russell at the Clover Inquest, 7th July 1892.
† For the complete letter see page 49.

Introduction.

Chronicle saying that he would pay 'Malone' for his services, the letter would "send a party to settle this matter."

Dr. Broadbent at once put the letter into the hands of the police, expressing the opinion that it was probably not worth notice, but a trap was laid. In the issue of the *Daily Chronicle* for Friday, 4th December, an advertisement was inserted in the 'agony' column inviting Malone to call. Two detective officers laid in wait in the doctor's house that day and until one o'clock on the Saturday, when Dr. Broadbent urged that it was useless to watch any longer.

Not only by Dr. Broadbent, but by the police authorities also, this anonymous letter was taken to be the handiwork of a lunatic, such letters at this time being frequently addressed to public and private persons. During the trial much adverse and undeserved comment was made upon the conduct of the Scotland Yard authorities in this matter, but they were subsequently entirely exonerated by Mr. Justice Hawkins.*

It may be that but for these letters Cream would have not only escaped detection, but even have been unsuspected of the murder of Matilda Clover.

X

At Chapel Street Berkhamsted there lived at this time with her mother a young woman named Laura Sabbatini, who had the misfortune to become acquainted with Cream, or, as she knew him, Dr. Neill. Both mother and daughter looked upon him as a respectable member of society, and after a short while Miss Sabbatini became engaged to be married to him somewhere towards the end of November or the beginning of December 1891.

On 5th January, 1892, Cream left his lodgings in Lambeth Palace Road, announcing that he was off to pay a visit to America. On the 6th he was with the Sabbatinis at Berkhamsted, and before leaving them he made a will (written in his own hand), which he declared he could not revoke, and by which he left all his possessions to Miss Sabbatini. He left the precious document in her keeping, and told her to write to him at an address in Quebec, which she did.

On the next day, the 7th January, 1892, he sailed from Liverpool for Canada on board the *Sarnia*.

---
* See Appendix I

Thomas Neill Cream.

XI

It is not necessary, indeed it would confuse rather than clear, this narrative, to give a detailed account of Cream's visit to Canada and the United States, but there are some important matters that must be touched on.

At Blanchard's Hotel, Quebec, Cream, who had arrived there on 20th January, met with John Wilson M'Culloch, a resident in Ottawa, who was a commercial traveller, representing a big grocery house, Messrs. Jardine & Co., of Toronto. This man made the acquaintance of Cream on or about 29th February, and was more or less constantly in his company until 8th March, seeing him as a rule several times a day. One Saturday afternoon M'Culloch mentioned to Cream that he was unwell, and was invited by the latter to his room. The doctor prescribed for him a couple of pills, which at any rate did him no harm. On another occasion Cream showed him a bottle containing whitish crystals, and said, "That is poison." When asked for what purpose he used it, he replied, "I give that to the women to get them out of the family way." M'Culloch said, "How do you do that?" and Cream answered, "I give it to them in these," showing a box containing a number of capsules, a box similar to that produced at the trial. He then brought out a pair of false whiskers and so forth, explaining that he wore them to prevent identification when operating. His talk, as was usual with men, turned largely upon his intrigues with women, and he also showed M'Culloch some indecent photographs. As this witness said, "He always had a loose tongue about women." Cream complained that he was bothered with his head and suffered from insomnia, adding that he dosed himself with morphia to gain relief.

During this visit to Quebec Cream, it seems, was in the habit of taking morphia—and probably opium—to such an extent that at times he appeared to be absolutely stupefied.

Later on in the year M'Culloch, reading in the newspapers of Dr. Neill of London having been identified with Dr. Cream of Canada, communicated with the police and was subpœnaed to come to England to give evidence at the trial.

While in Quebec Cream had made the acquaintance of Mr. M. A. Kingman, agent for the G. F. Harvey Manufacturing Company, of Saratoga Springs, N.Y. In February this firm of manufacturing

Ellen Donworth's Death

To the Guests
of the Metropole Hotel

Ladies and Gentlemen

I hereby notify you that the person who poisoned Ellen Donworth on the 13th last October is to-day in the employ of the Metropole Hotel and that your lives are no longer safe as long as you remain in this Hotel.

Yours respectfully
W H MURRAY.

London April 1892

The "Metropole" Circular.

Introduction.

chemists received from their Canadian representative an order for pills to be sent to Cream at Blanchard's Hotel, part of which order was for 500 1-16th grain strychnine pills. Later the firm was written to by Cream who suggested that he should be appointed their London agent, which application was negatived, but a further supply of pills was a few days later sent to him on his order.

It was during his stay at Quebec that Cream had printed there to the number of 500 what is known as the "Metropole" circular for distribution among the visitors at the Metropole Hotel, London.*

Cream wrote to Mr. Douglas Battersby, shipping agent of St. James's Street, Montreal, asking for information concerning the sailings of various liners with a view to booking a steerage berth for his return to England.

Going on to Montreal on 19th March Cream called on Mr. Battersby, a passenger agent, who described him as a "pussy little fellow" which scarcely seems felicitous as Cream was by no means small. Later Mr. Battersby received the following letter:—

Montreal, 22nd March, 1892.

D. Battersby, Esq.,
 Montreal.

Dear Sir,

I am expecting a parcel and some letters and papers at the Albion Hotel some time to day. Will you kindly get them for me and give them to the purser of the s.s. "Labrador," and ask him to take charge of them for me till I call on him in Liverpool for them. The parcel is a small one and you can either give or send it to the purser of the "Labrador" and much oblige

Yours truly,
Thos. N. Cream.

P.S.—I bought a ticket from you yesterday per s.s. "Britannic."

The parcel in due course reached Mr. Battersby who did not feel justified in handing it over as requested without having ascertained what it contained. "It might have been dynamite for all I knew," he said later. The parcel contained the copies of the "Metropole" circular. It was duly handed over to the purser of the "Labrador" and about the middle of April Mr. Battersby received this acknowledgment from Cream at Liverpool:—

---

* See reproduction opposite this page. This is one of the most amazing performances of this amazing man, and utterly purposeless.

Thomas Neill Cream.

R M S Britannic, Apr 7th, 1892

D Battersby, Esq ,
   Montreal, Canada

Dear Sir

   Received goods per " Labrador " all safe and your Letter Many thanks The " B " beat all previous records this time We had a fine run, and was two days in ahead of the " Labrador " I enclose 15 pence in English postage to reimburse you for the 25 cents spent Thanking you again for your kindness, I remain,

                  Yours truly

                                Thos N Cream

The draft of the circular was in Cream's handwriting!

Toward the end of March Cream, accompanied by Mr Kingman, paid a visit to Saratoga Springs being on his way via New York to England He there bought a case of medicines he had previously ordered and again endeavouring to secure the appointment as London representative was again refused But it was agreed that he should deduct a commission on any orders he might transmit to the company from England such orders to be accompanied by cash Cream seems to have been confident that he would make considerable money on these terms, and in order to enable him to conduct this business he received further moneys, to the tune of $1 100 00, from his father's estate

On 23rd March Cream sailed from New York on board the " Britannic " arriving at Liverpool on 1st April

XII

Cream reached London the following day 2nd April stayed for some time at Edwards Hotel Euston Square and on the 9th again took up his residence at 103 Lambeth Palace Road In the intermediate days he paid a visit to the Sabbatims at Berkhamstead

On 11th April what was justly termed by the Attorney-General an appalling event took place For some three weeks there had been lodging at 118 Stamford Street which dismal thoroughfare runs from Waterloo Road to Blackfriars Road, two " unfortunate " girls who had come from Brighton—Alice Marsh, aged twenty one, and Emma Shrivell, aged eighteen They occupied separate rooms on the second floor, each paying a weekly rent of 7s 6d On the night of 11th April, or, to be more precise at about a

Introduction.

quarter to two in the morning of 12th April Police-Constable George Cumley was passing along the west side of Stamford Street, which was on his beat, when some few yards from No. 118 he saw a man being let out of the house by a young woman. The man went away toward Waterloo Road, and the constable for the time thought no more of what was not an unusual occurrence in Stamford Street. Apparently he had a full sight of the woman, whom he afterwards recognised as Emma Shrivell. The man he described as about 5 feet 9 inches to 5 feet 10 inches in height, about forty-five to fifty years of age, wearing a moustache but not any whiskers, dressed in a dark overcoat with tall silk hat, and "I saw by the reflection of the street lamp that he had glasses, the light being on the same side of the street and immediately opposite No. 118. About three-quarters of an hour later Cumley saw a four-wheeled cab drive up to the house, from which descended Police-Constable William Leersfield, who had been summoned by George Vogt, the landlord of the house.

We must now retrace our steps. According to a statement made by Shrivell's friend Marsh had an acquaintance known by them as "Fred," who claimed to be a doctor, a man of stoutish build, dark, bald on top of his head, wearing glasses, and in height about 5 feet 8 inches to 5 feet 9 inches. He generally wore a black overcoat and a tall silk hat. He had been in the house with them that evening, and after a meal of bottled beer and tinned salmon had given them each three long thin pills (capsules no doubt). Cumley, to whom this statement was made, asked "Was that the man with the glasses that I saw you let out about two o'clock?" Shrivell's answer was "Yes."

The evidence of the landlady, Charlotte Vogt, was that she went to bed about eleven o'clock, when the house was all quiet. At half-past two she was awakened by a screaming and shrieking, and getting up, she found Marsh in the passage apparently in great agony. She at once sent her husband out for a cab and a policeman. She then heard Shrivell, upstairs, screaming "Alice!" Going up to her room she found the girl lying upon the floor, evidently in fearful pain. Again she heard Marsh shrieking, and, going down, found her lying on her stomach in the passage, her body twitching violently. Then her husband returned with the cab and Constable Leersfield, who confirmed Mrs. Vogt's statement that Marsh was lying on her face upon the floor, wearing only her nightshirt. He

Thomas Neill Cream.

administered an emetic of mustard and water. (Cumley gave evidence that Marsh was lying over the seat of a chair face downward.) Shrivell was found lying on the floor of her room fully dressed. The girls were placed in the cab and driven to St. Thomas's Hospital, but Marsh died upon the way. Shrivell lingered for six hours in agony, dying at 8 a.m., despite all efforts made to alleviate her suffering.

The inquest was held at St. Thomas's Hospital on 14th April and Dr. Wyman, the house physician, said that in his opinion the symptoms were consistent with death from poisoning by strychnine, but that an analysis of the contents of the stomach must be made. The tin in which the salmon had been contained had been examined, and it was proved that the contents had been wholesome. The theory of ptomaine poisoning had, therefore, to be abandoned.

At the adjourned inquest, on 5th May, Dr. Thomas Stevenson stated that his analysis showed that the girls had died from strychnine poisoning, but how administered he could not say. The jury's verdict was in accordance with this evidence.

XIII

Incidents, big and small, now crowd thick and fast. At 103 Lambeth Palace Road, there had been lodging for some time a young medical student of St. Thomas's Hospital, Walter Joseph Harper, a son of Dr. Joseph Harper, of Barnstaple. Mr. Harper when shown later a photograph of Cream, did not recognise the man, and indeed had no recollection of ever having seen him. But Cream took steps to learn all he could about the young doctor.

On Easter Sunday, 17th April, Cream showed great eagerness to read the report of the inquests upon Marsh and Shrivell in *Lloyd's Weekly Newspaper*, expressing his indignation at this cold-blooded murder.

The following day he went into Mr. Harper's sitting-room on the first floor, where Miss Sleaper was at the time, and asked questions about its tenant, as to where he lived, what kind of man he was and so forth. Then—or a little later (the evidence is confusing, but the date is immaterial)—he made to Miss Sleaper the astounding statement that Mr. Harper was the murderer of the girls in Stamford Street! He declared that the police held the proofs!

Death Certificate of Ellen Donworth

Death Certificate of Matilda Clover

Introduction.

That the girls had received warning letters urging them not to take anything that Mr Harper might give them. Miss Sleaper indignantly exclaimed that Cream must be mad, maybe she was not far wrong.

Then on Wednesday Cream went down to Berkhamstead to visit Mrs and Miss Sabbatini. The latter records that on this occasion he went to church with her; it was to attend a "service of song." Elsewhere it is stated that when paying these visits to the country he asked that he might have a Bible in his room.

On 26th April Dr Joseph Harper received at Barnstaple a letter, dated the 25th, and signed "W H Murray." There were enclosures, including a cutting from *Lloyd's Weekly News*, concerning Ellen Donworth's death. But why Ellen Donworth? For the letter itself said that the writer possessed incontestable proof that Mr W J Harper had poisoned the two girls in Stamford Street! The writer was willing to suppress this evidence on receiving the sum of £1500 sterling.*

In this case, as in the others, Cream seems not to have made any effort to follow up his threats, and cannot, as was surmised, have made his living as a blackmailer.

XIV

The deaths of Donworth or Marsh, and of Shrivell had been more than sufficient to arouse the energies of the police. They now received information of the remarkable circumstances attending the death of Matilda Clover, and on 30th April Inspector Harvey applied for and obtained an order from the Home Office authorising the exhumation of her body for the purposes of examination and the holding of an inquest in order to ascertain if the cause of death had been as stated in the death certificate. About this time Cream casually remarked to Miss Sleaper that it was just as well she had not—as he had suggested—gone round to Lambeth Road to make inquiries as to Clover's death, as there was going to be an investigation into the case.

There was also Police Sergeant M'Intyre hot upon the trail. From whom had he gained his information? From Cream himself

---

* See this letter on page 57

Thomas Neill Cream.

M'Intyre had been introduced to the doctor by a mutual friend and Cream, as was apparently his wont, soon became confidential. He showed him a letter which had passed through the post and which was addressed to the two girls at Stamford Street. It warned them to be careful of Dr. Harper, who would serve them as he had served Clover and Lou Harvey. This was the first M'Intyre or indeed any of the police had heard of Lou Harvey. Naturally they wanted to know more. A search was at once instituted for the record of the death of Lou Harvey, of which more anon.

On Saturday, 30th April, Cream paid his third visit to Berkhamstead, and on this occasion requested Miss Sabbatini to write some letters for him. When asked what was his reason for so doing he refused to give any. He dictated the letters, the first of which was addressed to "Coroner Wyatt," asking him to give an enclosed letter to the foreman of the jury at the inquest on Marsh and Shrivell. The enclosure repeated the ridiculous accusation against young Dr. Harper. Reference was made to George Clark, a detective of Cockspur Street, who had no knowledge whatever of Cream, and to him a third letter was dictated. All three were signed "W. H. Murray."

XV

One of the most important witnesses at the trial was John Haynes, who in the early days of April, 1892, had taken lodgings in the house of William Armstead, a photographer, who lived at 129 Westminster Bridge Road. There he met with Cream, and was quickly on terms of intimacy with him, receiving from him the confidences which Cream seemed fond of giving even to mere acquaintances.

Cream, as we know, was now beginning to be suspected of the police and was being carefully watched. As yet there was little concrete evidence against him, but there was an atmosphere of suspicion and a curiosity on their part to know more about him and his doings.

Mr. Armstead drew attention to the fact that his house was being watched, and Haynes asked Cream if it was he who was being shadowed. He received the reply "No, certainly not." The next day Cream did admit that he was being watched, and said that it was a mistake for another man who lived in the same

Introduction.

house as he did, and whose name was Harper, and so on, going into a vast amount—now and later on—of fabulous details. He added that Donworth, Clover, and Lou Harvey were murdered by the same unconscionable villain. He pointed out the house in which Clover had been done to death. He pointed out the house in which Lou lived, and had. Haynes warned Cream that he was elating on them so, and should give all this information to the police, but Cream said he knew of no possible use for it.

Constable Comley was anxious to meet Cream again, and was detailed to look out for him. On 12th May, between seven and eight in the evening, he saw Cream—that is to say, the man he had seen in Stamford Street—loitering outside the Canterbury Music Hall. He pointed to Police Sergeant Ward, who recognised the likeness to the man who had been described by Constables Coull and Eversfield. He watched Cream, who went away with a young woman, whom Cream did no poison. He told this girl that he lived solely to indulge in women.

On 17th May, Cream visited a girl friend named Violet Beverley, 1, North Street, Kennington Road. He prepared for her what he called " American drink," which somebody almost forced on her, she refused to take. He showed her a leather case containing a number of bottles of pills, and said he was a traveller for a New York drug house.

About 16th or 17th Mr. Cream admitted to Miss Sleaper that he knew her house was being watched; on one occasion he said he was being shadowed because he was an American, and on another that it was young Dr. Harper who was wanted.

Towards the end of May a dramatic little incident occurred. Cream and Haynes were riding on top of an omnibus, and when a short distance from Charing Cross they heard the newsboys shouting out, "Arrest in the Stamford Street case." Cream could not conceal his agitation. His companion persuaded him not to get down till they reached their destination. When they dismounted Cream eagerly bought the papers, gave them with a trembling hand to Haynes, and was greatly relieved when he found that the arrest was in connection with another case for which Stamford Street was then notorious.

Cream had given Mr. Haynes statements as to his movements while he had been in this country, but, curiously, had failed to

Thomas Neill Cream.

account for the date of the Stamford Street murders. The next day Cream met him in Lambeth Palace Road and said, "I am going away to-day at three o'clock. Will I be arrested if I do so?" To which M'Intyre replied, "I cannot tell you. If you walk across with me to Scotland Yard I will make inquiries." They went together half-way across Westminster Bridge, when Cream said, "I will not go any further with you. I am suspicious of you, and I believe you are playing me double." He turned back.

Meanwhile the police were busy searching for traces of the mysterious Lou Harvey, who Cream said had been murdered

XVI

On 26th May Cream, through his solicitors, Messrs Waters & Bryan, 17 East Arbour Street, wrote to Sir Edward Bradford, Chief Commissioner of Police, saying that he was being shadowed by detective officers, among them Sergeant M'Intyre, and complaining that his business was being injured. So indeed, it was.

On the same day Inspector Tunbridge of the Criminal Investigation Department, who had received instructions to make inquiry into the South Lambeth poisoning cases, called upon Cream at Lambeth Palace Road, at which interview Miss Sabbatini was present. Cream repeated his complaint, and then Tunbridge turned the conversation to Cream's business in this country. He gave a fairly accurate account of himself and his doings, among other things showing his visitor a case of medicines in which was a bottle of pills labelled, "1-16th grain strychnine," and explaining that they were intended for sale only to chemists and medical practitioners.

Then, on 1st June, Inspector Tunbridge went down to see young Dr Harper, who had now begun to practise at Braunton in Devonshire. A brief explanation was given as to why the inspector had called, and the two went over to Barnstaple to see Dr Joseph Harper. Reading the letter from Cream, Tunbridge at once grasped the fact that it was the clue he was looking for. It was in Cream's handwriting. Dr Joseph Harper readily agreed that Cream should be prosecuted for attempted blackmail; there was not yet sufficient evidence against him to permit of his being charged with murder

Introduction.

Cream had booked his passage for America, but on 3rd June a warrant for Cream's arrest was issued by Sir John Bridge at Bow Street Police Court, and at 5.25 p.m. on the same day Inspector Tunbridge arrested him in Lambeth Palace Road. The warrant was read to him, and he said, "You have got the wrong man. Fire away." Surely even in the drug-sodden brain of the wretched man it must now have dawned that his career was at an end?

In the *St. James's Gazette* for 24th October, 1892, appeared an article on "The Prisoner Neill," written by "One Who Knew Him." The writer states that he met Cream at the Adelaide Gallery Restaurant in the Strand. Cream, as usual, talked about women, also of music, of which he was fond. Money and poisons were other topics that interested him. He spoke, says the writer, with "a soft voice, though strong American accent, dressed with taste and care, and was well-informed and travelled as men go." He appeared to be a powerful man, his under-jaw heavy and protruding. He was addicted to gin, "tobacco and cigars," and chewing gum. He seldom legued or smiled. The writer adds—"He was of an exceedingly restless temper, always pacing about, even when drinking at a bar, and when sitting was always moving his legs like a dog dreaming, or fiddling with something on the table, and moving his head and rolling his eyes to watch every one who moved, the people who came and went, and even the waiters who attended on him. He appeared to hate being alone, for though he never seemed to enter with anybody, when my table was full he never went and sat by himself, but always managed to go and sit at an occupied table."

"Women were his preoccupation, and his talk of them far from agreeable. He carried pornographic photographs which he was too ready to display. He was in the habit of taking pills which, he said, were compounded of strychnine, morphia and cocaine, and of which the effect he declared was aphrodisiac. In short, he was a degenerate of filthy desires and practices. Almost from the time the question of the Lambeth poisoning case began to attract attention, and at any rate from the time he knew he was watched and guessed he was suspected, Neill became a changed man. Every trait in his character became exaggerated. He became more nervous and excitable. He

known to Londoners as "Gati-."

Thomas Neill Cream.

turned round and stood to see if men were following him; he made every excuse to turn down empty streets and to enter houses, he would suddenly turn round and walk back under pretence of having passed a tobacconist's, so as to see if he were followed, and would get into a cab quickly if he only saw a man crossing the street or saw any one turn and look after him. He had the air of a hunted man, and it would seem as if he was haunted in the night by the faces of the seven women and one man whom he had murdered, for he kept a candle alight in his room all through the night."

XVII

On Saturday, 4th June, at Bow Street Police Court, Cream was charged with attempting to extort money from Dr. Joseph Harper, of Barnstaple, Mr. Bernard Thomas prosecuting on behalf of the Treasury, and the accused being defended by Mr. John L. Waters. The case was adjourned and eventually did not close until the 28th. Meanwhile Scotland Yard was busy. With Inspector Harvey and Sergeant M'Intyre, Tunbridge paid another visit to Cream's room in Lambeth Palace Road, finding there many matters of interest, which he detailed in his evidence at the trial.

On 17th June Cream was identified at Bow Street by Masters and May as the man they had seen passing Hercules Buildings and entering Clover's house in Lambeth Road.

It will be remembered that the body of Matilda Clover was buried by the parish in Tooting Cemetery on 27th October, 1891. On 5th May, 1892, the grave was opened, and fourteen coffins had to be taken out of the ground* before that of Clover was reached and removed to the mortuary.

Dr. Stevenson† wrote—"In May 1892 the editor exhumed the body of Matilda Clover, who had died six months before from strychnine administered six hours before her death. The body, except as regards the face, neck, and fingers, was in an unusual state of preservation. Nearly all parts of the body, including the

---

* So stated by Mr. George R. Sims.

† "The Principles and Practice of Medical Jurisprudence," Taylor & Stevenson, Fourth Edition, 1894, Vol. I, p. 435.

Introduction.

fluids had an acid reaction. There was no rigidity, but the muscles were firm.*

The inquest was opened at the Vestry Hall, Tooting, on 22nd June before Mr A Braxton Hicks, coroner, and continued for three days, then being adjourned till 7th July, closing upon the 13th of that month. Mr John L Waters represented Cream, and Mr C F Gill and Mr Guy Stephenson, instructed by Mr Williamson, of the Treasury, assisted the coroner in his investigation. For the most part the evidence given was the same as that produced by the prosecution at the trial.†

When Mr C F Gill had called his last witness, the coroner said that in order to satisfy himself and the jury, Neill (Cream) must be sworn.

NEILL—My instructions are not to open my mouth.
CORONER—You must answer. All I wish to ask you is your name and occupation.
Mr WATERS—He does not want me to give evidence.
CORONER—I must know it from his own lips, and he must be sworn.
Mr WATERS—Under these circumstances he will consent to be sworn.
NEILL—I decline to say anything, sir, as if I answered, my instructions would not open my mouth. I am, doubtless, but I will not do so, sir.
Mr WATERS—I submit that this is a declared force, but Neill can be sworn, and then he will decline to give evidence.

Then Neill was sworn.

CORONER—What is your name?
NEILL—I decline to answer any question in regard to that.
CORONER—But you must tell me that.
NEILL—No sir. I have got my instructions as to what to do, and I shall abide by them whatever the consequences are.
CORONER—Is your name Thomas Neill Cream?
NEILL—I decline to answer that question.
CORONER—Are you a qualified medical man?—(No answer)

All of which surely was unnecessary and unseemly.

After twenty minutes consultation, the jury brought in the following verdict:—"We are unanimously agreed that Matilda Clover died of strychnine poisoning, and that the poison was administered by Thomas Neill with intent to destroy life. We therefore

---
* See Dr Stevenson's evidence at the trial pages 8 &c. Also Appendix VI
† See also Appendix V

Thomas Neill Cream.

find him guilty of wilful murder." An excited mob gave Neill an unkindly welcome on his leaving the Vestry Hall.

On 18th July Inspector Tunbridge charged Cream, then in custody, with the wilful murder of Matilda Clover, saying, "You will be charged with murder." To which Cream said, "What, in the Clover case?" Adding, when the charge had been read to him, "All right." Later on he asked, "Is anything going to be done in the other cases?"

On 21st July—the hearing closing upon 22nd August—Cream was brought up at Bow Street Police Court charged with the murder of Matilda Clover, Mr. C. F. Gill appearing for the Crown and Mr. Waters for the defence. The evidence was much the same as that given at the trial, and therefore need not be dealt with here. After a protest on the accused's behalf at so many several charges against him being dealt with at once, Sir John Bridge committed Cream to stand his trial for the murder of Matilda Clover, Ellen Donworth, Alice Marsh and Emma Shrivel, for attempting to murder Louisa Harris (otherwise Lou Harvey) and for sending letters to Dr. Broadbent and Dr. Harper threatening to accuse persons of crime, &c.

The police had not been able to find any evidence or proof of the death of Lou Harvey for the simple reason that the girl was alive! During the hearing at Bow Street, the magistrate received the following letter:—

PROOFS OF IDENTITY OF NEILL

Sir,

Met a man outside of St. James Hall Regent St. 12.30 one night in October about the 20th. Had been to the Alhambra and seen him there, earlier the same night. Went with him from St. James to an hotel in Berwick St. Oxford St. Stayed there with him all night left about 8 oc in the morning. Made an appointment with him to meet the same night at 7.30 on the Embankment. Met him same night opposite Charing X Underground R. Station. Walked with him to the Northumberland Public house, had glass of wine, and then walked back to the Embankment. Were he gave me two capsules. But not liking the look of the thing, I pretended to put them in my mouth. But kept them in my hand. And when he happened to look away, I threw them over the Embankment. He then said that he had to be at St. Thomas's Hospital, left me, and gave me 5s to go to the Oxford Music Hall, Promising to meet me outside at 11 oc. But he never came. I had told him that I was living at Townshend Rd St Johns Wood but I gave him the wrong number. I never saw him again till about 3 weeks after. When I had moved from St Johns Wood

Introduction.

to Stamford St. When I happened to be at Piccadilly Circus and I saw him I spoke to him, he asked me to have a drink, I had a drink in the Regent Ar St. He promised to meet me at 11 oc the same night He had not seemed as if he knew me while we were drinking. So I said to man don't you remember me. he said no. I said not that night when you promised to meet me outside the Oxford. He then said what's your name. I said Louisa Harvey. He seemed surprised, said no more, and walked quickly away. And at eert time about that night I saw him once again, about month afterwards with a young lady down the Strand, and I never saw him again. I never saw cease to say him give me capsules on the Lr bankment who could Identify him I had not troubled to read the case particular. H... right when I happened to read it in the star I was struck with the resemblance. So I got the Telegraph news no name of my n... mentioned so I was almost sure. He being under the impression that I took the capsules and after dropped dead in the stree.... sa..all

I could tell him that I was a servant. He wore Gold rimmed Glasses and had very Peculiar crosseyes stares as I can remember he had dress suit on and long m... knicks her his arm. He spoke with a fore n Twang. He asked me if I had ever been in America. I said no. He had an Old fashioned Gold Watch with a L... eye said was Chain and seal. Said he had been in the Army. I noticed he was very bars man he said he had... be a soldier.

I enclose photograph... from D... T.legrah of Saturday

Address
  Mrs Harris
    87 Up... North Street
      Brighton

She also wrote to the coroner at Tooting, to the effect that she thought she could give evidence that would be of use

XVIII

Here may be given some of the Letters written by Cream during the Bow Street proceedings, they shed light on the prisoner's frame of mind and temperament. The handwriting, it is said, was intentionally disguised so that it might not be compared to his hand with that of incriminating documents in the possession of the Treasury

On 28th June he wrote to Miss Sabbatini after her first appearance in the witness-box—

I was perfectly safe till you spoke against me, but how it will end now I do not know. You know, dear, you never saw me write a letter

Thomas Neill Cream.

in your life and yet you went on the stand and swore that my will and my letter which you gave to the authorities were in my writing.' Now, my dear Laura, you must correct this. The next time you are on the stand you must swear positively that you never saw me write and that you cannot identify any of my writing. If you do this you will help to save me. Mr Waters will tell you how to do it and correct the terrible injury you have done me. When the officers ask any questions about me tell them you don't know, as you don't remember. When they submit my writing to you and ask you if it is mine tell them " you do not know." For God's sake burn anything you have with my writing on. If you annoy me in any way or do me any injury in my time of trouble you are going to get into terrible trouble, and I cannot save you from it, but my solicitor and I will protect you as long as you are true to me and do me no harm. I may want the loan of some money from you till I get some from America. If you should run short dear borrow some from Winnie and I will make it all right with her by and by, you know. I paid her what you owed her before. Let me know dear the less money you can live comfortably on till I can get out of my troubles, as I want to make some arrangement for you.

Then on 4th July he wrote that he was delighted to receive her assurance that she would stick to him to the end. He knew her mother was prejudiced against him, but that did not trouble him in the least so long as she was true to him. Miss Sabbatini apparently reproached him with his threat to her, for he wrote—

I shall never threaten you my darling. All I ask of you dear is to say and do nothing that will hurt me or annoy my counsel. I would not have written as I did but I was afraid you could bring terrible trouble on your own head by your conduct. I shall say no more now, darling. In future say you don't remember or you don't know to every question you are asked about me. I do not blame you now, for I have found out it was mother made you tell about the letters. This is mother's gratitude for what I did for her. I cannot tell how long this will last. They are putting it off from week to week, trying to get evidence against me, but they cannot get any evidence that I committed murder or sent blackmailing letters to anyone. They are getting desperate and have sent more detectives to America to try and get evidence there. They have put more detectives on the case to try and get more evidence and I am sure they are watching you, and they will watch you till this is all over. They think you know a great deal more than you have told. They will be after you again, you may depend on that. I wish we could manage it so that we could get married then you could not testify against me, for a man's wife is never allowed to testify against him. Many thanks darling for your great kindness in lending me the £10. I wanted it badly till I get

---

* See Trial, page 118.

Introduction.

wrote from America. They searched all my trunks and clothing at 103 Lambeth Palace Road but they got nothing for their pains. I was ready for them. If the authorities had a strong case or a big pile of evidence against me they would not have put my case off till next Thursday, but they cannot prove that I committed any, now like Micawber they are playing a waiting game—waiting to see if something will turn up, but it wont, my darling. You need not be afraid of that. No, my dear Laura, you must cheer up, be brave, my darling. I would be glad to have you come to Holloway and see me, but I cannot hear you, my darling, and it is not safe for you to come because you are being too closely watched, they are trying hard to get more evidence against me. It makes me feel terribly bad also after you go away. I am so lonely without you. Why did you not let me know you were so fond of me when I was with you? Your letters are a revelation to me. I know now that you love me, but I never felt sure of it before. I was always fond of you. I could not help it. I became infatuated with you, and the longer I knew you the fonder I became. If I had known then as I know now that you are so fond of me, how much happier I would have been. It is that knowledge that is worrying me so much now, that I am away from you. I am glad that you are sticking to me, for if you were to forsake me I would gladly lose my life. I care nothing at all for life without you.

On 14th July he wrote—

Do not believe Sergeant M'Intyre's evidence that he swore to yesterday when he says I spoke ill of you to him. So help my God it is a lie. They are doing this to make you angry and get you to swear against me.

26th July, 1892.

My dear Laura,

Was at Bow Street yesterday, and heard *such good news* that I have not been able to sleep since. A member of Parliament sent me word that he had over two hundred witnesses to clear me if I wanted them. I am going to use some of them, as their evidence *will clear me*. Mr Waters will have some news for you on Saturday or Monday next. Be sure and look your best in Court next week as my friends are always in Court now.

Yours for ever,

NEILL

On 5th August Neill wrote—

My darling Laura,

I really do not understand you. Last week you found fault with me because I did not recognise you in Court, and on Tuesday I could not get you to look when I turned round. What do you mean by it? I cannot write from Holloway unless you acknowledge receipt of every letter I send you. How am I to know the police are not getting hold of my letters if you do not let me know you are receiving

Thomas Neill Cream.

them? I am very ill with bowel complaint, and when I think of the harm you have done me in giving up my will and letter to the police, it makes me wild. I hope to God I will never meet your mother again."

Finally this—

London 16th August 1892

My dear Laura,

The fact that I have never been seen with Donworth, Clover, Marsh or Shrivell ought to satisfy you that the authorities cannot prove I murdered them. Constance Linfield swore I was not the man she saw with Donworth. Lucy Rose refused to identify me as the man she saw with Clover on the night of her death.

Policeman Comely refused to swear I was the man he saw coming out of Marsh and Shrivell's house on the morning of their death. Now how are they going to prove I murdered them. Dr. Stevenson's evidence is very favourable to me, and it alone would clear me in the Clover or Marsh and Shrivell case. The strychnine pills I bought from the Harvey Drug Company were sold to a passenger on the "Britannic" and we have sent for him to prove it. So, you see I have a complete answer to that. Three witnesses at the Coroner's inquest swore falsely and the authorities knew it and did not call them at the Police Court. Robert Taylor, Clover's uncle was one of them. If the authorities could prove I murdered these girls do you think my case would have dragged as it has done since last June. The blackmailing case has become very weak through your evidence that you could not swear to my writing.

The longer the authorities delay the matter shows they cannot get the evidence they want and require to convict. Be sure and send every pill box and every bottle you have with the labels of Priests or the Harvey Drug Company to Mr. Waters at once. Do not degrade yourself by conversing with Ward or Tonbridge. We caught Haynes and Tonbridge swearing falsely last week. Love to yourself and dear little girl from

Yours in &c.,

NEILL.

The whole story is like the plot of an Elizabethan tragedy of horrors. As one walks through the drab streets of Lambeth to-day the shadow of this sinister man still haunts them.

XIX

Cream was tried at the Central Criminal Court, Old Bailey, on 17th October 1892, and succeeding days before Mr. Justice Hawkins. Read with what has gone before and with what follows in the Appen-

---

* The above extracts are reprinted from *The Daily Telegraph*, 24th October, 1892.

Introduction.

dices* it completes the material for painting a full-length portrait of Thomas Neill Cream. His demeanour in Court was as callous as has been that of the majority of murderers at their trial.

From the legal point of view the trial presents only one point of considerable interest. Cream was indicted for four murders and other crimes, and the indictment charging him with the wilful murder of Matilda Clover was proceeded with. With the exception of the blackmailing letters written by Cream the evidence against him was by no means strong, nor indeed was it in the other cases of murder and the case of attempted murder. The prosecution—as also the defence—realised that the strength of the case against Cream lay in the cumulative power of the evidence against him which could be produced only if the evidence in the other cases was held to be admissible when the case of Clover was being tried. There can scarcely be a doubt but that the admission by the Court of this evidence hanged Cream. The Attorney-General argued that the evidence he desired to call was admissible on the grounds that he could thus prove that the accused was in possession of strychnine, that the death of Clover was a death due to the administration of strychnine, that it would show that in the other cases the accused had pursued the same course as it was alleged he had done in the case of Clover, and that it was a systematic course of action, and, also, on the ground that the accused himself had grouped all these cases together and attributed the murders to one hand in his letter to Dr Harper. The defence met these arguments with the usual contentions. Mr Justice Hawkins gave his decision promptly in favour of admitting the evidence and refused to reserve a case.

The admission or rejection of such evidence is dealt with fully in the introduction to the volume in this series devoted to the Trial of George Joseph Smith, edited by Mr Eric R. Watson. There is quoted this interesting passage from a letter written by Mr Justice Hawkins to Mr Justice Wills over:— "I dissent from the suggestion that such evidence . . . can only be admitted in corroboration of a *prima facie* case which a judge would be justified in leaving to a jury if it stood alone." The "Laws of England" says that such evidence when admitted is so admitted in order to show . . . not that

---

* See Appendices II and III.

Thomas Neill Cream.

the defendant did the acts which form the basis of the charge but that, if he did such acts, he did them intentionally and not accidentally, or inadvertently, or innocently." When lawyers fall out it sometimes happens that a criminal comes to the halter. Those who wish to follow the matter further are referred to the volume in the series named above.

A minor point arose as to the admissibility of dying statements, which came up in the evidence of Lucy Rose who was with Clover at her death. (See page 71.)

The scientific evidence as to the finding of strychnine in the bodies of the deceased girls was clear and raised no new points.

It took the jury but a few minutes to decide upon their verdict of "Guilty." If there had been any doubt in their minds as to what decision they should come to it must have ceased to exist after the judge's summing up.

XX

According to the late Mr. George R. Sims, Cream on his return to Holloway after his counsel's speech on his behalf sang and danced in his cell, confident that he would be acquitted. The judge's summing up must have staggered that confidence, the jury's verdict shattered it. He did not dance and sing in the condemned cell at Newgate.

On the application of his solicitors a respite of seven days was granted, in order to allow time for the arrival from America of evidence which it was asserted would prove that Cream was insane. But on the night of 12th November the following letter was received by Messrs. Waters & Bryan:—

Whitehall, 11th November

Gentlemen,

With reference to your further letters of 9th and 10th inst., I am directed by the Secretary of State to inform you that after the most careful consideration of the affidavits submitted by you on behalf of Thomas Neill, now lying under sentence of death in Newgate Prison, and of all the circumstances of the case, he has been unable to discover any sufficient grounds to justify him consistently with his public duty, in advising Her Majesty to interfere with the due course of the law.

I am, Gentlemen,
Your obedient servant
GODFREY LUSHINGTON

Messrs. Waters & Bryan, Solicitors,
15 Temple Chambers, Temple Avenue, E.C.

Introduction.

An extraordinary story was put about—and promptly and authoritatively contradicted—that Cream had made confession of his crimes to Mr. Waters. Cream was not the type of man that confesses.

Night and day he was kept under careful observation, there being an absolute reason for this customary precaution in the fear that he might attempt suicide. This precaution, so the *Daily Telegraph* of 16th October, 1892, observed, was based upon a remark which he is said to have uttered on Friday after leaving the dock without saying a word to Mr. Justice Hawkins, who had passed sentence of death upon him. As he was being removed Neill's exclamation was overheard, "They shall never hang me." His impending fate appeared to occasion him no distress of mind. He took his dinner and tea as usual, and conversed with the warders in his usual free style, without making reference to the murders laid to his charge. At nine o'clock he is said to have slept well, and was on Saturday quite composed and quiet. His demeanour is that of a man who does not realise his awful position, but he was expected to have shown his true feelings when the verdict was given. In fact, he had declared that he intended "to give it to Hawkins," and his silence in the dock surprised people who have been closely in contact with him. Neill's behaviour whilst at Holloway has mirrored his reckless indifference, but he seems to have mainly depended upon that Mr. Geoghegan's eloquent advocacy and the strenuous efforts of Mr. Waters, his painstaking solicitor, would have caused the jury to disagree. It is felt no regret that the verdict came as a blow to the prosecution, for from the first the strength of the case was regarded as being very largely in the compilation, in the chain of testimony, which would have been innocuous if the evidence had been strictly limited to the Clover murder. So long as doubt remained as to the legal counsel bar of the evidence bearing alike on the deaths of Marsh and Shrivell and other crimes, Neill, it was clearly perceived by the authorities, had more than a chance of escaping capital punishment. The accused himself appears to have nourished this expectation, and before his removal from Holloway his protestations of release were so strong that he treated the Governor to a violent outburst of foul language because that official gave orders that he should be taken to the Old Bailey in the clothes which he wore when arrested. Neill then threatened what he would do when set at liberty once more. Through-

35

Thomas Neill Cream.

out his detention he had suffered from anxiety and sleeplessness. When Mr. Geoghegan had delivered his fine speech for the defence — upon which the Attorney General and Mr. Justice Hawkins have privately congratulated him — the accused's hopes of acquittal ran high, and that night in his cell, he sang and danced wildly. This was on Thursday. On Friday afternoon he knew that his doom was sealed, and then it was that he declared he would never go to the gallows, which if he could only reach the high windows of his condemned cell he would himself see as the permanent stead, a few feet distant, on the other side of the prison yard in Newgate.

"Do you think that Neill will commit suicide?" as the question put to one of the leading officers who have been engaged in bringing the murders home to the accused.

"No, was his answer; he is utterly reckless of other people's lives, but he is particularly careful of his own neck. He does not mind how many he kills, but he won't kill himself" — and this opinion was given as the result of some months of the closest study and personal observation.

On the Monday night — his last night — he was very restless, uneasy, silent, pacing up and down the cell for nearly an hour as though endeavouring to steel himself. When at last he lay down he was unable to sleep, tossing from side to side, only occasionally falling into a doze broken by startings. He rose soon after six o'clock, haggard and worn, his cheeks colourless, his eyes mournful, moving his feet and hands twitching nervously. He ate no breakfast. He wore the clothes in which he had appeared in the trial, black coat and dark trousers. He neither confessed his crime nor admitted the justice of his sentence.*

It was stated that he acknowledged to his gaolers the justice of his sentence and admitted that he had murdered many other women.

There were present at the execution Mr. P. K. Metcalfe Deputy Under-Sheriff of the county of London, Lieut. Colonel Milman, Governor of Newgate and Holloway, Colonel Smith Commissioner of the City Police, Mr. Gilbert Medical Officer of Newgate and Holloway, the Rev. Mr. Merrick the Chaplain and other officials. Billington was the executioner. The culprit's demeanour was calm and composed, and it is understood that he made a short statement

---

* See *The Mercury, Advertiser*, 15th November, 1892.

Introduction.

thanking the officials for their kindness to him since he had been under their charge. The length of the drop was 5 feet. A crowd assembled outside the prison to witness the hoisting of the black flag, the appearance of which was greeted with cheering. An inquest was afterwards held in one of the Courts in the Sessions House in the Old Bailey before Mr. Langham, the coroner for the City of London. Lieut.-Colonel Milman and M. Gilbert gave evidence stating that the execution was successfully carried out, and the jury returned a verdict accordingly."

XXI

That Cream was legally guilty of murder there is no question. He knew what he was doing; he utilised his medical knowledge to attain his ends; and he understood clearly that his acts were illegal. It was hopeless to prove insanity in the legal sense of the term. But was Cream sane from the point of view of the defence and psychologist? Unfortunately, the materials for studying the mentality of this highly abnormal man are scanty and inadequate, and do not provide a sufficient basis for fully diagnosing his case. Nor does it serve any good purpose to write him down as a 'moral monster,' which is a slipshod phrase used usually to cover ignorance. What it would be really interesting and helpful to know is how he became what he was. Some maintain that a man is insane who deliberately acts contrary to the regulations imposed upon him by the society in which he lives, refusing stubbornly to earn a living by reputable means. But that does not carry us very far, even if true. What we need to know is how the criminal becomes a criminal, and in Cream's case, as in most others, the evidence is insufficient to justify a definite conclusion. Though there is no justification for entering here upon a discussion of controversial points of psychology, it will be interesting to review some of the incidents and factors of Cream's career, or rather to give a sketch of his mentality, a full portrait being impossible, rather to state the problem than to attempt any solution of it. Cream must be classed among the habitual murderers. He began his criminal career as quite a young man in Canada, and practised it continuously

* See *The Times*, 16th November, 1892.

Thomas Neill Cream.

until the hangman put an end to his activities with the exception of the years when he was incarcerated in Joliet prison.

In the child is to be found the key to the psychology of the man, and of Cream's childhood and ancestry we know nothing. The criminal grows from the soil and the physical and mental nutriment with which he is nourished, and also inherits something from his ancestors, how much and exactly what we do not know. But it is not till he is a young man entering college that we have any sidelights upon the character of Cream. There on the one hand he was a successful student in the medical school and must have possessed at least average mental capacity; on the other hand he was extravagant in his habits and somewhat of a fop. So are many young fellows who after college settle down into decent citizens. But even during his undergraduate days Cream entered on his career of crime, commencing with arson, presumably requiring money to pay for his extravagances. As soon as he was qualified to practise as a medical man he became a professional abortionist. Why did he avoid the obvious, normal career before him? Later in his life his relations deemed him to be mad, using a loose term as a convenient explanation of conduct that was otherwise inexplicable.

It must not be forgotten that Cream was more than a murderer, far more than that. As we know, he commenced his career with arson, going on to the practice of abortion, to the filthy trade of blackmail, and then to murder on an almost wholesale scale. Lacking the materials for making a study of the genesis and development of his criminal genius, we must be content with a brief survey of his adult conduct, his physique, and his mentality.

There is no reason to doubt that he was on the whole bodily sound enough; we have no specific complaint from him but only vague complainings of ill-health and that he suffered from sleeplessness due to headaches. Mr. Aitchison the optician, in an affidavit stated that he found Cream to be suffering from hypermyopia, or extreme short-sightedness, of lifelong duration, that this tended to bring about a nervous breakdown and to induce an almost insatiable craving for opiates. He added that the frequency with which he appears to have taken these opiates coupled with the size of the doses, accentuated the defect itself and produced changes in his moral nature both startling and repulsive. The phrase "of lifelong duration" is highly significant. Any defect of eyesight that is not

Introduction.

properly corrected by glasses almost always results in uncertainty of temper, sleeplessness, nervous headaches, and other troubles. These in turn are more than apt to produce an unstable condition of mind, especially in the young. The mental effect of any defect of the senses is bad. To a boy at school defective eyesight or hearing is a handicap; it sets him apart and makes him seem unusual and apparently stupid to the unobservant and inconsiderate. Thus a mental conflict is set up, too often with disastrous results. The spirit of Ishmael enters into the boy.

To assuage the pain of the headaches and to alleviate the insomnia resulting therefrom Cream resorted to drugs, chiefly morphia, with the invariable disastrous results. He became a drug fiend. The witness McCulloch stated that he saw Cream taking morphia, and that on occasion he seemed to be stupified with drugs. Other witnesses testified to this habit. The morphia habit produces a morbid condition of mind and a debasement of the moral nature; memory becomes weakened, and in many cases there are delusions and hallucinations. In Cream there were the unrestrained and super-normal lustful desires in a bad soul. According to another statement he was in the habit of taking pills "compounded of strychnine, morphia and cocaine," declaring that they possessed aphrodisiac properties. The evil effects of cocaine are notorious, among them being mental apathy and moral degeneration.

Apparently strychnine fascinated Cream, not only did he use it medicinally himself, but most probably also to procure abortion, for which purpose, like all other drugs, it is valueless, as it has no specific action upon the uterus. It was probably sheer love of inflicting pain that led Cream to select this drug for despatching his victims. His medical knowledge must have made him acquainted with other poisons equally noxious and much more difficult to trace.

Cream was devoid of all sense of social obligation and without sympathy with or understanding of the suffering of others. It could be helpful to have known if as a child he displayed this insensibility, if he was abnormally cruel or addicted to obscenity, lying and boastfulness. He possessed the traits and characteristics common to habitual murderers, boastfulness, lying, cunning, hypocrisy, remorselessness. He was talkative to a degree fatal to his safety. As for example, he was reckless in his confidences to casual acquaintances on board the "Sarnia" when on his way from

Thomas Neill Cream.

Liverpool to Halifax in 1892, giving it out as his opinion that London was the best place to live in and constantly talking about the women of the street in that city. He said that he had made a special study of poisons and boasted that he habitually took morphia. He admitted that he had practised abortion on many women. It is said that he drank to excess during the voyage. Similar testimony was given at the trial by M'Culloch, Haynes and others. He was described as a degenerate of "filthy desires and practices."

It need scarcely be said that there is no adequate motive for murder, nor for legal purposes need any motive be found. The motive sometimes attributed to Cream was his desire to procure money by blackmail. But in England in no case did he follow up his blackmailing letters by any attempt to extort money, nor the murder of the women was not necessary to provide material for threatening letters. In only one of his murders was it clearly proved that his motive was the gaining of money, namely, the murder of Stott in America. These letters, as also many of his conversations, seem to have been sheer bravado.

His actions were probably governed by a mixture of sexual mania and Sadism. He may have had a half crazy delight in feeling that the lives of the wretched women whom he slew lay in his power, that he was the arbiter of their fates. It is, of course, possible but I think not probable, that he wreaked vengeance on these "unfortunate" women because he had acquired in early life disease from contact with a prostitute. Sensuality, cruelty and lust o power urged him on. We may picture him walking at night the dreary, mean streets and byways of Lambeth, seeking for prey, on some of whom to satisfy his lust, on others to exercise his passion for cruelty; his drug sodden, remorseless mind exalted in a frenzy of horrible joy.

Whatever exactly he was, the halter was his just award.

Thomas Neill Cream

Leading Dates in the Cream Case

1850	27 May—Thomas Neill Cream born at Glasgow
1854 5	Family emigrates to Canada
1872	1 October—Enters McGill College, Montreal
1876	31 March—Graduates
	Marries Flora Eliza Brooks
	October—Pays first visit to London
1878	March—Returns to Canada
1880	23 August—Accused of Murder of Julia Faulkner at Chicago
1881	1 November—Imprisoned with life sentence for murder of Daniel Stott, at Chicago
1891	31 July—Released and returns to Canada
	1 October—Lands at Liverpool
	5 ,, —Reaches London
	6 ,, —Meets Masters and May
	9 ,, —Meets Matilda Clover
	13 ,, —Murder of Ellen Donworth
	20 ,, —Murder of Clover
1892	7 January—Sails for Canada
	23 March—Sails from New York for Liverpool
	24 ,, —Reaches London
	11-12 April—Murder of Marsh and Shrivell
	3 June—Arrested on charge of blackmailing
	21 July—Charged with murder &c. at Bow Street
	17 October—Trial at Central Criminal Court commences
	21 ,, —Found guilty and sentenced to death
	15 November—Execution at Newgate

THE TRIAL

WITHIN THE

CENTRAL CRIMINAL COURT

OLD BAILEY, LONDON

MONDAY 17th OCTOBER, 1892

Judge—

Mr JUSTICE HAWKINS

Counsel for the Crown—

THE ATTORNEY-GENERAL (*Sir Charles Russell, QC, MP*)

The Hon BERNARD COLERIDGE, QC, MP

Mr HENRY SUTTON

Mr CHARLES FREDERICK GILL

(Instructed by the Director of Public Prosecutions)

Counsel for the Prisoner—

Mr. GEOGHEGAN

Mr H WARBURTON

Mr CLIFFORD LUXMOORE DREW

Mr W HOWEL SCRATION.

(Instructed by Messrs Waters & Bryan)

First Day—Monday, 17th October, 1892.

Thomas Neill, thirty-eight,* was indicted for the wilful murder of Alice Marsh, Ellen Donworth, Emma Shrivell and Matilda Clover; also for sending to Joseph Harper a letter demanding money with menaces without any reasonable or probable cause; for sending a similar letter to William Henry Broadbent; and for attempting to administer to Louisa Harris a large quantity of strychnine with intent to murder her.

The prisoner pleaded "Not Guilty."

The indictment charging the prisoner with the wilful murder of Matilda Clover was proceeded with.

Opening Speech for the Crown

The ATTORNEY-GENERAL† said that the prisoner, whose name was Thomas Neill Cream, stood indicted under the name by which he was better known in this country, namely, of Thomas Neill, with the murder of a young woman named Matilda Clover on 20th October, 1891, the means employed being the administration of strychnine. Matilda Clover lived at 27 Lambeth Road, and belonged to the class of persons known as "unfortunates." She had one child. The prisoner would appear from a baptismal certificate found amongst his effects to have been born about 19th May, 1850,‡ and he would therefore now be about forty-two years of age. His father seems to have been a native of Scotland, living in Glasgow, but he emigrated when the prisoner was a child to the Continent of America, and lived for a considerable time in Quebec, Canada. The prisoner appeared to have received a medical education in America, and styled himself, probably having received some American degree, a Doctor of Medicine.§

---

* Actually aged forty-two.

† At first Cream sat composedly on a chair in the corner of the dock, but during the Attorney-General's opening speech his attitude became one of keen and close attention. His mouth twitched and his hands shifted uneasily. At the time of the trial he wore a full moustache and beard of reddish brown. His face was pale.—*The Daily Telegraph*, 18th October, 1892.

‡ Actually 27th May, 1850.

§ See page 2 of Introduction.

Thomas Neill Cream.

Attorney General

He arrived in this country from America on 1st October, 1891, at Liverpool and a few days later came on to London, putting up at Anderton's Hotel in Fleet Street. While living at Anderton's Hotel he met in the streets a young woman named Eliza Masters. He accompanied her to her place of abode, Orient Buildings, which front upon Hercules Road, and later, in her company, he went to Gatti's Music Hall. At the music hall Eliza Masters met a friend named Elizabeth May. Both these persons belonged to the class already referred to. After leaving Gatti's Music Hall they went in the direction of Ludgate Hill. Prisoner left them, saying that he was going up Fleet Street to his hotel, and told Eliza Masters that he would write to her in a few days appointing to pay her a further visit. He appeared to have been looking out for lodgings, and on 7th October he went to lodge at the house of Mrs. Sleaper, 103 Lambeth Palace Road. On 9th October Eliza Masters received a letter, since destroyed, stating that the writer would come to see her between three and five o'clock that afternoon. The writer identified himself by referring to their companionship at Gatti's Music Hall, and he added in the letter something that would prove to be significant, namely, that the letter was not to be destroyed, as he wanted to get it when he came to see her.

Having received this letter and expecting this visitor, Eliza Masters and her friend, Elizabeth May, to whom she mentioned the expected visit, were on the lookout before the coming of the visitor, and as they watched from their window they saw on the opposite side of the street a young woman, the murdered woman, known as Matilda Clover, walking along in the direction of Lambeth Road. She was carrying a basket, and wore an apron with strings over her shoulders. She was known to Eliza Masters and Elizabeth May by appearance, but not by name. Following Matilda Clover was the visitor whom Eliza Masters and Elizabeth May were expecting, the prisoner at the bar. There was no doubt of his identification. He was following the girl, and he was seen to turn round as if recognising the fact that she was being followed. When he had passed the house the two young women, their curiosity being excited, came down into the street and followed Matilda Clover and the prisoner. They saw the girl go to the door of No. 27 Lambeth Road, saw the prisoner follow her to that door, saw the girl stop upon the threshold of that door until he came up, and saw both go into that house

Opening Speech for the Crown.

Attorney General

The two young women, Masters and May, waited in the street to see whether the prisoner would come out, and as he did not they went back, after waiting about half an hour, to their residence in Orient Buildings. It did not appear that either of the young women met the prisoner again except on one occasion a few days later, when May saw him going past Orient Buildings in the direction of Lambeth Road.

They had no evidence of what transpired between 9th October and 20th October, but on 20th October, the day on which it was alleged Matilda Clover was murdered, a circumstance of grave importance came to the knowledge of the servant at No. 27 Lambeth Road, where Matilda Clover lived with her child. That house was tenanted by a Mrs. Vowles or Phillips, and the rooms which Matilda Clover occupied were two rooms on the second floor. The servant of the house was named Lucy Rose. On the morning of 20th October Lucy Rose, the servant, found in Matilda Clover's room an open letter, addressed to Matilda Clover, which she read. Its purport was to invite Matilda Clover to meet the writer of the letter outside the Canterbury Music Hall at 7.30 that evening, 20th October. In that letter, as there had been in the letter addressed to Masters, was also an injunction that Matilda Clover should not destroy the letter, but should bring it with her when she was keeping the asked-for appointment, together with the envelope in which it was enclosed. Clover asked Rose to help her to put her child to bed, and appeared to have left the house in time to keep the appointment at 7.30. Later, the exact hour not being fixed but probably between eight and nine o'clock, Clover returned to 27 Lambeth Road, accompanied by a man. She and her companion were let in by Lucy Rose, who would give a description of him. She described him as a tall, broad man, of some forty years of age, with a heavy moustache and no whiskers. The jury would see photographs of the prisoner at that time, at which time he did in fact wear a heavy moustache, and no whiskers or other hair on his face. It would appear that after Lucy Rose had let in these two persons Clover went out, returning and bringing, it was supposed, some bottled beer. A little later Lucy Rose heard the door open and Clover apparently letting the man out of the house who had been her companion; she also heard some word of good-night spoken between them. There was no direct evidence that the prisoner—supposing him to be as the prosecution said he was, the

Thomas Neill Cream.

Attorney General

man who was let into the house—met Clover again that evening. But she undoubtedly went out later. Lucy Rose went to bed at ten o'clock that night, and according to the evidence of Mrs. Vowles or Philips, she saw Matilda Clover come in at a later period in the night. Mrs. Vowles retired to bed, but there was no accurate means of fixing when Clover did so. It was probable that she did not go to bed immediately on returning to the house.

At three o'clock in the morning the house was aroused by the shrieks of one in agony. Mrs. Vowles and Lucy Rose went to the room in which Clover lived and found her in great pain, lying across the bed, her head wedged in between the mattress and the wall, and obviously suffering the greatest agony. There was no doubt that Clover was given to excess of drinking like so many of her class, and there was equally no doubt that Mrs. Vowles and Lucy Rose thought that drink was the cause of her illness. Matilda Clover made at that moment certain statements which he would touch further just then. A doctor was sent for, and the assistant of a doctor, a gentleman of the name of Coppin, arrived. He did something to give her relief, and he also appeared to be under the impression that the girl was under the influence of drink. His treatment did not produce the hoped-for effect, and after intervals of agony and convulsions, which there was no doubt were of such character and such as would have been caused by a fatal dose of strychnine, Matilda Clover expired—after suffering for over four hours—at 8.45 a.m. on 21st October.

On 22nd October, the next day, Dr. Graham gave a certificate under circumstances of the grossest culpability. He certified that he had attended Matilda Clover during her last illness, but he really had not attended her at all on that occasion. The illness began in the early morning of 21st October and ended at 8.45 a.m. on that day. He had not attended her or seen her. He certified that her age was stated to be twenty-seven years, that she died on 21st October at Lambeth Road, and that to the best of his knowledge and belief the primary cause of her death was delirium tremens, and the secondary cause syncope. On 22nd October Matilda Clover was buried at Tooting by the parish authorities. They had reached this stage. Matilda Clover's wretched and obscure life was closed. She was lying in a pauper's grave, thought of and remembered by few. Only one person living could know that a fearful tragedy had been enacted in her case.

Opening Speech for the Crown.

Attorney General

and that person was the one who had administered to her the fatal dose of strychnine which resulted in her death.

In this same month of October a startling event, indeed, took place. The exact day in October the witness who spoke to it, Miss Sleaper, the daughter of the prisoner's landlady, could not tell. But the fact itself fixed the date as closely following upon the event of 21st October. The prisoner told Miss Sleaper there was a young girl in Lambeth Road, a young girl with a child, who, he suspected, had been poisoned, and he wanted Miss Sleaper to go to Lambeth Road to inquire whether in fact she was dead. Miss Sleaper was at first disposed to yield to this request. But later on it seemed to her to be altogether so strange that she declined. At a later period the prisoner referred to the fact of her having so declined.

Another extraordinary thing occurred a little later. There had been no suggestion by any one of foul play in the case of Matilda Clover, still less any suggestion of strychnine as being the cause of her death. Yet, on 28th November, 1891, the prisoner wrote this letter in the assumed name of M. Malone—

London, 28th November, 1891.

D. W. H. Broadbent

Sir,

Mrs. Clover, who until a short time ago, lived at 27 Lambeth Road, S.E., died at the above address on 20th October (last month) through being poisoned with strychnine. After her death a search of her effects was made, and evidence was found which showed that you not only gave her the medicine which caused her death, but that you had been hired for the purpose of poisoning her. This evidence is in the hands of one of our detectives, who will give the evidence either to you or to the police authorities for the sum of 2500*l*. (two thousand five hundred pounds sterling). You can have the evidence for 2500*l*., and so that you save yourself from ruin. If the matter is disposed of to the police it will, of course, be made public by being placed in the papers, and ruin you for ever. You know well enough that an accusation of that sort will ruin you for ever. Now, sir, if you want the evidence for 2500*l*., just put a personal in the *Daily Chronicle*, saying that you will pay Malone 2500*l*. for his services, and I will send a party to settle this matter. If you do not want the evidence, of course, it will be turned over to the police at once and published and your ruin will surely follow. Think well before you decide on this matter. It is just this—2500*l*. feeling, on the one hand, and ruin, shame, and disgrace on the other. Answer by personal on the first page of the *Daily Chronicle* any time next week. I am not humbugging you. I have evidence strong enough to ruin you for ever.

M. MALONE.

Thomas Neill Cream.

Attorney General

Dr Broadbent is, as the jury knew, a man of very high eminence in his profession, a man upon whom a threat of that kind would have no effect, would probably have no other but the opposite to the desired result. But the prisoner had only recently arrived from America, and might not have known what the position and standing, and still less have known the character, of Dr Broadbent were. It might be that he thought that what he said in the letter would be sufficient to insure his being bought off from making the accusation. The importance, however, of the letter was this—that they had there in the handwriting of the prisoner the statement of death by strychnine poisoning, and that at a time when no one else living but the person who administered the strychnine could have known that it had been the means of causing Clover's death.

It would appear that in November, 1891, the prisoner had made the acquaintance of a young lady of respectable position, the daughter of a lady living at Berkhamstead. In the month of December he proposed marriage to that young lady, and was accepted by her. On 6th January, 1892, he made a will in her favour, which, he told her, was irrevocable. It was not so in fact. On 7th January, 1892, he sailed from Liverpool for America and Canada. In the latter country he made the acquaintance of a gentleman of the name of M'Culloch, who would be called. Both had been staying for some time at Blanchard's Hotel in Quebec. They became, apparently, intimate, the prisoner being there confidential in his statements to Mr M'Culloch. He showed him a case of medicines and bottles of pills, together with certain capsules, to which further reference would be made, and also a bottle which apparently contained a very large quantity of strychnine. In reference to the use to which the pills were put, they would find from the evidence of Mr M'Culloch that the prisoner said he used them for the purpose of preventing childbirth. He described the life he had been leading in London in connection with women—women of the class already referred to, and mentioned also that he had been in the habit of using disguises, false whiskers, or things of that kind. While in America he had been in communication with a drug company called the Harvey Drug Company for the purpose of becoming their agent for the sale of their medicines in this country. He appeared to have purchased from that company a considerable quantity of their medicines, principally pills. On 2nd April, 1892, he again returned to London. After some days spent chiefly in the country

Opening Speech for the Crown.

Attorney General

he returned on 9th April to reside as he had done before at 103 Lambeth Palace Road and there he continued to reside until the time of his arrest.

Certain appalling events took place before the end of April 1892. The death of a woman called Donworth or Linnell had occurred in October of the previous year, that death being caused by poison, that poison being strychnine. Then on 11th April, 1892, occurred two other appalling deaths—those of Emma Shrivell and Alice Marsh. All those three persons—Donworth, Marsh, and Shrivell—were members of the "unfortunate" class and all had lived on the south side of the river, not far from the neighbourhood of Lambeth Road, Orient Buildings and Lambeth Palace Road. These matters had naturally been the subject of conversation, and towards the end of April it came to the knowledge of the police that another woman of the same class, about whose death there had been no previous suspicion entertained—namely, Matilda Clover—had met with her death under remarkable circumstances. Matilda Clover's death having come to the knowledge of Inspector Harvey he immediately applied for and obtained an order from the Home Office on 30th April, 1892, authorising the exhumation of the body of Matilda Clover for the purposes of medical, scientific examination. Just about this time the prisoner said to Miss Sleaper, referring to his former request, that it was perhaps just as well that she had not gone round to inquire about the girl's death, because there was going to be an investigation into that case.

About this time the prisoner made the acquaintance of a man named Haynes, who lived at the house of a Mr. and Mrs. Armstead, 129 Westminster Bridge Road. The prisoner had been there on more than one occasion for the purpose of being photographed. In this way he came to know Mr. and Mrs. Armstead, and through them their friend, Mr. Haynes. Mr. Haynes would tell them that on 4th May, 1892, the prisoner told him that a young Dr. Harper had poisoned Matilda Clover, Alice Marsh and Emma Shrivell, that he had also poisoned Lou Harvey, that he (the prisoner) knew Marsh and Shrivell well, and had often warned them against Harper, and cautioned them against taking anything that Harper should give them to take. Up to that moment in the stages of the story the name of Lou Harvey had not occurred. But Lou Harvey was alive and well, and would appear as a witness. Later on he stated

Thomas Neill Cream.

Attorney General

systematically his reasons for suspecting Harper in relation to Lou Harvey. Haynes's curiosity was excited. He asked where Lou Harvey had lived, and he was shown by the prisoner No 55 Townshend Street, St John's Wood, as the house in which the murdered Lou Harvey had lived.

On 3rd June, 1892, the prisoner was arrested on the charge of sending a threatening letter to Dr Harper,* to which charge his answer was, "You have got the wrong man. Fire away." He was at Bow Street on that charge off and on from the 4th to the 28th of June. Meanwhile, following on the exhumation of the body of Matilda Clover, Dr Stevenson having had portions of the viscera—stomach, liver, and so forth submitted to him, had made an analysis with the result that he discovered the presence of strychnine and came to the conclusion that a fatal dose had been administered, and that it was the cause of her death. On various days between 2nd June and 13th July an inquest was held on the body of Clover at Tooting, and Neill was present during the proceedings. He (the Attorney-General) made no comment, but merely stated the fact that it was conveyed to Neill that he had an opportunity, if he desired to take it, of giving evidence at that inquiry. Indeed, the coroner went the length of asking him questions, which Neill declined to answer. The verdict of the coroner's jury, on the inquisition upon which the prisoner is arraigned here as well as upon the direct indictment, was "wilful murder." The prisoner was then brought before the magistrate at Bow Street, and after a protracted inquiry he was committed for trial for the various offences with which he was now charged.

The jury would observe that the prisoner, in certain letters had referred to the cases of Donworth, Marsh, Shrivell and Harvey as murder by poisoning. He must make some statement with reference to the facts which it was proposed to prove in relation to those cases. It would be convenient if he now stated broadly the grounds on which, after anxious care, his friends and himself had thought that those facts ought to be laid before the jury. They did not know, they could not anticipate, what might be the special points upon which his friend, whose valuable assistance the prisoner possessed, might seek to rely. They submitted—and if objection was

---

* Father of the above named "young" Mr Harper

Opening Speech for the Crown.

Attorney General

taken at a later stage by his friend it would be discussed—they contended that evidence of those facts was admissible in order to prove that Neill was in possession of and was dealing with strychnine; that strychnine was really the cause of the death into which they were inquiring so as to negative any suggestion of accident; that Neill was brought into similar relations with Marsh and Shrivell so as to support the identity of the prisoner; that the motive was to create an opportunity of making false charges against other persons. Lastly, he would submit, if there should be any question, that the evidence proved from the systematic and deliberate mode of procedure of the prisoner that he understood in all its gravity the nature of the act he was committing, if he, in fact, did commit the act. The statements of the prisoner himself rendered it impossible to exclude this evidence.

The first of these cases in the order of date was the case of Ellen Donworth. He wished at once to say that the prosecution admitted that the evidence, the direct evidence, was not sufficient to connect the prisoner with the murder of Ellen Donworth. He would have been quite content to have passed this case, but his learned friend had intimated that he desired all the circumstances to be submitted to the jury.

These were the facts. Ellen Donworth lived at 8 Duke Street, Westminster Bridge Road. On 13th October, in consequence of a letter she had received, she had gone out between six and seven p.m. Later on the same night she fell down in the street, obviously in great agony. She was treated with care at her home, and then taken to St. Thomas's Hospital in a cab, but died on the way. She made in her agony certain statements in which she referred to a man. He would not detail those statements, because a question might arise as to the proof of the necessary conditions which would make them admissible. But he was entitled to say that she did make a statement, and that she did in connection with that statement give a description of a man. On 15th October an inquest was held upon her. On 19th October the prisoner wrote the following letter to Mr. Wyatt, the deputy coroner:—

London, 19th October, 1891.

G. P. Wyatt, Esq., Deputy Coroner,
East Surrey.

I am writing to say that if you and your satellites fail to bring

Thomas Neill Cream.

Attorney General

the murderer of Ellen Donworth *alias* Ellen Linnell, late of 8 Duke Street, Westminster Bridge Road to justice that I am willing to give you such assistance as will bring the murderer to justice, provided your Government is willing to pay me 300,000*l* for my services. No pay if not successful.

A. O'Brien, Detective.

The inquest was held and on 22nd October the jury found a verdict of death by poisoning with strychnine and morphia by some person unknown.

On 5th November 1891, the prisoner wrote a letter to Mr. Frederick W. D. Smith M.P., son of Mr. W. H. Smith 186 Strand, signed "H. Bayne" in these terms:—

Sir,
On Tuesday night, 13th October (last month) a girl named Ellen Donworth, but sometimes calling herself Ellen Linnell, who lived at 8 Duke Street, Westminster Bridge Road, was poisoned with strychnine. After her death, among her effects were found two letters incriminating you which, if ever they become public property will surely convict you of the crime. I enclose you a copy of one of the letters which the girl received on the morning of 13th October (the day on which she died). Just read it, and then judge for yourself what hope you have of escape if the law officers ever get hold of those letters. Think of the shame and disgrace it will bring on your family if you be arrested and put in prison for this crime. My object in writing you is to ask if you will retain me at once as your counsellor and legal adviser. If you employ me at once to act for you in this matter I will save you from all exposure and shame in the matter, but if you will wait till arrested before retaining me, then I cannot save you as no lawyer can save you after the authorities get hold of those two letters. If you wish to retain me just write a few lines on paper saying "Mr. Fred Smith wishes to see Mr. Bayne the barrister at once." Paste this on one of your shop windows at 186 Strand next Tuesday morning, and when I see it I will drop in and have a private interview with you. I can save you if you retain me in time, but not otherwise.

Yours truly,
H. Bayne

Mr. Frederick Smith

In that letter was enclosed a document addressed to Miss Ellen Linnell and signed "H. M. B." which stated that the writer had written to her and warned her that Frederick Smith of W. H. Smith & Son was going to poison her, and that the writer had seen Frederick Smith prepare a medicine and saw him put enough strychnine in it to kill a horse and if she took any of it she would die

Opening Speech for the Crown.

Attorney General

On 16th November a letter enclosed in an envelope in the prisoner's handwriting, was sent to Mr. Horace Smith, the magistrate at Clerkenwell, stating that he had enough evidence to hang Mr. Frederick Smith and that he would make it hot for the police if they did not take action in the matter.

At the inquiry into the case of Ellen Donworth at Bow Street one of the witnesses who were called to speak to the identity of the prisoner not only did not identify him, but came to the conclusion which she expressed, that Neill was not the man she had seen in company with Donworth.

The next case to be laid before you was that of Lou Harvey, *alias* Harris, a very remarkable and important case. She resides at 44 Townshend Street, St. John's Wood, with a painter and glazier named Harvey, whose name she took, her real name being Louisa Harris. About 21st October 1891 she saw the prisoner and entered into conversation with him at the Alhambra. Afterwards she met him outside St. James's Hall, Piccadilly, and went with him to a hotel in Soho, where she passed the night with him. Next morning the prisoner noticed, or affected to notice, certain spots on her forehead, and he told her he would give her some pills which would have the effect of taking them away. He made an appointment for that purpose to meet her on the Embankment the following evening at 8 o'clock. She told Harvey, who thought it was a strange business. She went to keep the appointment accompanied by Harvey. The prisoner was there. Harvey stood some little way off. The prisoner told her that he was a doctor at St. Thomas's Hospital and produced some pills, which she described as "long pills," and which he asked her to swallow. She took them in her hand and attempted to swallow them, but really transferred them to her other hand. The prisoner asked her to show him her hands, that he might be convinced she had followed his instructions. She let the pills fall from her hand and showed him her hand. The prisoner then somewhat hastily bade her " Good night," and offered to call her a cab. She expressed a wish to go to a music hall as he had suggested, but the prisoner said he could not go with her as he had an appointment at St. Thomas's Hospital, but would join her at 11 o'clock. She kept the appointment and was at the music hall, but the prisoner did not turn up. Some time later she again met the prisoner, but on that occasion he apparently did not recognise her. She told him who she was, and in view of what subsequently happened

Thomas Neill Cream.

Attorney General

it is pretty clear that he did not know her again, for they found him at a later date telling Haynes that Lou Harvey had been poisoned, and that she had dropped down dead outside a music hall. And he pointed out the house in Townshend Street, St. John's Wood, as the place where Lou Harvey had lived. But an extraordinary thing in relation to this matter was that the woman, who lived at 44 Townshend Street had given him 55 as her address, and it was No. 55 that was pointed out by the prisoner to Haynes. These facts were communicated to the police by Haynes. Inquiries made by the police resulted in finding a living Lou Harvey, not a dead one. It was not until the evidence of Haynes was given before the Coroner, in which the name of Lou Harvey came out, that this young woman most properly communicated with Sir John Bridge and told the story which he had narrated to them.

He now came to the last of these tragical instances—the deaths of Alice Marsh and Emma Shrivell. Marsh and Shrivell, who lived at 118 Stamford Street, occupying two rooms on the second floor. On 9th April, 1892, as we know, the prisoner, as the jury would remember, returned to take up his permanent abode in Lambeth Palace Road. As Miss Sleaper's evidence would show, two days later, contrary to his custom, he dined early, and said he had an engagement and would be late that night. Early next morning, 12th April, at 1.45 a.m., a police-constable named Cumley was on his beat in Stamford Street, within a few yards of No. 118, the door was opened and a man was let out by a young woman and came into the street. The constable would describe that man to the jury. The description of the man was fixed in his recollection by a circumstance of a fearful nature which occurred a short time later. That circumstance was this—Between 2 and 3 a.m. on the same morning Police-Constable Eversfield was called by the landlord of 118 Stamford Street to that house. When he arrived there he found the two women, Alice Marsh and Emma Shrivell, suffering intermittent agony with tetanic convulsions which lasted for a minute or a minute and a half, then ceased, and then recurred, accompanied by rigidity of the muscles, the signs and symptoms of strychnine poisoning. A certain description was given by one of the women and a certain statement made which he forbore to give to the jury at that moment for the reason he had already given. The women were put into a cab and taken to the hospital. Marsh died in the cab on the way. Shrivell

Opening Speech for the Crown.

Attorney General

died in the hospital after prolonged suffering at about 8.15 that morning, 12th April 1892. An inquest was held on 13th April, and the proceedings were fully reported in the press.

On Easter Monday, 18th April, Neill proceeded to make a series of detailed inquiries from his landlady's daughter, Miss Sleaper, as to the position of a young gentleman, Dr. Walter J. Harper, who was living as a lodger in the same house. That gentleman had just obtained his degree as a doctor of medicine. He was the son of Dr. Joseph Harper of Barnstaple. Apparently, although living in the same house, the prisoner and he had not become acquainted. On 25th April the prisoner wrote and forwarded by post to Dr. Joseph Harper a letter bearing that date. It was signed, "W. H. Murray," and was as follows:—

London, 25th April 1892

Dr. Harper, Barnstaple.

Dear Sir,

I am writing to inform you that one of my operators has indisputable evidence that your son, W. J. Harper, a medical student at St. Thomas's Hospital, poisoned two girls named Alice Marsh and Emma Shrivell on the 12th inst. and that I am willing to give you the said evidence (so that you can suppress it) for the sum of 1500*l* sterling. The evidence in my hands is strong enough to convict and hang your son, but I shall give it to you for 1500*l* sterling, or sell it to the police for the same amount. The publication of the evidence will ruin you and your family for ever, and you know that as well as I do. To show you that what I am writing is true, I am willing to send you a copy of the evidence against your son, so that when you read it you will need no one to tell you that it will convict your son. Answer my letter at once through the columns of the London *Daily Chronicle* as follows:— "W. H. M.—Will pay you for your services.—Dr. H." After I see this in paper I will communicate with you again. As I said before, I am perfectly willing to satisfy you that I have strong evidence against your son by giving you a copy of it before you pay me a penny. If you do not answer it at once, I am going to give evidence to the Coroner at once.

Yours respectfully,

W. H. MURRAY.

The constable who saw the man leave 118 Stamford Street at once gave a description of him, and on 12th May he saw Neill in the Lambeth Palace Road and formed the opinion that he was the same man he had seen on the early morning of 12th April leaving 118 Stamford Street. Observation was kept on the movements of the prisoner, who appeared towards the latter part of May to have

Thomas Neill Cream.

Attorney General

complained to Sergeant McIntyre of being watched. Prisoner also told the sergeant that Shrivell had received two letters of warning against Harper. On one occasion, hearing the newsboys shouting out news of an arrest, the prisoner wished to stop the omnibus on which he was riding, and, after showing great signs of trepidation, purchased a paper, and appeared to be pleased that the news was in reference to another case and not to that of the murdered girls.

At the prisoner's lodgings after his arrest was found a curious bit of paper. The writing on it was in pencil, and the full purport of what was written might not have been ascertained. On one of the metals "M. C." were two dates, and the third date 20th October, the date of the death of the girl Clover. On the same paper, in connection with the words "L. S." was found writing in the prisoner's hand of two dates—one 11th April, which was the date of Shrivell's death. There was also found in his possession a paper with the address of Marsh and Shrivell, and it would be proved that he had on more than one occasion said that he knew them well.

Now, as regards the facts, there could be no doubt that Clover, Marsh and Shrivell died of strychnine poisoning. The question was, who administered it? That the prisoner had access to strychnine there was no doubt. From the evidence of Lou Harvey and from other circumstances, probably in each case strychnine was administered in gelatine capsules in which the strychnine, in states of pills, were placed. The prisoner had in his possession many minute pills containing from one-sixteenth to one-twentieth part of a grain. Half a grain might be a fatal dose. The evidence would show that as many as 20 of these pills could be put into one of these capsules, and there would be no difficulty, therefore, in administering a fatal dose. How did the prisoner get the capsules and strychnine? Early in October he ordered from a chemist a considerable number of gelatine capsules, and those supplied in the first instance being too large, he required them to be changed. Some were then supplied a little more than half the size of the original capsule. That the prisoner had strychnine would be apparent from what was found in his possession, and signing himself "M.D." as he claimed he was entitled to do, there would have been no difficulty in his obtaining strychnine. Returning again to the case of Matilda Clover, it was clear that the prisoner knew and visited her, that she died of poison, that the person who administered that poison did so with murderous

Opening Speech for the Crown.

Attorney General

intent that the late Mrs. Donworth, the indeed assistant Coroner, Dr. Graham, all treated this as a case of death caused by drink, that there was no suggestion by any one of strychnine poisoning, that no living person knew or could have known that she had been poisoned and poisoned by strychnine, except the man who administered it; and yet within a short time of her death they had the prisoner attempting through Mrs. Sleaper to make much of... they had his letter to Dr. Broadbent in which, in his own hand, the statement was clearly made that the death was caused by strychnine. What explanation there could be of this fact he could not guess.

The prisoner had the great advantage of the assistance of his learned friend and able colleague, Mr. Geoghegan. He would no attempt—he could not successfully attempt—to anticipate what his defence would be. But one thing at least he might say, that, remarkable—in many directions, in accordance—as some circumstances of this strange case might be, one thing at least stood out apparent and distinct. It was recorded under the hand of the prisoner's own pen that if he was the man who was guilty of the crime laid to his charge, he well knew and understood the nature and quality of his act.

Evidence for the Prosecution

JOHN HAYNES examined—I am a civil engineer, lately... of the Sir Walter Raleigh New Street, Grand... Houndsditch... 1889 and 1891 I was in Chicago, America, and I knew the prisoner very well, he was a practising physician there at the time. I knew him by the name of Thomas Neill Cream.

MISS BEARDS examined—In October 1891 I was book-keeper at Anderton's Hotel, Fleet Street. This (produced) is the hotel register. I find that on 5th October a Dr. Neill came to the hotel, and he is marked off on the 7th as leaving.

JAMES AITCHISON examined by Mr C. F. Gill—I am an optician at 47 Fleet Street. On 9th October 1891 the prisoner came to me and I examined his eye. He told me that he came from America. I found his left eye was very much more defective than his right. It

Thomas Neill Cream.

turned inwards towards the nose, giving him a decided squint. He ordered two pairs of spectacles which were supplied to him on 17th October. I saw him again in April this year.

ELIZABETH MASTERS, examined by the ATTORNEY-GENERAL—In October, 1891, I was living at Orient Buildings, which face into the Hercules Road. Turning out of Orient Buildings and to the left you come to the Lambeth Road. I had three rooms on the second floor. In the next room to me lived Elizabeth May. Early in that month I met the prisoner at Ludgate Circus. I think it was on a Tuesday. He asked me to have a glass of wine. We went to the King Lud. From there he accompanied me to Orient Buildings. It was a very wet night. From Orient Buildings we went to Gatti's Music Hall. I there met Elizabeth May. I had promised to meet her before I went. I introduced her to the prisoner. The prisoner was wearing a dark mackintosh and a square topped felt hat. At the music hall he told me he had come from abroad to claim some property. I cannot recollect if he said what he was. He said that in his younger days he was a student at St. Thomas's Hospital. He showed me a photograph of his mother and one of himself. He said he was staying at a hotel in Fleet Street. While he showed me the photographs he took off his hat. I think he had glasses on at the time. I noticed a peculiar look in his eyes, and that he had a squint. I think he put his glasses on in the music hall. He, May and I went from the music hall together to Ludgate Circus. Before we left the music hall I gave him my address, and I expected to see him again, because he told me he would write to me when he got settled in his apartments.

That was on a Tuesday, and on the following Friday, 9th October, I received a letter, which I destroyed after keeping it about three months. In the letter he told me that he was going to call that day between three and five o'clock, and that I was not to be so cross as I was on the Tuesday night. I knew it was from him, because I did not expect a letter from any one else, and because he told me it was from the gentleman I went to the music hall with. The letter said I was not to destroy it, but to keep it till he called, as he should expect to see it again that afternoon. I told May I expected him and showed her the letter. When the time came between three and five o'clock, I and May were sitting at the window looking out into the street for this gentleman to come. On the same side of the street

Evidence for Prosecution.

Elizabeth Masters

as our house I saw Matilda Clover come carrying a basket, and wearing a white apron with shoulder straps and a hat. She was going towards the Lambeth Road. I did not know her to speak to or by name, but I had noticed her pass the house three or four times and knew her by appearance. No. 27 Lambeth Road is ten or thirty yards from us, I should think, round the corner. (Shown a photograph.) This is a photograph of the woman I saw that day. I have no doubt about it. I noticed the prisoner following her, and I saw her turn round and smile at him. He had on a silk hat and dark clothes. I put on my hat and asked May to do the same, and we followed to the corner to see where he went. I stood at the corner and saw Clover stand at the door of No. 27, where she lived, with the handle of her basket looking towards the prisoner, who had followed her. He came up to the door, followed Clover into the house, and then the door was shut. I waited there for quite half an hour, but he did not come out.

Who was the man who went in with her?—The prisoner. I then went away. I did not see him again until I saw him at the Police Court. May told me that she had seen him again. I remember hearing afterwards that Clover had died from a dream of means.

Cross-examined by Mr. Geoghegan.—I did not see the prisoner from October, 1891, to 17th June, 1892, eight months later. Inspector Tunbridge asked me to go to Bow Street police station to identify a man. He said he heard I had been to the music hall with a man whom I had seen go with the woman Clover.

When you went to Bow Street police station did you expect to find at the Court the man you had seen going by?— Yes. After I had been two or three minutes at the station I was called in by some one to look at a number of gentlemen, or men, standing in a court room or passage. All the persons had their hats on. I walked up and down in front of twice, and had a good look at them, and I failed to identify any one. I cannot tell you now many men there were. I could not say if there was a police-constable among or close to them. I don't know if a police was there. I don't know who was there. I don't know that I spoke to Tunbridge. I left the room and then I believe Elizabeth May was called in after me. I was in another room. When she came out Tunbridge called me in again. I don't know who was there, or whether they were

61

Thomas Neill Cream.

Elizabeth Masters

the same number, or whether they were the same persons. Their hats were off.

I think you were called to identify the man you had seen passing your house with a silk hat on?—Yes. I identified the prisoner with his hat off as the man I had seen at Gatti's Music Hall. Going from Carnot Buildings there is a public-house on the right-hand side where the Hercules Road comes into the Lambeth Road. I stood in my doorway and watched—not at the public-house door—I could not see 27 Lambeth Road from my door. I followed to the corner of Hercules Road, and then stood at the corner. 27 Lambeth Road was on the opposite side of the road some way down—the same side as the Masons' Arms.

When you saw the men following the girl in Hercules Road on what side of the road were they?—They were both on the same side of the road as our buildings.

On which floor is the window which you were looking out from?—On the second floor.

Was it open or shut?—It was shut.

I suppose all you got was a glimpse of them as they went by?—Yes, and then I went to the top of the steps and watched him. May was told to go to the police station at the same time as I was, and we went there together.

You both knew that you were going there to identify the men?—Yes.

And you would mention the matter as you went there?—Yes.

Did you ask her what the man was like?—No, I did not. She seemed to know better than I could. I think she knew better than I did.

Will you tell us what happened at the music hall when you went there with the prisoner?—May was sitting there, and I asked her and Neill to come and have a drink.

Were the prisoner and you along with Elizabeth May during the greater part of the performance?—No. I and the prisoner were sitting apart from May. The prisoner was my friend, and had nothing to do with May.

Re-examined by the ATTORNEY-GENERAL—I noticed that the postmark on the letter I got was Lambeth. When I went in to the identification there were a number of persons with hats on. I walked up and down and did not recognise the prisoner. On the second occasion I went in the persons' hats were off, and I then had no

Evidence for Prosecution.

Elizabeth Masters

difficulty in recognising the prisoner. I and May followed Clover and the prisoner to the corner, where we stood till they went into the house and the door was closed. After that I walked up to the door into which they had gone, and I saw the number 27 on it.

ELIZABETH MAY examined—In October last year I was living in the same building as and in the next room to Masters. I recollect being at Gatti's Music Hall one night at the end of September or in October. I saw Masters there in the prisoner's company. I spoke to them coming out. Afterwards we all three went together in a cab to Ludgate Hill, and had a drink at the King's Head. I identify the prisoner as the man. He was then wearing a hard silk hat with a square top.

A few days afterwards Masters told me something about a letter, which she showed me and asked me to read. I knew she was expecting a letter, because I heard the prisoner say "I can send it to you in a day or two." I do not remember what was in the letter, except that it was signed with two initials. I saw the sealed envelope next afternoon. In the evening of the day before I next saw Masters and I was at her window watching for the girl that was to call when we saw Clover pass, with a white apron with straps, and carrying a basket in her hand. I did not know her name, but she passed the house daily, and I recognised her as a person I had seen before. (Shown photograph of Matilda Clover.) This is a photograph of the girl I saw pass. The prisoner was following her. I have no doubt of that. The girl turned round and smiled. Masters and I put our hats on and followed them to the corner of Hercules Road and Lambeth Road. Clover was still going down Lambeth Road and the man was still following her. She stopped at the door, the prisoner went up to her, they both went in. I accompanied Masters up to see what the number was; it was No. 27. I knew that Clover lived at 27 by seeing her go into that house before. I and Masters waited there for over half an hour. No one came out, and we went home.

On the second occasion that I saw the prisoner he had on a silk hat and a dark suit. As far as I remember, he had no beard, but only a moustache. I cannot remember whether I saw the prisoner once or twice after that before I saw him at Bow Street, but I saw him passing my house going towards Lambeth Road.

How often do you think you saw him after that night in Gatti's

63

Thomas Neill Cream.

Elizabeth May

Music Hall?—I may have seen him twice. I am quite positive that I saw him passing towards the Lambeth Road. On that third occasion he had a silk hat on. I went with Masters to see whether I could identify the prisoner at Bow Street. I was shown a number of persons wearing their hats. I recognised the prisoner with his hat on. I do not know that I saw him afterwards there with his hat off. Soon after the occasion on which I and Masters followed Clover and the prisoner I heard Clover was dead.

Cross-examined by Mr. GEOGHEGAN.—I had a drink with Masters and the prisoner at the bar in the music hall, and then they went away again to look at the performance and left me.

The gentleman was with Masters and not with you?—That is so.

Were you with them again in the music hall?—Yes, I was with them again before the performance was over. We had another drink, and then I left the hall with them and we took a cab.

Did you see the prisoner at the Coroner's Court?—Yes.

Was he then sitting in Court between two warders?—Yes.

Were you brought there to identify him?—No.

Did you hear him speak?—Yes, but I could not remember his voice again.

It did not recall him to you?—No.

When you saw Matilda Clover and the prisoner pass your house on which side of the road were they?—They were on the same side of the way as the window in Orient Buildings which I and Masters looked from.

I suppose that both you and Masters had the same opportunity of seeing as you looked from the window?—Yes.

How many persons were present when you picked out the prisoner at Bow Street?—I should think there would be sixteen to twenty. I was waiting for ten minutes before I was brought into the room where the persons were. When I saw the prisoner there he had a few days growth of beard. I knew I was looking at a man who had not been able to go to the barber's or shave himself, but it was not sufficient to hide him from me.

Were there any other unshaven people there?—As far as I can remember, there were no other unshaven or unshorn people among them.

Did all the other men look respectable?—I cannot say

Evidence for Prosecution.

Elizabeth May

Did they all have top hats on?—I did not notice if they all had top hats.

Did you not see some of them whispering and chattering together?—No. I did not see a gaoler there. I cannot recollect if there was a policeman.

What did Inspector Tunbridge ask you to do?—He asked me to pick out the man who had been in Gatti's Music Hall, and I went in and picked out Neill.

Is that all?—Yes, that is all that took place.

Did you know Ellen Donworth?—No.

Did you hear anything about her falling down dead?—Yes, I either read or heard about that.

I suppose it caused a sensation—I did not take any note whether it caused a sensation or not.

Re-examined—I had an opportunity of seeing the prisoner at the music hall, at the King Lud, and passing our house. I saw he had cross eyes, a squint.

By the COURT—I first met the prisoner at Gatti's and had a drink with him. Then he and Masters went to look at the performance. We had another drink with him before we left Gatti's. He and Masters went from Gatti's in a hansom cab back to Ludgate Hill. At Bow Street Tunbridge asked me to step inside and see if I could recognise the man I saw at Gatti's. That was all he said. After that I went and looked at the men, and recognised the prisoner. That is all that took place.

WILLIAM HENRY BROADBENT, M.D., examined—I practised at 34 Seymour Street, Portman Square, on 30th November, 1891, when I received this letter by post; this letter is dated 28th November, the postmark on the envelope is " 30th November, London, W.," and on the postage stamp is the mark ' S E "

London, 28th November, 1891

Dr W. H. Broadbent
Sir,

Miss Clover who until a short time ago lived at 27 Lambeth Road, S E died at the above address on the 20th October (last month), through being poisoned by strychnine. After her death a search of her effects was made, and evidence was found which showed that you not only gave her the medicine which caused her death, but that you had been hired for the purpose of poisoning her. This evidence is in the hands

Thomas Neill Cream.

Dr William Henry Broadbent

of one of our detectives, and will give the evidence either to you or to the police authorities for the sum of 2500*l* (two thousand five hundred pounds) sterling. You can have the evidence for 2500*l* and in that way save yourself from ruin. If the matter is disposed of to the police it will, of course, be made public by being placed in the papers and ruin you for ever. You know well enough that an accusation of that sort will ruin you for ever. Now sir, if you want the evidence for 2500*l* just put a personal in the *Daily Chronicle* saying that you will pay Malone 2500*l* for his services and I will send a party to settle this matter. If you do not want the evidence of course it will be turned over to the police at once and published and your ruin will surely follow. Think well before you decide on this matter. It is just this—2500*l* sterling on the one hand, and ruin, shame and disgrace on the other. Answer by personal on the first page of the *Daily Chronicle* any time next week. I am not humbugging you. I have evidence strong enough to ruin you for ever.

M. MALONE

Cross-examined—I gave the letter to the police immediately I received it on 30th November.

The Court adjourned.

Second Day—Tuesday, 18th October, 1892

WILLIAM NIXON REECE examined—I am a police inspector of L Division. I prepared this plan of the district, it is correct. I have made twelve copies of it. It is to the scale of 1½ inches to 300 yards from measurement. It is a compass of about 2 miles or 1 square mile.

Cross-examined by Mr. GEOGHEGAN—I see on the plan the main entrance to Waterloo Station, and opposite to it are the Wellington and Lord Hill public-houses. Going down Waterloo Road on the left-hand side you come to Morpeth Place, and at the corner of the Waterloo Road and Morpeth Place is the Artisans' Dining Room and Coffee-house. I am stationed at Walworth and the district was strange to me till I went to make the plan. It is about a minute's walk from the Lord Hill public-house to Morpeth Place. I do not know if Ellen Donworth came from the Lord Hill and fell down dead. From where the New Cut intersects the Waterloo Road, near the centre of the plan, it would take fully a quarter of an hour to walk to the Lord Hill, 118 Stamford Road, and the Masons Arms—I could do it in a quarter of an hour easily.

JOHN GEORGE KIRKBY, examined by Mr. C. F. GILL—I am assistant to Mr. Priest, a chemist, of 22 Parliament Street. At the beginning of October 1891—before the 12th—the prisoner came into our shop. He said he was a medical student at St. Thomas's and gave his name as Thomas Neill. He told me he was attending a course of lectures at St. Thomas's Hospital. He asked me for some nux vomica, and that being a schedule poison I asked him for his name and address, and gave him a piece of paper, and he wrote this order—"One ounce 10 to 20 drops diluted with water," and "sulphate of quinine," and signed it "Thomas Neill, M.D., 103 Lambeth Palace Road." I supplied him with the nux vomica. A day or two afterwards he asked for some empty gelatine capsules. I told him we did not keep them in stock. He asked me to get them for him. On the same day Mr. Priest gave me an order, dated 12th October, to go to Maw, Son & Thomson, wholesale chemists, to get a box of capsules. I got a box of 100 12-grain capsules there the same day. The next day Neill came to the shop

Thomas Neill Cream.

John George Kirkby

and I showed him the capsules. He looked at them and said that they were too large; he wanted some about half the size. I afterwards went to Maw, Son & Thomson and changed the capsules, and got a box of No. 5 capsules, which were a little less than half the size. Neill did not say what he wanted the capsules for.

What are these capsules generally used for?—They are used for putting powders and solids into, in order as far as possible to render the medicine tasteless. The No. 5 capsule produced is similar to those supplied to the prisoner. A day or two afterwards Neill came to the shop again and I gave him the capsules, in a box similar to this. After that he came to our shop on different occasions up to the following January. I supplied him from time to time with nux vomica in quantities of from 1 to 4 ounces; the last time I supplied him with it was on 20th December, I see by the order. Upon each occasion I took from him a written order. This one and the first one I had from him are the only orders I have been able to find. We do not register them; it is not necessary. It comes under the second schedule and so long as it is labelled poison with the name and address of the seller it is quite sufficient.

Cross-examined by Mr GEOGHEGAN—Before 20th October I had never sold to Neill more than one ounce of nux vomica. What I sold him was the British Pharmacopœia strength, i.e. a grain of strychnine to one ounce of nux vomica. Nux vomica contains brucine. The capsules are American. They are not used for taking castor oil or sandalwood oil; sandalwood oil is sold in flexible capsules. All you want in a capsule is that it shall melt. If oil were put into one of these it would not be tasteless. All these are used for pills, powders and solids; they are not commonly used by medical men in London. We have different kinds of capsules prescribed, sometimes we prescribe these. English people prefer English capsules and foreigners prefer foreign ones. I asked the prisoner whether he was a qualified medical man. I looked through the Medical Register. I did not find his name there.

Are you in the habit of selling poisons to persons whose names you cannot find in the Register?—No. On 20th December when the prisoner gave me his last order, I sold him four ounces of nux vomica.

I suppose he would deal with you for other matters besides nux vomica and the capsules?—Yes. He used to buy an ounce, I think, of opium, not always once a week, but at least once a fortnight

Evidence for Prosecution.

John George Kirkby

Are you bound to register the sale of opium and laudanum?—Yes

Is there an entry in your books of the sale to the prisoner?—Yes. I have not the books here. There is only one entry of a prescription with opium in it.

Should there not appear in your books the times and amount of the nux vomica you sold to Neill?—No. For a sale across the counter we would not book it. The sale of opium or laudanum appears because it was a prescription and I copied it in.

By the COURT—I wrote this date "20th" at the time of the purchase. As a rule I always date the orders. It was an omission on my part not to have dated this other one.

I suppose a registered medical man has more facility of purchasing poison than a man who is not registered?—Yes.

What would you do if a stranger came and represented he was a medical man and you found he was not in the Register?—I should not supply him with poison if it was in the first schedule. A person might die from poison in the second schedule, but I should see whether the man could write a Latin prescription or not. He might be a medical student if his name was not in the Register. I did not register in our books every purchase that the prisoner made. I registered the opium because it was a prescription, and there were other ingredients. I did not register the prescription with nux vomica in it because no sulphate of quinine was mixed with it. It was an independent item. And I should not have registered the other but that he had it two or three times, and to save trouble of looking it up I took a copy of it in the book; it was not necessary to register it. I should not register it in the book ordinarily if it was for a medical man. I have no reason to give why I did not register it when I found he was not in the Register. I could not say whether my practice is followed by other chemists.

LUCY ROSE, examined by the ATTORNEY-GENERAL—I live now at 19 Merrow Street, Walworth Road. In October, 1892, I was living as a servant to Mrs. Phillips (who is also known as Mrs. Vowles) at 27 Lambeth Road. I was there five weeks in all; I left a fortnight after Matilda Clover died. She was living there when I went into the service, occupying the top floor consisting of two rooms. She was 27 years old and had a little boy about two years old living

Thomas Neill Cream.

Lucy Rose with her. (Shown a photograph.) This is a photograph of her. There was no other young woman living in the house besides Clover then. The household consisted of Mrs. Phillips, myself, Matilda Clover, her child, Mr. Vowles and Mrs. Phillips' grandson, who was a child of about nine, I think. Matilda Clover was not allowed the use of a latch key, she would let herself out and be let in by me or someone else in the house. I recollect the night on which she died. The previous day I went into her room and found an open letter of hers on the table, with the envelope. I could see that it had come through the post; I did not notice the post-mark. I read the letter. I was in the house from the time I read the letter on the morning of the day before the death, until after the death. After the death I looked for the letter carefully, and could not find it.

The ATTORNEY-GENERAL proposed to ask the witness as to the contents of the letter.

Mr. GEOGHEGAN objected that the suggestion of the prosecution was that the letter told the woman to return the letter and envelope to the writer, and that the writer was the prisoner. No notice to produce had been served.

Mr. JUSTICE HAWKINS considered that there was no proof of similarity of handwriting or any other evidence to connect the prisoner with the letter.

The ATTORNEY-GENERAL did not press the evidence.

Examination continued—Between seven and ten in the evening before Clover died I let her in. I do not know what time she had gone out. When I let her in a gentleman was with her. There was the light of a small paraffin lamp in the hall. The gentleman was tall and broad and had a heavy moustache; he had no other hair or whiskers on his chin or face except the moustache. I should say he was about forty. He was wearing a large coat with a cape to it, and a high silk hat. I had never seen him before. She had seen the prisoner and did not recognise him. Soon after they came in Clover went out for some beer, leaving the man in her rooms, and she returned. After that the gentleman went out, Clover did not go out, she bade the man " good-night " at the door. I heard her say " Good-night, dear " as she let him out. I did not see him then. Later I know she went out herself, because she asked me if I would

Evidence for Prosecution.

Lucy Rose

listen to her baby. That was about an hour, I should think, after the man left. I went to bed about ten, and she had gone out at that time. After going to bed I went to sleep. I was awoke about three o'clock by loud screams. I slept in the back room, under where Clover slept. I called the landlady and went into Clover's room, and found her lying across the foot of the bed with her head fixed between the bedstead and the wall. She told me she had been poisoned by pills given her by the gentleman. She was apparently in great agony. During her agony she screamed as if in great pain. There were moments when she appeared to have relief, and then the fit came on again. When the fits were upon her she was all of a twitch. She said once she thought she was going to die, and she said she would like to see her baby.

Did she make a statement how she had been poisoned?

Mr. GEOGHEGAN objected.

The ATTORNEY-GENERAL submitted that he had laid the foundation for asking what statement exactly the deceased had made as to how she had been poisoned.

Mr. GEOGHEGAN contended that the mere fact that a person said, when in great pain, that she thought she was going to die did not imply that settled sure feeling that there was no possible chance of recovery such as could render a dying declaration admissible.

Mr. JUSTICE HAWKINS said the point had been before him more than once, and he did once allow such a declaration. But he held that before a dying declaration could be admitted it must be proved that at the moment the person made the statement she was in such a condition that her immediate death was probable; she must be labouring under a mortal disorder, which mortal disorder she believed would be the immediate cause of death.

The ATTORNEY-GENERAL did not press the point.

Examination continued—When the fit or agony was on her, her eyes rolled about terribly. I remained in the room with her, in and out of the room, the whole of the time until her death. These intermittent fits continued up to the time of her death. She died at a quarter to nine the same morning. In her moments of relief she was quite calm and collected; it was in one of those moments of relief that she made the statement about dying and her desire to see the child. Her words were, 'I think I am going to die, and I should like to see my baby.' The landlady went for medical help

Thomas Neill Cream.

Lucy Rose

Mr Coppin, assistant to Dr M'Carthy, came, I think about seven, he only stayed a few minutes. Clover had been drinking the previous night. I noticed it. Mr Coppin sent some medicine. The first drop I gave her she turned all black. We sent Mrs Phillips' grandson for it. As she got worse, Mrs Phillips went again for Mr Coppin, but he did not come. Clover was getting worse, during that early morning she vomited a good deal. Dr Graham came for the first time in the middle of the day, he gave the certificate of death. He had not seen her that morning, not until she was dead. She was buried at Tooting on 27th October by the parish. I think Mr Measures was the undertaker. I do not think any information of her death was given to the police. I do not remember the date when the police first came to me to make inquiry about Matilda Clover, I think it was about seven months after her death. I attended the inquest; it began on 22nd June, and the verdict was given on 13th July. Until the inquest I had heard nothing about strychnine in connection with Matilda Clover. She sometimes went out to market for herself, with a basket. She then generally wore a grey dress and a large apron with shoulder straps to it.

The ATTORNEY-GENERAL—I do think that the evidence falls short—just short—for me to press the point of the dying declaration.

Mr JUSTICE HAWKINS—It is on the line.

Cross-examined by Mr GEOGHEGAN—When I left Mrs Phillips I went to live at another house in Lambeth Road about three minutes' walk from there, and I stayed there seven or eight weeks. Clover was in the habit of bringing men to 27, it is four doors from the Masons' Arms. I believe the first eight houses after the Masons' Arms took in lodgers. There were other lodgers at Mrs Phillips when I first went there who took men home with them.

I was examined once before Mr Hicks, the Coroner, then before Sir John Bridge, at Bow Street, and then recalled. I gave evidence in Court three times. Before I gave evidence in Court a gentleman called on me and asked what I knew about the matter, and took it all down in writing, he only called once. I made a statement to Inspector Harvey and another gentleman.

The man I saw had a coat with a cape on it.

While Clover was in great agony a cup of tea was given to her, and she drank it. Just before her death she was wearing a brand-new pair of boots, they had been purchased at Lilley's in Westminster

Evidence for Prosecution.

Lucy Rose

Bridge Road. They were pawned the day after her death. I remained with her till she died. I saw her die. Besides the tea and medicine she had some soda and milk; it did not stay on her stomach. She drank some of it. She had no difficulty in swallowing. I did not see her corpse taken away, I was not in the house, I was with Mrs. Phillips' daughter. A person from Lambeth Walk laid her out, I don't know her name. I should know her again if I saw her.

I saw the letter on the table, and read it from beginning to end.

She told me she had bought the boots at Lilley's; she did not say a gentleman had bought them; she said the gentleman was with her at the time. I did not see her buy them. I saw her the day she bought them, in the morning, and again in the evening; she bought them in the evening when she was out. She was drunk when she came home. She said the gentleman had given her the money to buy them.

The gentleman left earlier than ten o'clock. She came back about half-past ten. Mrs. Phillips said it was about that. I heard Mrs. Phillips give evidence before the Coroner. Clover always had to knock at the door when she came in, no matter what time she came home. I did not wait up to let her in, Mrs. Phillips did. I did not see clearly the man she brought home.

Re-examined by the ATTORNEY-GENERAL.—When she went out to a neighbouring shop she sometimes left the door ajar. I used to leave it open when I went out. Clover was the only woman lodging in the house in October. There was no one else there when she died. I think there had been about a week before. There was no man in the house that I saw on 20th October except the man I have described. I was in the house all the day and all the evening and night. I think Sergeant Ward first spoke to me about Clover's death. Inspector Harvey saw me after that. My first statement was made to Inspector Harvey and another gentleman. Clover complained of her throat, she said she seemed as if she had something sticking in her throat and if she could get it up she thought she should be better. I think she vomited after taking all the things.

Mrs. EMMA VOWLES, examined by Mr. COLERIDGE.—In October last I was living at 27 Lambeth Road, at that time I had a lodger named Matilda Clover. She occupied some upper rooms with her child. About three o'clock in the morning of 21st October I was

Thomas Neill Cream.

Mrs Emma Vowles called by Lucy Rose, and I went and saw Clover lying across the foot of the bed. I saw her vomit. I did not stay with her long. I went to fetch Dr. Graham, he did not come, Mr Coppin came. I was not present when Clover actually died. I gave a description of her death to Dr. Graham, and it was in consequence of what I told him that he gave his certificate of death from delirium tremens and syncope. I had seen her about an hour before her death. I next heard about her when Inspector Harvey came, five or six months ago. Up to that time no suspicion had arisen in my mind as to her death by strychnine, I had heard no suggestion of that kind from any one. I remember the inquest in June; I think that was the first time I heard anything about her death by strychnine.

Cross-examined—I still live at 27 Lambeth Road, and still take in lodgers. I have lived there about two years and nine months, during that time I have taken in lodgers.

Mostly women?—Not mostly women. I don't take many women in. This was the first death that occurred in my house.

Do your neighbours on both sides take in lodgers?—Yes.

Did you know that Clover had friends who used to visit her before Lucy Rose came to you?—No. I never saw any persons that used to visit her. I know she had a friend named "Fred," the baby's father, visiting her, he was constantly in the habit of coming to see her. She did not stay out late then, only for the last four months.

Had she a key?—Yes, I gave her a key to let herself in with.

When did you usually go to bed yourself?—I went to bed at all hours because I used to sit up for my husband, he is a cabman, he drives a day cab, he is seldom in before twelve, sometimes two.

Do you give all your lodgers keys?—Yes.

Who were your lodgers?—One was a cabman and his wife and little child, and there was another woman.

Did she bring men in?—I never knew her to do so.

Did Matilda Clover bring men in?—I don't think she did either. As far as I remember, I never saw the prisoner before the inquest, he was then between two warders. The man named "Fred" was in the habit of coming to see Clover. They had a quarrel, and I heard Fred say he would never put foot inside the house again. He was a slight, fair man, and wore a light suit. She was cut up about it, she was very anxious to make it up with him if she could meet

Evidence for Prosecution.

Mrs Emma Vowles

him. Her rooms were not let again for months after her death. I saw her body after death. My rooms used not to be long empty, but since her death I have not let so well. I don't remember how long it was after her death before a lodger came, it was a long time. The neighbour in the next house on my left is named Payne, I only know her to say "Good morning." The person on the right I did not know to speak to.

Re-examined—The father of Clover's child, Fred, is a very slight fair young man, with light blue eyes, and I should take him to be thirty-two or thirty-four.

Is he like the prisoner?—No, he is not at all like him.

When did the quarrel that you have referred to take place?—About four weeks before her death. I don't think she had seen him since the quarrel up to the time of her death. She used to speak to me about him very much.

There seems to be some misapprehension about the latchkey?—I did not let her in on the Monday that she died. She had her own latchkey. She was in the passage when I got upstairs. I was going to bed with a light in my hand. My husband had not come in, and I was going to my room to wait up for him. I went up after Clover. I had no means of knowing what time she went to bed. The child slept with her in the same bed.

By the COURT—I saw no man at all in my house that night. I was not long in Clover's presence before she died, only the short times between, I don't suppose more than one-half hour altogether. I had not been in her room for an hour before her death. I had been out twice for the doctor. I registered her death. I said when I registered it that I was present at her death. It was want of thought. I registered it the night she died. She spoke reasonably to me when I saw her, she was very sick when I was in the room. Dr Graham asked me what the symptoms were before her death. I told him she was trembling, and was very sick.

FRANCIS COPPIN, examined by the ATTORNEY-GENERAL—I live at 138 Westminster Bridge Road. I am assistant to Dr. M'Carthy. On the morning of 21st October, about seven o'clock, I was called in to 27 Lambeth Road. I saw Lucy Rose there. As far as I recollect, Mrs Phillips took me up to see Matilda Clover. She was lying on a bed. She was not in a fit at the time I saw her first

Thomas Neill Cream.

Francis Coppin

She had a quick pulse, was bathed in perspiration, and trembling. I was with her about ten or twelve minutes. She had a convulsion while I was there. There was a twitching of the body. She had vomited previous to my being there. I saw the vomited matter there. I gave her some medicine to stop the vomiting. I concluded that she was suffering from epileptic fits, convulsions due to alcoholic poisoning. I had been told by Mrs Phillips that she had been in the habit of drinking. That helped me to form an opinion as to what she was suffering from. I was examined at the inquest on Matilda Clover. I had heard before that that a girl had taken two pills. I did not hear of strychnine until three detectives came to me, that was before the inquest, I should think about the end of April or the beginning of May.

Cross-examined—The word "poison" was not mentioned to me in connection with this woman's death. I have had fourteen years' experience in this part of London, and a good deal of experience of drink in its various forms. I had no doubt that this woman was suffering from excessive drink.

Are you acquainted with the symptoms of strychnine poisoning?—Yes. Nothing in her appearance suggested that to me. I should put the symptoms described down to delirium tremens from convulsions, that sometimes occurs. There was nothing to point out to me that she died from anything but delirium tremens.

What medicine did you prescribe?—Carbonate of soda.

Re-examined by the ATTORNEY-GENERAL—I am not a qualified practitioner. I have never had a case of strychnine poisoning. I can say from my reading that intermittent convulsions and twitching of the body are indications of poisoning by strychnine. They are "tetanic convulsions." I was told by Mrs Phillips that she had been drinking. I was prepared to accept the idea of drinking. I asked the girl what she had been drinking and how she was, and I examined her.

Was that all that you asked her?—Yes. I was with her for about ten or twelve minutes, during that time there was one convulsive fit. I saw Dr Graham before he gave his certificate. I told him I thought it was drink.

By the COURT—When I saw her at seven in the morning I thought she would die, but not so quickly. I thought she was in a dying con-

Evidence for Prosecution.

Francis Coppin

dition About an hour after I saw her, soon after eight, Mrs Phillips came round to ask me to go again immediately I sent a messenger to Dr Graham to tell him to go, as he had been attending her for twelve days previously I did not go myself I inquired of Mrs Phillips when the vomiting, twitching, and so on commenced, and I heard it was about three, I think

Dr ROBERT GRAHAM, examined by the ATTORNEY-GENERAL—I am a registered medical practitioner I knew Matilda Clover She had been to consult me on several occasions, the first being about twelve days before her death During the twelve days I saw her about eight or nine times. I had been prescribing for alcoholism bromide of potassium and sedative medicines, as for a woman who had been taking drink On each of the eight or nine occasions she came to my place the last time was on 19th October I do not keep entries of club patients in my book, she was in a club I fix the 19th merely from memory That was the last occasion I saw her alive, and it was at my own place On the morning of 21st Mrs Phillips came twice, the first time I was out at a case; it was half-past four She came again at half-past six I was engaged at a labour and was just going out to it for the second time, and could not go, so that I did not see Clover at her house till I saw her dead. I sent Mrs Phillips to Dr M'Carthy as I could not go myself I said, "You had better call in another medical man, as I cannot come," and I suggested Dr M'Carthy, in the Westminster Bridge Road After the death I saw Mrs Phillips and Mr Coppin I already knew Clover had been in the habit of drinking, that was what I treated her for From both Mrs Phillips and Mr Coppin I got the information which I put in this certificate, which I gave

In giving such a certificate in this way I suppose you were aware you were guilty of a very grave dereliction of duty?—I am not aware of it

By the COURT—I suppose you knew you were bound to put the truth in it?

Examination resumed—In that certificate I stated, " I certify that I attended Matilda Clover during her last illness'—I had not seen her on her death-bed—' such person's age was stated to be twenty-seven years, that I saw her on 21st October 1891" I say

Thomas Neill Cream.

Dr Robert Graham

I saw her when she was dead, and I made examination of her body "To the best of my knowledge and belief the cause of her death was, primarily, delirium tremens secondly syncope" That means delirium tremens resulting in or causing syncope, which means failing of the heart's action

Cross-examined by Mr GEOGHEGAN—When Clover came to consult me she had all the symptoms of a person who had been drinking to excess I gave her a sedative—bromide of potassium—which is the usual thing to give in such cases If a person has undergone a course of sedatives and then drinks brandy, it would have a marked effect on her Brandy does not go with bromide of potassium in the case of a person in a weak state of health

What would happen if such a person took an excessive amount of spirit, after a dose, say of 15 grains of bromide?—The two things acting on one another in the body of a person in a weak state of health would produce a kind of fit if the person took an excessive amount of spirit If a person took 15 grains of bromide of potassium, and then took brandy on the top of it, it would have a very marked effect on him On one occasion when I attended this woman in my surgery she was taken quite faint

Would you say that she was a strong person?—She was not a strong woman by any means and her mode of life was not conducive to her health

Re-examined by the ATTORNEY GENERAL—I stated at the inquest that on one occasion at my surgery she felt faint, I gave her a glass of water, which restored her; she seemed refreshed Bromide of potassium is a nerve sedative I should say it was a thing commonly prescribed in cases of drink I have made no statement to the solicitor for the defence

By the COURT—When you say "marked effect," what do you mean?—I mean that with a person who drank excessively of spirits the bromide would not have the effect of subduing the convulsion altogether, if there was a convulsion

Would it have the effect of producing a convulsion?—No, I do not say that

Were you informed by Mrs Phillips that this last illness commenced with screaming, great agony, twitching, tetanic spasms, and so on?—No I asked how she came home and what condition

Evidence for Prosecution.

Dr Robert Graham

she was in, and I was told that she had drunk nearly a bottle of brandy. Mrs Phillips told me that, that she came in and she had been drinking heavily that night, she was drunk and rolling about. I asked Mr Coppin the symptoms he had noticed. I did not learn from anybody that between 3 a.m. and the hour of her death she had been in torture. Nobody told me that she had been or that she had not been. I did not ask Rose, she was absent taking the child downstairs. I asked Mr Coppin and the landlady, and she said she was simply shaking. I said before the Coroner that from my knowledge I thought it was quite possible that she had a fit of delirium tremens, and that syncope had supervened.

JOHN MEASURES, examined—I live at Regency Place, Kennington Cross, and am foreman to Mr Mouatt, the undertaker, of Waterloo Road. I had the conduct of Clover's funeral. The body was buried by the parish on 27th October at Tooting cemetery. The coffin had a plate with "M Clover, 27 years." I made the coffin. I was present on 5th May when the grave was opened, and on 6th when the coffin was opened. I identified the coffin and the clothes on the body.

Cross-examined—I myself took the body and put it into the coffin.

ELIJAH GEORGE STEERS, examined—I am assistant cemetery-keeper at the parochial cemetery at Tooting. There was an order from the parish for the burial of Clover, and I was present when the body was buried. In consequence of an order from the Home Office the body was exhumed on 5th May, and removed from the grave to the mortuary at the cemetery.

JOHN HARE, examined—I am a labourer at Lambeth cemetery. I live there. I was present when Clover's coffin was taken up. I opened it in Dr Stevenson's presence. He having taken from the body what he wanted it was reburied.

EMILY SLEAPER, examined by the ATTORNEY-GENERAL—I live with my mother at 103 Lambeth Palace Road. She sometimes lets rooms. On 6th October last year the prisoner came and looked at a room and arranged, and on the 7th he came in. He said he had been staying at Anderton's Hotel and his luggage was marked with the label of that hotel. He had one room, the second floor front

Thomas Neill Cream.

Emily Sleaper

He said he had means. He said nothing about what his profession was, beyond telling us that he was Dr. Neill. He saw no patients at our house, and so far as I knew he did not practise his profession at all. He said that he came to England on account of his health. When he came he wore a brown mackintosh and a felt hat with a flat top.

Some time after he came to stay at Lambeth Palace Road he asked me to take a letter for him round to Lambeth Road; he mentioned the number, but I forget it. He said he knew a young lady there, and he thought she had been poisoned; he wanted to find out if she was dead or not. A name was mentioned, but I could not remember it. He said that the young lady had a child. I said I would go at first, but afterwards I refused. I said I had better not, and he said himself that perhaps I had better not. I think he said he would go himself.

Did he tell you anything about what he had ascertained?—He did not about that time tell me anything about what he had ascertained or say anything in reference to her, not until later on.

Did he tell you that he knew who had poisoned the young lady whom he knew in Lambeth Road?—Yes, it was Lord Russell. The Russell case was going on in the Divorce Court at that time. He continued to live in our house until he left to go to America, as I understood, on 5th January. On 7th April he returned and took the one room. On the 9th he came in, and he remained there until he was arrested. Easter Sunday this year was on 17th April. He made no reference then to the letter he had wanted me to take to Lambeth Road. It was not till he was being watched, in May I should think, that he referred to his former request and said it was a good thing that I did not go round to the house, as they were going to exhume the body. I asked him how he knew, and he said he had sent a Mr. Haynes round—I had seen Mr. Haynes—I understood him he had sent Haynes to make inquiries about the girl, so I thought, about the time the body was to be exhumed. My attention was not called to Clover's death at the time it occurred; I did not know anything about it. The prisoner never had dinner at home except on Sunday, but on Monday, 11th April, after he returned he had the dinner which had been ordered in for the Sunday. On the Monday he dined at half-past six. He said he had a late appointment and went out at ten. What time he came back I do not know.

Evidence for Prosecution.

Emily Sleaper

Do you remember hearing something about the inquests on Alice Marsh and Emma Shrivell?—Yes; we take *Lloyd's* newspaper, there was a report of those inquests in it. I could not say if it was on Easter Sunday. The prisoner asked me for the paper, he wished to read the inquest on those two girls. He said it was a cold-blooded murder. In April we had also lodging in our house a young medical student named Harper. He had been lodging with us for three years, he was a son of Dr. Harper, of Barnstaple. On the day after he asked for *Lloyd's* newspaper the prisoner came into Mr. Harper's rooms, which were on the drawing-room floor. I was there. The prisoner asked me several questions about Mr. Harper, and looked at his medical books. I could not remember the exact questions now he asked me. I did not refuse to answer him. He asked me where Mr. Harper lived and what kind of gentleman he was. I told him that he was very quiet. I felt no difficulty in answering the questions he put to me. Later on he told me that it was Mr. Harper who had poisoned the girls in Stamford Street. I said that he was the last man in the world to do such a thing, that he must be mad. He told me not to tell any one. He said the police had the proofs. I asked him how he knew, and he said that he had a detective friend from America. He said each of the women had had a letter before their death warning them not to take the stuff that Mr. Harper would give them. I understood him to say that the police had the letters.

I noticed that the house was being watched on the Sunday when the prisoner was away, that was in May, about 16th or 17th. I could not give the exact time, but some time about the middle of May. The prisoner said he was aware that the house was being watched. I told him they were watching him. He said they had made a mistake, that they were suspicious of him because he was an American. On one occasion he said that they were after Mr. Harper. That was after the occasion in May that I have spoken to, I think. Later I asked him why he took an interest in the inquest which was going on, and he said the man ought to be brought to justice. When he went away from Saturday to Tuesday he gave me on the Saturday, 30th April, a cash-box to take care of. That was before the house was being watched. When I became aware the house was being watched he asked me to give him the cash-box back. He gave me with the cash-box a note-book, they were wrapped up in a newspaper in one parcel. The cash-box was locked

Thomas Neill Cream.

Emily Sleaper

I think it was on the Friday after his return that he got the cashbox from me. I was aware at that time that the house was being watched, he mentioned it to me first. When I gave him the parcel he tore the note-book up and asked me to burn the pieces, and I did so. Later on a detective came to the house to make inquiries and desiring to know the prisoner's movements. I then wrote this paper at the prisoner's dictation, he being in bed at the time—

I arrived in Liverpool on the 1st of October 1891, came ashore on the 2nd October, spent three days in Liverpool, arrived in London on the 5th October, put up at Anderton's Hotel, spent two or three days there then removed to 103 Lambeth Palace Road, where I remained till the 6th of January, 1892, on which night I returned to Liverpool on my way to America. There I remained until the 23rd of March, on which day I sailed from New York for Liverpool. I arrived in Liverpool on the 1st of April in London on the 2nd of April returned to Liverpool on the 4th or 5th of April, spent two or three days in Liverpool after which I returned to London, put up at Edwards's Hotel,* spent two or three days there, then went down into the country where I spent several days after which I came to live at 103 Lambeth Palace Road, where I still reside

THOMAS NEILL

That 25th May was the first date, as far as I know, on which any detective had come to the house to inquire. I asked the prisoner to write some letters for me in relation to a relative of mine, and he afterwards handed me these documents, one is in the form of a letter to Dr Souttar, and the other is a draft advertisment † After he was arrested I received from him, from the prison, this letter (produced) which I afterwards handed to Inspector Tunbridge There was a cupboard in the prisoner's room. (Shown box.) I have seen a box like this in it. I opened the box empty capsules were in it, such as these. When he was arrested on 3rd June the capsule box was not in the cupboard. I had failed to see the capsule box in the cupboard for about a week before his arrest. That would be after the house was being watched. Up to that time the box had been there the whole time the prisoner was staying with us. I had occasion to go to the cupboard. When Tunbridge came I pointed out the things belonging to the prisoner, and Tunbridge took them away

---

* In Euston Square
† See letter reproduced opposite page 175. Further details on this point are not procurable

Evidence for Prosecution.

Emily Sleaper

Cross-examined by Mr. GEOGHEGAN—When the prisoner came in October he had no patients and no visitors, as far as I could see, and no acquaintances. He had no sitting room. As far as I could see he was thrown on himself and his own resources for amusement and occupation. He told my sister in my hearing that he suffered from his heart and brain, and had been advised to take a long voyage for his health. He suggested to me that he was unable to sleep at night.

Was he in the habit of dosing himself with opium?—I know that during October he was taking opium. He took a dose of medicine in water, and ate a lump of sugar afterwards. I do not know how often he took it.

Did he appear to be ill during October?—Yes.

How did the name of Lord Russell come to be mentioned?—I read the Russell divorce case in the *Daily Telegraph*. It was while I was reading it he mentioned that Lord Russell was the man who had poisoned the women.

Did the prisoner appear to be a very inquisitive man?—Yes.

Thrusting himself into persons' affairs with which I had nothing to do?—Yes, so far as I could judge. I know that of the few acquaintances he had in London Haynes was an ex-detective, whom he had met casually at a photographer's in the Westminster Bridge Road, and M'Intyre, a police officer connected with Scotland Yard.

When the prisoner went away for the few days did he tell you where he was going?—Yes, he said he was going into the country to Berkhamstead; he told me he was engaged to be married, and he said he was going down to where his sweetheart was staying. Before he gave me the cash-box and note-book I had seen him open the cash-box. I think he used to keep it in his portmanteau, and the note-book as well; I never saw it about.

Was the newspaper parcel containing the cash-box and note-book tied up at all?—No.

There was nothing to prevent you reading the note-book if you had had the curiosity to do so?—No.

Did the prisoner ever give you any medicine in a capsule?—I once complained of being ill, and he gave me medicine, not in a capsule.

Re-examined by the ATTORNEY-GENERAL—In October he complained of not being in good health, and of sleeplessness, and he was

Thomas Neill Cream.

in the habit of taking laudanum. He did not continue that practice later on, it was only the first time he stayed with us, afterwards he seemed to have got better. He took very little at our place, he only dined on Sundays. He used to take milk and toast for his breakfast.

Dr. THOMAS STEVENSON,* examined by the ATTORNEY-GENERAL—I am lecturer on medical jurisprudence at Guy's Hospital and one of the analysts employed by the Government. On 6th May, in consequence of instructions from the Home Office, I went to the cemetery at Tooting; a grave was there pointed out to me by Steers, from which a coffin had been taken. The grave was in a very dry place, and there had been no wet on the coffin. Measures was also there. I noticed on the coffin a plate with the name 'M. Clover, 27 years.' The coffin was opened in my presence, and I examined the body, assisted by Mr. Dunn, senior demonstrator at Guy's Hospital. The body was that of a well-developed female of apparently between the ages of 25 and 30, as I judged. For the most part it was in a very good state of preservation. I proceeded to a closer examination by dissection, external and internal. I opened the large cavities, the abdomen, chest and heart. The brain was free from any tumour or hæmorrhage, it was much decomposed. I could detect no sign of disease, either there or in the upper portion of the spinal cord. There was no sign of disease in the heart, stomach, bowels, spleen, liver, or kidneys. The bladder was empty. The womb was unimpregnated; it was that of a woman who had borne a child or children. The stomach was empty. I found no indication of any disease in the vital organs that went to account for her death.

I then, for the purposes of analysis, removed as much of the brain as I could, the stomach, the upper portion of the duodenum (the first portion of the small bowel), the whole of the liver, both kidneys, the spleen, the heart, and nearly half a pint of fluid which had drained into the cavity of the chest during the examination. The entire portions so removed weighed 114½ ounces. I proceeded to analyse those for the presence of poison generally, but especially for alkaloidal poisons, of which strychnine is one. I detected strychnine in the stomach, liver, the fluid in the chest, and the brain. The kidneys and spleen I reserved for other purposes of

---
* See Appendix VI

Evidence for Prosecution.

Dr Thomas Stevenson

analysis. I obtained from the stomach, liver, brain, and fluid from the chest an appreciable quantity of strychnine which I tested on a frog, injecting it beneath the skin of the frog's back. It had the characteristic results of strychnine poisoning from which it died; it had tetanic convulsions, was very rigid, the forelegs were clasped across the chest, it had peculiar croaking peculiar respiration, and, in fact, quite characteristic symptoms. I made, eventually, a quantitative analysis in which I obtained a weighing from the same viscera, that is, I took the portion obtained from nearly the whole of the stomach, about one-third of the liver, a quarter of the brain, and half of the chest fluid, and I obtained from those together, about two pounds of material, one sixteenth of a grain of strychnine. That one sixteenth would represent an average medicinal dose, one-twelfth is the maximum medicinal dose. In my judgment, from the evidence I have heard in the case to-day about the woman vomiting frequently, and from my finding her stomach empty, and from the quantity that I did find, and the indications I found, it points conclusively to a larger and fatal dose having been administered. I have no doubt that, taking into account the vomiting and the length of time, it did point to a much larger dose. A little above half a grain has killed, but one grain is usually about a fatal dose.

I was not present when Lucy Rose and Mrs Vowles were examined. Twitchings, convulsions, and rigidity, with intermittence, I should say, would at once suggest the taking of strychnine. Those convulsions and spasms are tetanic, they are not at all the symptoms you would find in the case of delirium tremens. There are very marked differences, in delirium tremens the mental faculties are obscured and perverted, in strychnine spasms they are often very acute and are not at all impaired, except perhaps just at the very last moment of life. In strychnine poisoning after twitchings the whole body, as a rule, becomes rigid and often arched backwards, the patient has a sense of being suffocated, due to a fixing of the muscles of the chest, and generally in half a minute, or more often in two or three minutes, all the spasm passes off, the patient is perfectly sensible, bathed in perspiration and free from spasms. Mr Coppin referred to Clover being bathed in perspiration; that is a symptom of strychnine poisoning. It is also a sign of delirium tremens, but the patient will remain bathed in perspiration continuously for hours throughout the whole of a bad case of delirium tremens. The case

Thomas Neill Cream.

Dr Thomas Stevenson

described, of the spasms being intermittent and the patient being collected and calm during the intervals of freedom from pain, would not be consistent with its being delirium tremens; the patient is generally not calm but flurried, excited, tremulous, and certainly there is no real intermission of the symptoms. I mean, a patient is not in a state of ease at one minute, and then in two or three minutes more in a state of violent convulsion. Assuming the case to be one where there are those violent agonies, and spasms followed by minutes of freedom from pain, calmness and collectedness, that would be a symptom of and would point to strychnine poisoning. The symptoms point to strychnine poisoning, and my analysis and post-mortem examination lead me to the same result. Bromide of potassium is given to allay nervous irritation and excitement; it is often given in delirium tremens as a sedative. I cannot say whether it would make any difference if the bromide was taken after drink or drink after bromide; all I can say is that if the man were to take drink after a sedative it might start delirium tremens.

On 4th July I received from Inspector Tunbridge this case of pills* and a box containing several kinds of coated pills. I examined the whole of these pills and analysed some completely. The case contained fifty-four bottles of pills, and of those bottles seven contained strychnine, all in medicinal quantities, taking pill by pill. The bottle, No. 2 in the case, was full, and contained 160 pills. I analysed them twice and found 1·22 grain in each pill; they are labelled "Strychnine, 1-16 grain, poison," but they are a little short of that quantity. Twenty-two of them would make up a complete grain, and eleven of them would make half a grain. Rather less than half a grain has been a fatal dose, but certainly approaching a grain would be a fatal dose. I do not think that there is any poison that quite approaches in the character of its crystals the appearance of strychnine; to a skilled eye there is something rather characteristic, but I would not, with all my knowledge, establish an opinion by mere examination by eye. I think an ordinary observer might easily mistake the crystals for those of some other substance. I also had produced to me a box of capsules, one of them was given to me called a five-grain capsule, and into that I put a score of these pills—these pills contain other matters; they weigh about three-parts of a grain each,

---

*See illustration opposite this page

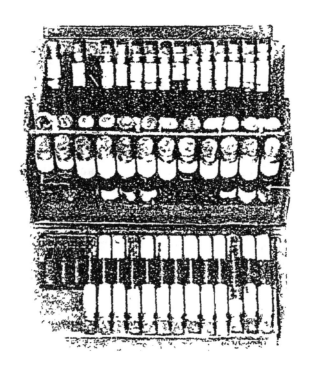
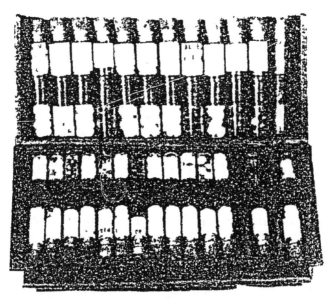

Cream's "Sample" Case of Medicines

Evidence for Prosecution.

Dr Thomas Steverson

the chief part of them is milk sugar and a little excipient to make the mass stick together, and then there is the strychnine. Strychnine in small quantities is given in nervous diseases, generally as a tonic; it is very largely given as a medicine in small doses, but not frequently in 1-16 of a grain. I got the twenty pills into the No. 5 capsule without powdering or breaking them up. By powdering them you could get a few more in, not many more I think. If strychnine crystals themselves were put in of course, there would be a great deal more strychnine. I don't know if I tried with a five-grain capsule, but you could get more than five grains of strychnine into it because strychnine is heavier than many powders; you would be able to get into a five-grain capsule seven or eight grains of strychnine generally, if the strychnine crystals were powdered up and put in with no other matter.

The time at which a fatal dose of strychnine begins to operate varies according to the mode in which it is taken and the condition of the patient. If it is taken in a capsule, first the capsule must take time to dissolve. I have experimented with them in warm water and I find it takes a quarter of an hour at least before they soften and give way. Then the form in which the strychnine is put in the capsule affects it; if it is in a hard pill mass it will not operate so quickly as if it is in loose powder; it would dissolve more slowly. If it is given in a liquid the symptoms are produced more quickly. The time also varies greatly according to the contents of the stomach, and the state of the stomach, as to the period of digestion, acidity of the stomach and many conditions affect it. The margin for the beginning to operate of a fatal dose is from two minutes, but from ten to twenty minutes is the usual time when it is taken in any article of food; it may vary from two, five, or ten minutes up to three-quarters of an hour; and, when the patient is asleep, longer than that, two or three hours exceptionally. Generally it is about three-quarters of an hour after it comes in contact with the stomach that it begins to operate. The time that it takes to operate fatally would depend upon the dose, and the condition of the stomach, and whether it is retained in the patient or not. I heard that this woman on her death-bed vomited frequently; that in my judgment would probably have the effect of sending out in the vomit some portion of the strychnine taken.

Cross-examined by Mr GEOGHEGAN—I think all these little

Thomas Neill Cream.

Dr Thomas Stevenson

bottles were full when they were brought to me. Certainly this one containing the 168 pills was. I took some out to experiment with.

Did you hear Dr Graham say to-day that he had attended Matilda Clover for drink?—Yes.

What effect would excessive drinking have upon her nervous system?—Her nervous system would be very much upset. I cannot say exactly what the effect of alcohol would be, but if a person were on the verge of delirium tremens I should think it would render that person more susceptible to the effect of strychnine.

I suppose it is a question of degree?—Yes. I think a person like that would be affected sooner than a person living a temperate and healthy life.

When do the symptoms first show themselves from the time that the pill or draught has first been swallowed?—Usually within half an hour.

If the patient has been asleep I suppose it may be retarded for some time?—Yes, it may be retarded for two or three hours. I have never known it retarded for two hours by sleep alone, but it has been when opium or morphia has been taken.

Did you discover any morphia in your post-mortem examination?—No. I know of no instance of its being found so long after death. I can give an instance of death occurring from strychnine $5\frac{1}{4}$ hours afterwards. The first case I gave evidence in in this witness-box was the case of Silas Barlow in 1876.* Barlow had poisoned his mistress with nux vomica containing strychnine, and she died in $5\frac{1}{4}$ hours. The fatal dose was not known, but very little was found in the body after death.

Was that an exceptional case?—No, I do not think it was an exceptional case, I think there are two cases where death occurred after six hours.

Was there medical attendance in Barlow's case?—I can hardly tell you. I gave evidence, but I did not make the analysis. I think there was no medical attendance till after death, but I cannot be positive. I think in the other two cases there was some medical attendance. I don't know about sedatives—my impression is that

---

* *Reg.* v *Silas Barlow*, alias *Silas Smith* C C C., November, 1876. The poison was administered in the form of vermin killer, mixed with a decoction of sarsaparilla.

Evidence for Prosecution.

Dr Thomas Stevenson

a doctor was called in who tried to do something to alleviate their sufferings. There is no remedy for strychnine, nothing to alleviate it really.

What about chloroform?—Chloroform would prolong life. Injecting morphia does not seem to delay the progress much, but chloroform or chloral does allay the spasms and so protract the time before death will occur. When I heard of the evidence given before the Coroner and the magistrate of the twitching of the body, the convulsive spasms, the perspiration, and other matters, it at once conveyed to me the idea of poisoning by strychnine, without the finding of strychnine. When I made my post-mortem examination I had not heard of the symptoms, but I may say that I had heard of strychnine.

Did you confine yourself to strychnine?—No, not at all. Before I injected into the frog I had performed the colour test. The frog presented the symptoms of strychnine poisoning.

Of course there is a difference between a frog and a human being in that the frog is a cold-blooded animal and a human being is warm-blooded?—Yes. But the frog is a very delicate animal for symptoms. I do not know that it is very susceptible, but it is satisfactory at all events, and probably it does not give so much suffering as experimenting on a rabbit or a dog.

Is not brucine one of the component parts of nux vomica?—Yes

Is it possible to separate strychnine from brucine when you get small quantities such as a grain or two?—Yes, it is only a delicate and difficult chemical operation to do so.

Did you find any brucine in this analysis?—No. There is no difficulty in detecting brucine in the presence of strychnine. I do not know if I should have detected brucine if it had been present, because I do not know anything about the detection of brucine some months after death.

What about prussic acid?—You can detect prussic acid months after death.

Did you find any prussic acid?—No

Do you think you would be able to detect disease of the spinal cord after the body had been for some months in the ground?—In many cases I should not expect to be able to do so, but in some cases I should.

Would disease of the spinal cord cause tetanic spasms?—It might. Mr Coppin described the spasms as of a peculiar kind

Thomas Neill Cream.

Dr Thomas Stevenson

Is a vegetable poison usually more difficult to discover than a mineral poison?—Yes, it is generally more difficult.

Do you put it that the colour test in strychnine poisoning is uncertain and fallacious?—No, but it must be confirmed by other experiments, proof that it is an alkaloid, separating from the material in a particular manner, giving the colour test with several reagents appropriate for strychnine, and the fact that it does produce the physiological test on the frog. As a rule we are not justified in resorting to experiments on animal life till we get some strong presumptive evidence justifying it, and giving good ground for thinking it desirable to do it. I found strychnine obscurely crystalline.

I suppose other substances will present the same appearances as strychnine?—Yes. I would not in such small quantities rely on the crystalline form. The form of the crystals does not in this case enable me to pronounce positively, nor does the colour test by itself. The action on the frog shows either strychnine or brucine I think. I injected the fluid into the frog after subjecting it to bichromate of potassium, and the action on the frog helped me to the belief that strychnine was what was injected. It confirmed absolutely in my mind the presence of the poison.

The capsules which have been shown you are merely gelatine, are they not?—Yes.

And quinine is sometimes taken in such capsules?—Yes, drugs nauseous to the taste are put in them and taken by patients.

Would you say that there is anything exceptional even in a non-professional man possessing them?—Probably there is not. I do not think they are very much used in London. They are used.

Is it not the case that they are all made in America?—One always goes to an American firm for them I believe, or else the retailer gets them from an American firm.

You said that you found one-sixteenth of a grain of strychnine?—Yes, I found one-sixteenth of a grain of strychnine absorbed in the body. It would be excreted in the urine. Of course, it is distributed through all the parts of the body, and as I operated on a great part of the body I might have got the greater portion from the abdominal viscera.

The heart was normal?—Yes.

And the lungs?—I should think the lungs had been a little congested.

Evidence for Prosecution.

Dr Thomas Stevenson

Would you not expect in death from strychnine poisoning that the heart would be contracted?—No. It is very variable, sometimes it is full, and sometimes it is contracted. Symptoms of strychnine poisoning which are always present are the spasms attended with clearness of intellect, with remissions, and so on. I take the aggregate of the symptoms, I put the whole thing together, and say that, drawing the inference from the aggregate number of circumstances, I come to the conclusion that it was strychnine poisoning.

There have been many cases of strychnine poisoning tried?—Yes.

There was the well-known case of William Palmer?*—Yes. That case was in the infancy of our knowledge of strychnine.

Was there not a great deal of conflict of knowledge about that case?—No, I would not say that. We knew little of strychnine then. It was the first homicidal case in which it was used, and some time after I had the first suicidal case. Of late years we have had many cases. I have been through the Palmer case lately.

The body generally was rigid, was it not?—No, it was flaccid. The arms and legs were rigid.

Is not one symptom of strychnine poisoning rigour after death?—Yes, but it is not always present. It depends whether the patient dies in a spasm or in an interval of remission. When a person died in a state of exhaustion the body would be flaccid in strychnine poisoning.

Is not rigidity invariable?—No, it is very common, but it is not invariable.

You will agree that the time between which the poison was taken and death is very important?—Yes, I think it is. It did not exceed the extreme maximum time.

What is the common time?—Three-quarters of an hour is the common time.

May not an inexperienced person make a mistake in the colour test?—I think that may be so if the drugs are not pure. The colour I rely on is a purple-violet, which then passes through a play of colours that I cannot explain. I know nothing else that gives that precise play of colours.

---

* See " Trial of William Palmer " in the ' Notable Trials Series

Thomas Neill Cream.

Dr Thomas Stevenson

Re-examined by the ATTORNEY-GENERAL—I suppose the length of time in which a fatal dose will prove fatal depends on the mode in which it is administered?—Yes, and to some extent upon the condition of the patient and upon the quantity administered. Death is generally more speedy from a very large dose. If by vomiting the patient has got rid of a portion of the dose, that would be a reason for expecting that the patient would live longer or would recover. If the patient died in one of the paroxysms, I should expect rigidity of the body after death, and that that rigidity would last for some time. It would generally disappear in a week or two after death; but in Palmer's case some portions of the body remained rigid from 21st November, when he died, to early in January when the body was exhumed. In the present case over six months had elapsed.

As regards the absence of brucine, so far as it is valuable at all, what would it indicate?—It would be an indication that the strychnine had not been administered in the form of nux vomica. I have not experimented in the direction of tracing brucine after death, and I do not know any one who has.

Will you tell us again how you arrived at the result that strychnine was the cause of death in this case?—I arrived at the result that strychnine was the cause of death, not taking each matter as isolated, but as cumulative and supporting each other: the appearance, the colour test, the fact that it was an alkaloid, the crystals, and, finally, the action on the frog. The frog is an animal which remains rigid long after death, and it may be made rigid though many other of its vital portions are cut off first. I cut the head off, and then made the body rigid. Having considered the matter carefully in the light of my experience I have given the result I arrived at. When I was proceeding to make this examination I had heard of strychnine—that was after I had made my examination of Marsh and Shrivell. I received the order from the Treasury on 4th May, and that mentioned strychnine. That was after I had made an examination of Marsh and Shrivell, and the day before I gave evidence at the inquests on those persons.

JOHN WILSON M'CULLOCH, examined by the Hon BERNARD COLERIDGE—I live at 374 Slater Street, Ottawa, in Canada. I am a traveller for Robert Jardine & Co, Toronto, in coffee, spices,

Evidence for Prosecution.

John Wilson M'Culloch

baking powder, and extracts. At the end of February this year I was staying at Blanchard's Hotel Quebec, from the evening of 29th February to the afternoon of 8th March. I there made the prisoner's acquaintance. I knew him as Dr Cream. He occupied a room upon the same floor as I was, and next door to me. I saw him several times each day. A day or two after I got here, on Saturday afternoon I felt unwell. I mentioned it to the prisoner, who took me to his room and gave me a pill, which he took from a bureau drawer, a dressing-case—the pills were in bottles. He gave me an anti-bilious pill and a blue mass pill. He showed me some photographs. Next day I had conversation with him on business after dinner. He asked, with reference to my samples, if he could handle them to advantage in London. Before that we had conversation about each of our businesses. He took me to his room and showed me some samples he had received from the States of pills and patent medicines. They were all in bottles; there were about eighteen or twenty bottles various. He opened his tin trunk and took out a cash-box, and from the cash-box he took a wide-mouthed bottle about 3 inches long by 1 inch in diameter. It contained whitish crystals and was about one third full similar to the contents of the bottle now shown to me. He asked me referring to the bottle did I know what that was? He said "That is poison." I said, 'For God's sake, what do you do with that?" He said "I give that to the women to get them out of the family way." I said "How do you do that?" He said, "I give it to them in these," showing me a box containing eighteen or twenty capsules. It was a box exactly like the one that is now shown to me and the capsules were the same, but I did not see the cover, because he laid it on one side. The capsules were about five-eighths of an inch long. He stepped back to the trunk and produced a pair of false whiskers or divided beard without moustaches. I said, "What do you use these for?" He said, "To prevent identification when operating." Previous to that he had led me to believe that he procured abortion. We had several conversations about his visit to London, and during one of them he told me that he had had lots of fun in London with the women. He mentioned Waterloo Road, Westminster Bridge Road, London Road, and Victoria Road, and said he had met as many as three women on one night, between the hours of 10 p.m. and 3 a.m., and had been in their company, and had

Thomas Neill Cream.

John Wilson M'Culloch

used them, and had paid no more than one shilling to each. He and I drove round on Sunday evening. 6th March, he pointed out where his sisters, brothers, and other relatives lived, and were in business, and where he had worked as a boy in his father's shipyard.* He told me that he was over there to secure his share of his father's estate, as his father had died about a month or so previous. A photograph he particularly showed me he said was that of a lady, Laura Sabbatini, to whom he was engaged to be married in London. He showed me no photographs of his relatives, but photographs of other women he did show me. There were several photographs on a bureau, and those were the only ones I paid much attention to. He showed me some jewellery in the tin box—bracelets and brooches, and I think there was a necklace. He told me he had gotten them back from a lady to whom he had been engaged, but who had got married during his absence in the States. He said they were very valuable. These pills are very similar to the pills he showed me, this is not the sample case nor the bottles I saw.

Cross-examined by Mr Geoghegan—I met him as a visitor staying at the same hotel. I was not introduced to him; he was a casual acquaintance made in the hotel sitting room.

How long were you with him?—About eight and a half days. We only once went out for a drive together. We were a good deal in each other's company in the evening, and grew chatty and friendly.

Did you ever see him take morphia pills?—Yes, I saw him take morphia pills on one occasion. He said he had these pills because his head was bothering him. I told him that he ought not to take so many.

When was this?—This would be on Thursday, 3rd March.

Was that previous to the conversation about the women in London and about practising abortion?—Yes.

Did he spend a good deal of money?—Yes, he spent a good deal of money, not only in mine, but in everybody's company.

Were you continually associating with him?—No, I was not. I saw him at meal times and at night. If he entered a room I did not get up and leave it.

---

*Should have been "lumber" yard.

Evidence for Prosecution.

John Wilson M'Culloch

I did not believe a word he said about the abortion at the time. He made a statement about it two days before he showed me the pills, I believed him at that time. I still continued to speak to him. There was only one room to sit in, and I sat in the same room with him, although I knew he was a professional abortionist. I was not going to stand outside. I chatted and talked with him in the same way.

Did he go to some queer places in Quebec?—I do not know. I did not go with him.

Did he tell you that he had been to some brothels in Quebec?—No, he did not.

Did he show you some improper and indecent photographs?—Yes.

What did he say to you about his head?—He said his head bothered him so that he could not sleep at night, and that in consequence he took morphia to relieve his brain.

How is it that you come to remember all these conversations? Do you keep a record of them in your diary?—No, I do not keep one. I have no memoranda of it. I trust to my memory.

Have you been brought over to London specially for this case?—Yes.

Re-examined by the ATTORNEY-GENERAL.—I had read in the papers an account of the identification of Thomas Neill with Dr Cream, the person I know, in connection with the inquest, and thereupon I identified him as the person I had met in Quebec, and I wrote a letter to the Chief of Police at Montreal, on the advice of friends. After doing so a communication was made to me through Inspector Jarvis,* who was out in America on this matter, and I was subpœnaed to come here and give evidence.

What did you and the prisoner usually talk about?—He talked part of the time about some musical instruments that I helped him to purchase. That brought us together.

Did you continue to be friendly with him to the end?—No, I lost confidence in him on Monday afternoon, through a conversation about an American who had come over there with plenty of money, and the prisoner said he ought to have had that man's money, and I asked him how that was, and he said, " I could give that man a pill and put him to sleep, and his money would have been mine." I said,

---

* Of Scotland Yard

Thomas Neill Cream.

John Wilson M Culloch

"You would not kill the man for 2000 dollars, would you?" and he said, "I ought to have done it," and he regretted he had not done so, and I shunned him then

GEORGE PERCIVAL WYATT, examined—I am a Coroner for the county of London and Surrey. About 19th October of last year I received this letter and envelope, and enclosed in the letter was the other letter and envelope to the foreman of the jury:—

London, 19th October, 1891

To G. P. Wyatt Esq.,
    Deputy Coroner,
    East Surrey

    I am writing to say that if you and your satellites fail to bring the murderer of Ellen Donworth *alias* Ellen Linnell, late of 8 Duke Street, Westminster Bridge Road, to justice that I am willing to give you such assistance as will bring the murderer to justice provided your Government is willing to pay me 300,000*l* for my services. No pay if not successful

    A. O'BRIEN, Detective

About the 2nd or 3rd May of this year I received the following letter, with enclosure:—

London, 2nd May, 1892

Dear Sir

    Will you please give the enclosed letter to the foreman of the Coroner's jury at the inquest on Alice Marsh and Emma Shrivell, and oblige
    Yours respectfully

    WM. H. MURRAY

London, 2nd May

To the Foreman of the Coroner's Jury, in the Cases
    of Alice Marsh and Emma Shrivell

Dear Sir

    I beg to inform you that one of my operators has positive proof that Walter Harper, a medical student of St. Thomas's Hospital, and a son of Dr. Harper of Bear Street, Barnstaple, is responsible for the deaths of Alice Marsh and of Emma Shrivell, he having poisoned those girls with strychnine. That proof you can have on paying my bill for services to George Clarke, detective, 20 Cockspur Street, Charing Cross, to whom I will give the proof on his paying my bill
    Yours respectfully,
    WM. H. MURRAY

ALFRED DYKE ACLAND, examined—I am a member of the firm of W. H. Smith & Son, having among other places of business 186 Strand. On 6th November 1891 I received this letter, dated 5th

Evidence for Prosecution.

Alfred Dyke Acland

November, and the envelope; it had been through the post, it is addressed to Frederick Smith, but I opened it. I handed it to our solicitors—

London, 5th November, 1891.

Mr. F. W. D. Smith,
   c/o William H. Smith & Son,
      186 Strand.

Sir,
      On Tuesday night, 13th October (last month), a girl named Ellen Donworth, but sometimes calling herself Ellen Linnell, who lived at 8 Duke Street, Westminster Bridge Road, was poisoned with strychnine. After her death, among her effects were found two letters incriminating you, which, if they ever become public property, will surely convict you of the crime. I enclose you a copy of one of the letters which the girl received on the morning of 13th October (the day on which she died). Just read it, and then judge for yourself what hope you have of escape if the law officers ever get hold of these letters. Think of the shame and disgrace it will bring on your family if you are arrested and put in prison for this crime. My object in writing you is to ask if you will retain me at once as your counsellor and legal adviser. If you employ me at once to act for you in this matter, I will save you from all exposure and shame in the matter; but if you wait till arrested before retaining me, then I cannot act for you, as no lawyer can save you after the authorities get hold of these two letters. If you wish to retain me, just write a few lines on paper, saying "Mr. Fred Smith wishes to see Mr. Bayne, the barrister, at once." Paste this on one of your shop windows at 186 Strand next Tuesday morning, and when I see it I will drop in and have a private interview with you. I can save you if you retain me in time, but not otherwise.

      Yours truly,

            H. BAYNE.

Dr. JOSEPH HARPER examined—I am a medical man, practising in Barnstaple. I received this letter of 25th April 1892, on 26th, with the three enclosures of Ellen Donworth's death, and the cutting from *Lloyd's Weekly News*. The following is the letter:—

London, 25th April, 1892.

Dr. Harper, Barnstaple.
Dear Sir,
      I am writing to inform you that one of my operators has indisputable evidence that your son, W. J. Harper, a medical student at St. Thomas's Hospital, poisoned two girls named Alice Marsh and Emma Shrivell on the 12th inst., and that I am willing to give you the said evidence (so that you can suppress it) for the sum of 1500*l.* sterling. The evidence in my hands is strong enough to convict and hang your son, but I shall give it you for 1500*l.* sterling, or sell it to the police for the

Thomas Neill Cream.

Dr Joseph Harper

same amount. The publication of the evidence will ruin you and your family for ever, and you know that as well as I do. To show you that what I am writing is true, I am willing to send you a copy of the evidence against your son, so that when you read it you will need no one to tell you that it will convict your son. Answer my letter at once through the columns of the London *Daily Chronicle* as follows:—"W H M—Will pay you for your services.—Dr H." After I see this in paper I will communicate with you again. As I said before I am perfectly willing to satisfy you that I have strong evidence against your son by giving you a copy of it before you pay me a penny. If you do not answer it at once I am going to give evidence to the Coroner at once.

    Yours respectfully,
        W H MURRAY

My son, Walter Joseph Harper, was pursuing his medical studies in London for some years at St Thomas's Hospital to qualify for his degree. He qualified in March or April. I showed him the letter and its enclosures when he came back to Barnstaple.

Dr WALTER JOSEPH HARPER examined—I am the son of the last witness. I recollect my father showing me the letter and its enclosures. I resided for some time at 103 Lambeth Palace Road, Mr Sleaper's. I was then studying at St Thomas's Hospital. Last Easter I was at Bromley from Saturday to the Tuesday. I had never spoken to the prisoner. I knew him by sight.

HENRY JOHN CLARK, examined—I keep a private inquiry office at 20 Cockspur Street, Charing Cross. On 5th May last I received an envelope like the one which is now produced. I handed it over to Inspector Harvey about three weeks afterwards.

Mrs FANNY PAYTOR, examined—I reside at 57 St Paul Street, Lewes Road Brighton. I am married. Alice Marsh was my sister. The writing on this piece of paper traced to the prisoner, now shown to me, is my sister's. Also that on the other pieces.

JOHN HAYNES examined by Mr C F Gill—I am an engineer and am at present out of employment. About the beginning of April last I went to lodge at 129 Westminster Bridge Road, the house of Mr Armstead photographer. I was there introduced to Neill. He afterwards told me that he was agent for the Harvey Drug Company

Evidence for Prosecution.

John Haynes

He showed me a case of samples, which I have since seen. I was to an extent a good deal in his company. I went about with him in the daytime, and in the evening sometimes. On one occasion Mr Armstead made a communication that we were being followed, that his house was being watched. I asked Neill if it was he they were following and he said, 'No certainly not.' I said "I cannot go to the music hall with you to-night without making inquiry." That was about 11th May. Instead of going to the music hall that night I went to make inquiries. The following day I told Neill that he ought to have told me the evening we were together that he knew he had been followed for some time. He said that he had been followed for another man who lived in the same house as he; he said his name was Walter Joseph Harper, a medical student at St Thomas's. I asked him why they followed Harper; he made a verbal statement at that time, and afterwards a written statement which I took down in his presence with his permission. This verbal statement was as nearly as possible the same as was afterwards reduced to writing. These are the rough notes I took at this time at the Cafe de Paris, in Ludgate Hill, where we went to dine together—

Walter J Harper MRCS, LRCP student at St Thomas's, at one time well known among a low class of people B T, lived at time of murder at 103 Lambeth Palace Road, father an MD at Barnstaple (B St), been supplying son with ample means while in London, promising son partnership on account of &c. W J H got girl at Mutton's, at Brighton, in trouble some time back, procured abortion for her. Stamford Street girls aware of this H visiting them, they threatened him, blackmail, victims W J H weeks before tried to purchase strychnine, telling him of his trouble asking what he could do under the circumstances, be well to get rid of them &c., person suspecting wrote girls warning, anonymous letter, &c., is fairish, 5 8, slim, thick brown moustache, haughty and distant in manner gentlemanly, &c, &c. Ask Sidney Jones, consulting surgeon, Thomas's. Issued invite to H to wedding of daughter. Left day before inquest suddenly, leaving property behind 118 Stamford Street Mrs E Vogt. Did girls receive anon letter before affair? J H—A B H *

The name of the terrace is underlined. 'B T' is Blythe Terrace—that is to show she lived there and "B St" is Bear Street. "On account of " &c means on account of old age. That was given to me to make inquiries by Neill. He gave me the names of Marsh and Shrivell, who he said, received anonymous letters before death,

---

* It need scarcely be said that this statement was a lie from beginning to end

Thomas Neill Cream.

John Haynes

before taking poisons from Dr. Harper. That was given to me in order that I might investigate it if I wished to prove his statement. After making the statement he mentioned incidentally at the time that Harper had not alone poisoned Marsh and Shrivell, but other three women; he mentioned the names Ellen Donworth, Matilda Clover, and Lou Harvey. Some time after the first meeting he told me that Matilda Clover lived at 27 Lambeth Road. He went with me and pointed out the house to me. He said she had been poisoned with strychnine, and that her body should be exhumed and the poison would be found. He asked me to make inquiries that very morning; he waited outside till I made inquiries. I inquired if Matilda Clover had died there from poisoning. He said Lou Harvey had been poisoned by Harper at a music hall, and that she had fallen dead either at the music hall or between two music halls which he named, I think the Royal and the Oxford. He said Lou Harvey resided at 55 Townshend Road, St. John's Wood. I went with him there; he pointed me out the house where she had resided, 55 Townshend Road. I made inquiries. He said the reason Harper had told him of the victims in the different cases was that Marsh and Shrivell were acquainted with Harper at Brighton. He said that he was on terms of the greatest friendship with Harper, and that Harper, being in trouble, had asked him to procure strychnine for the purpose of poisoning those girls. He said he had written an anonymous letter to Shrivell and Marsh, warning them not to take medicines of any kind from Dr. Walter J. Harper.

Have you made any other notes?—I have, for my own purpose, they are at home, 129 Westminster Bridge Road. Apart from these notes, I wrote a statement which I gave to the authorities. I can find my other notes.

Mr. Justice HAWKINS—Then let us have them. Let an officer go with the witness at once to secure them.

The Court adjourned.

Third Day—Wednesday, 19th October, 1892.

JOHN HAYNES recalled further examined by Mr C F GILL—After I had been to Townshend Road with the prisoner, I went there with Sergeant M'Intyre and pointed out the house to him. When Neill made his statements to me about young Mr Harper I told him it was a very grave matter, and asked him how it was he had not communicated what he knew to the authorities, and that I thought it my duty to do so. He said it would be very foolish of him to think about doing such a thing, as there was more money to be made out of it by seeing Walter J Harper's father at Barnstaple. I said to him that this was not America, and he could not do as he pleased here, that it was a penal offence. He said that he did not care

I remember being on an omnibus with him towards the end of May, and hearing the newspaper boys calling out "Arrest in the Stamford Street case." Neill appeared agitated, and called my attention to the boys; and he wanted to get down and buy papers We were then some hundred yards from Charing Cross coming west I remonstrated with him as to getting down, and said, 'We shall be at Charing Cross directly, and then you can buy a paper." When the bus stopped at Charing Cross we got down and he purchased all the evening papers all that the vendor had and he gave me several to read. He asked me to read that item of news, it referred to an arrest in what was known as "The Stamford Street Road to Ruin Case", it had nothing to do with the murder of Marsh and Shrivell When I read it to him he appeared to be much relieved.

I was with him on 3rd June, the day of his arrest, until five minutes before he was arrested. I learned of it later on in the evening. He wanted to send for me but was not allowed. His arrest took place in the early part of the week following the omnibus incident. I produced at the inquest the pencil notes which are now shown to me. I went with Inspector Harvey to Westminster Bridge Road last night and found there a telegram and a note with it, and this little memorandum on the back of a letter. It had been in my pocket for weeks and it is rubbed. It is the name and address of Matilda Clover in Lambeth Road. The note was a private affair of my own. The telegram has nothing to do with the case, it is from the prisoner to myself

Thomas Neill Cream.

John Haynes

Cross examined by Mr Geoghegan—I have travelled a good deal in America as well as other places in the world. I was introduced to the prisoner at Mr Armstead's, the photographer. During the progress of our acquaintance we frequently discussed America and some prominent people there. He told me that he had travelled in various parts of America. When we spoke about this blackmailing I believe I told him that it was punishable with penal servitude, and that the truth was immaterial.

Where had you acquired that legal knowledge?—I acquired it in travelling about the world a good deal for forty years. I am an engineer out of employment.

You say that you are an engineer out of employment; would you mind writing down on this piece of paper the name of the firm for whom you last worked, and the date? I am not attacking your veracity in the questions I ask, as I believe you are here anxious to tell the truth?—I will with the greatest pleasure, write where I was last employed, and by whom. (The witness wrote down the name of a firm of engineers in America, also the date.) I may tell you I never thought I should be a witness against Neill. This refers to a firm of engineers in America, where I was working in January, 1891.

Have you ever been a detective?—I have not.

Or a private inquiry agent?—Yes, in London and elsewhere, making inquiries for the British Government.

Did you tell the prisoner you had been so employed?—Yes.

Where?—In America and elsewhere.

You knew Le Caron?—Yes, very well.

You have been in communication with him?—Yes.

And you had conversation with the prisoner about the matter?—I can't remember. But it is quite possible when I mentioned the name.

And when he heard you had been working for the British Government he grew most confidential?—Yes.

The Court—Naturally so.

Cross-examination resumed—And so he told you all you wished to know?—I did not desire to know anything.

And you suggested that what he had said ought to be laid before the authorities?—Yes.

And he said "Certainly"?—No, he did not say that.

Evidence for Prosecution.

John Haynes

But did he try to prevent you doing so?—He did. He said more money could be made elsewhere.

Did you get from him about a dozen photographs of Mr. Harper?—No, I received one photograph of young Mr. Harper from him, and that was one he had stolen from one of the albums in the house where Mr. Harper lived, from Miss Sleaper's album.

How many did he steal?—He told me only one.

And you received it?—Yes.

Then you received stolen goods?—I received that.

You took all you have told us down in writing, and the more you wrote the more confidential he grew?—Yes.

He told you Lou Harvey had dropped down dead in a music hall?—Yes.

Did he not say that he had at a subsequent period met her in the street?—No.

If he had told you that, I suppose it would have done away with the poisoning story and would have destroyed your interest in him?—Yes.

You have a claim, if I mistake not, on the British Government?—No.

On the late Home Secretary?—No.

You never told the prisoner so?—No.

You were anxious to get an appointment in the London police, were you not?—No; I knew Mr. Soames.

He is the solicitor for *The Times*, is he not?—Is he?

Did you ever write to Sir Edward Jenkinson?—Yes. He gave me a testimonial.

Did you recommend yourself to him as an engineer?—I did not.

As a private inquiry agent?—I did not. I was introduced to him. It was not my idea to obtain employment in the London, or Liverpool, or any other police.

Where did your conversations with the prisoner take place?—At the Café de Paris,* Ludgate Hill, and other places.

Did you always carry pencil and paper with you?—I am always provided with pencil and paper. I openly jotted down everything.

Have you seen the prisoner constantly taking drugs?—Yes, on many occasions.

Do you know what those drugs were?—I did.

---

* Since departed, now a tea shop.

Thomas Neill Cream.

John Haynes

Was morphia one?—It was. He took morphia, strychnine, and opium.

PATRICK M'INTYRE, examined by Mr C. F. GILL—I am a police sergeant in the Criminal Investigation Department. About the beginning of May I made the acquaintance of the prisoner. I was introduced to him by Mr William Armstead, a photographer of Westminster Bridge Road. Neill told me that he was a doctor of medicine, that he had studied at St Thomas's Hospital, and had been at Edinburgh and Dublin, and afterwards had gone to America. About 19th May he spoke to me about being followed, and asked me to make some inquiries. At that time I knew of no suspicion attaching to him. I made some inquiry then and saw Inspector Harvey and Chief Inspector Mulvaney about the matter. On 19th May Neill and I were in the Pleasant public house in the Lambeth Palace Road. I was waiting there until he went to his lodgings at 103 Lambeth Palace Road to fetch his case and some letters for the purpose of showing that he was a *bona fide* commercial traveller. Inspectors Harvey and Mulvaney were with me. Neill produced his case and some correspondence, and opened it. There was some conversation with regard to it, and then Harvey and Mulvaney went away, and I was left with Neill. He said to me that a few nights previously he had met a "rip" in the Westminster Bridge Road who had informed him that she was sent after him by the police for the purpose of ascertaining who and what he was as they suspected him in connection with the Stamford Street poisoning cases. That was the first mention of the matter by him.

After that were you in communication with your superiors?— Yes. About mid-day on 24th May I went to Neill's house at Lambeth Palace Road. He arranged to meet me that evening at 7.30. He did not keep the appointment, and I went to see him at eight in the evening. He had sent Miss Sleaper to say he could not keep the appointment, he was ill in bed. I found him in bed when I went at eight, he then said that about a week before the last inquest (that was the one upon Marsh and Shrivell) he was leaving his lodgings at 103 Lambeth Palace Road in the morning when he was stopped in the street by a man who said he was a detective, and gave his name as Murray. The man questioned him as to Dr Harper and as to Dr Harper's associations with women. He then produced a letter, addressed to Shrivell and Marsh at Stamford Street, the letter having

Evidence for Prosecution.

Patrick M'Intyre

passed through the post. The purport of the letter was to warn the girls to be careful of Dr. Harper, as he would serve them as he had done the girls Clover and Harvey.

By the Court—You knew of no man named Murray in the force?—I did not, my lord.

Examination continued—How did he describe Murray?—He said he was a man of about forty years of age, 5 feet 8 inches, or 5 feet 9 inches in height, that he wore a dark cut-away coat, light trousers, and a hard felt hat, and had a heavy moustache and straggling grey hair.

Did you ask him if he had a photograph of Murray?—I did.

Did you ask him if he knew a man named Clark, a detective?—I asked him if he knew Clark, but not as a detective. The prisoner said he did not.

Did you say anything to him as to his handwriting?—I said I had seen my superior, and had been instructed to get a specimen of his writing.

Did you take a piece from some paper in the room and ask him to write on it?—I took a piece from some notepaper on the table, and he wrote on it in my presence. (The paper was produced.)

You will find, if you look at it, that it bears the watermark "Fairfield—Superfine Quality."?—Yes, I have seen it.

(His lordship inspected the paper, holding it up to the light in order to see the watermark.)

You have seen the letter sent to Dr. Harper?—Yes, the same mark is on the letter as on the paper.

(Mr. Geoghegan said he did not contest the handwriting being that of the prisoner, or the watermark on the letter. It was an American watermark, and not known in England.)

Examination continued—You had some further conversation with him?—I did.

And did he speak to you about Shrivell and Marsh?—Our conversation was not confined to these two. We talked over all the poisoning cases.

Did you say anything to him as to his knowledge of those girls, and how they had come to their death?—I said "Doctor,* you appear to be pretty well posted in these matters. The matter of King's

---

* An American brand.

Thomas Neill Cream.

Patrick M'Intyre

Cross was spoken of, where a man was in custody or had been charged. The prisoner said, "Yes, I have followed the matter closely in the *British Medical Journal*. Being a medical man, I take an interest in matters of this kind."

Had you ever heard of Clover up to the time the prisoner said Murray had spoken of Harper and said the other girls would be served in the same way as Clover and Harvey?—No. I asked him if he would let me have a general record as to where he had been since he had been in this country and where he had stayed at. He said he would do so if I called the following morning. I called the following morning and found Miss Sleaper in his room writing this document as to his movements. I read it over in his presence, and told him that he had not accounted for the date on which the Stamford Street poisoning case occurred. He said, "So soon as I get out of bed and I am able to look up some dates, I will be able to fix my whereabouts at that particular time, but I think I was at Berkhamstead."

Next day I met him in the Lambeth Palace Road. He said, 'I am going away to-day at three o'clock. Will I be arrested if I do so?' I said, "I cannot tell you; if you will cross with me to Scotland Yard I will make inquiries." We proceeded together about half-way across Westminster Bridge when he stopped and said, ' I will not go any further with you, I am suspicious of you, and I believe you are playing me double. You sent a 'tip' after me to meet me outside the *British Medical Journal* office." I pointed out that that was a matter of impossibility, as I was not aware that he was going there. He walked back with me as far as the corner of Stangate, and said he would consult a solicitor as to the annoyance caused to him by the police, being followed and so on, and he asked me if I could recommend him one, and I said no, I could not, as it would not be consistent with my position to do so.

How did you come to make his acquaintance in the first instance?—I made his acquaintance by accident.

Were you one of the officers entrusted to make inquiries with regard to Lou Harvey?—Yes, and I did so with the view of tracing the death and the body, and getting some traces of her. Haynes went with me and pointed out a house, 55 Townshend Road, where I made inquiries but I could not succeed in finding any trace of such a person. I made other inquiries, and inquiries were made by other officers of police, with regard to Lou Harvey.

Evidence for Prosecution.

Patrick M'Intyre

What did the prisoner tell you with regard to his business?—The only thing he showed me with regard to the Harvey Drug Company was a letter which he gave to me open in the public-house. I do not remember his mentioning the name of any person with whom he did business.

Cross-examined—I think you are attached to the Criminal Investigation Department at Scotland Yard?—Yes. Throughout the London Divisions there are a number of divisional detectives. Information of any crime in London would come first to the local police, and would be forwarded to Scotland Yard. I do not know anything about the divisional police. On 1st November I received a letter about Clover's death.

Did that letter come from Scotland Yard?—I do not know. Inspector Tunbridge would know more about it than I do.

The ATTORNEY-GENERAL intimated that Inspector Tunbridge would be called, who would be able to speak on that matter.

Cross-examination continued—Do you know Haynes?—Yes, I have known him for some years.

As an ex-detective or secret agent?—No.

As what?—I first knew him as an engineer on board ship.

But from January, 1891?—He only returned from America six months before.

Is he a friend of yours?—Yes.

Did you ask him what he had been doing there?—I knew he was in the Home Office Department as a secret agent to make inquiries about a certain class of suspected persons.

You yourself were connected with the dynamite explosions, following suspected persons in London?—Yes.

When Neill told you that Detective Murray had stopped him in the street and told him this story, did you express disbelief?—I thought that some person was trying to blackmail him. I did not believe it was a detective.

When did you first speak to Haynes about it?—About that time. Early in May, the first or second week.

You used to see Haynes constantly, with the knowledge of the prisoner?—Yes.

I suppose that you conveyed to Chief Inspector Mulvaney what the prisoner had said?—Certainly. I said I would make inquiries, and I introduced the prisoner to Chief Inspector Mulvaney.

Thomas Neill Cream.

Patrick M'Intyre

We have heard about getting introductions through a photographer. Now he is getting into a higher class of society and making the acquaintance of chief inspectors of police. Was the poison mentioned when Mulvaney was in his company?—I don't think so.

Did he tell you he was connected with the women who were poisoned?—Yes. That was after the conversation with Haynes. I first heard from the prisoner about Lou Harvey.

Who told him he was suspected?—A woman told him. That was before the Charing Cross incident.

Had Haynes mentioned Lou Harvey to you?—I presume so. He took me to see the house.

Did Haynes show you a photograph?—The prisoner gave me a photograph of Dr. Harper. I do not know that Haynes showed me any, but he may have done so. He has been in the habit of showing me photographs. My official duty has brought me into connection with him before this matter, in relation to suspected people from America.

GEORGE HARVEY, examined by the ATTORNEY-GENERAL.—I am an inspector with the L Division, and am stationed at Lambeth. I have had charge of the inquiries respecting the deaths of the four women, Ellen Donworth, Alice Marsh, Emma Shrivell, and Matilda Clover. I first heard of the death of Matilda Clover on 28th April of the present year. I first heard the cause of her death after the arrest of Neill on another charge at Bow Street Police Court. He was arrested on 4th June and taken to Bow Street. Up to that time I had not heard any suggestion from any one as to her death being caused by strychnine. I first heard of the letter to Dr. Broadbent during the inquiry at Bow Street, on one of the remands.

The magisterial inquiry began on 21st July, and the prisoner was committed for trial on 22nd August. The first time he was before the magistrate at Bow Street was on 4th June on a charge of blackmailing.

The Broadbent letter was sent to Scotland Yard. Was it ever forwarded to you?—It was not. Assuming that the letter went to Scotland Yard and I had thought proper to make inquiries about it, it would have been forwarded to me.

When did you first begin to make inquiries about these cases?—In April I sent Sergeant Ward and other officers to make inquiries,

Evidence for Prosecution.

George Harvey

and they reported the suspicious deaths of Donworth, Marsh, and Shrivell. I was not then aware of the death of Clover.

How was it you heard of Matilda Clover's death?—I had sent my officers to all parts of London to make inquiries of prostitutes. Sergeant Ward made a report relating to Matilda Clover. In consequence I went and saw Lucy Rose at 58 Lambeth Road on 28th April. I took a statement from her relating to Matilda Clover's death. I also went to 27 Lambeth Road and saw the landlady, Mrs. Phillips, or Vowles. In consequence of the information I received from those persons I communicated with the Treasury, and an application was made to the Home Secretary with a view to the exhumation of the body of Matilda Clover. The order was made on 5th May, and the body was exhumed on the 6th.

You recollect the report of Dr. Stevenson as to Clover's case. Was there, before that time, any suggestion as to the cause, or any kind of suspicion raised with reference to the death of any of this class of persons except Donworth, Marsh, and Shrivell?—None whatever.

Cross-examined—Is Waterloo Road in your district?—Yes. As you go down Waterloo Bridge Road from the Strand the station* is on the right and Morpeth Place is on the left, almost immediately opposite the station. There is a large lamp at the corner. Morpeth Place is a place consisting of bad characters. Going down Westminster Bridge Road the Canterbury Music Hall is on the right as you go under the railway bridge, and Gatti's Music Hall is on the left, within about 200 or 300 yards of the Canterbury.

Do you remember what was said about the death of Donworth?—Yes, I remember the death of Ellen Donworth on 13th October of last year. She staggered and fell in the road by the Lord Hill public-house, within about 30 or 40 yards of Morpeth Place. Her death caused a fearful sensation in South Lambeth; it was called "The Lambeth Mystery." I was present at the inquest.

Was a man named Slater under examination in November?—Yes.

Was he under remand at the time of the inquest?—I am not sure whether he was or not. I took some of the witnesses in Donworth's case to identify him. He was a tall man, with drooping shoulders and straggly beard. There was a general worn out appear-

---

* Waterloo Station

Thomas Neill Cream.

ance about him. He was not stout. His age would be about forty or forty-five. One of his eyes had been injured, and that gave him a rather peculiar look. The witnesses failed to identify him as the man seen with Donworth, and the Treasury did not carry the case further. He then went to Clerkenwell, and my division had nothing more to do with him.

By the COURT—He was a jeweller's traveller.

ALFRED WARD, examined—I am a sergeant in the L Division. I had instructions to make inquiries relating to the deaths of Marsh and Shrivell but not as to Donworth specifically, but inquiries among that class of women. On 28th April I made a report to Inspector Harvey of certain information I had obtained the day previous, the 27th. Up to that time I had not heard any suggestion of foul play in relation to Matilda Clover. On 27th April I had an interview with Lucy Rose. That was the first and only occasion I had seen her, and the first occasion on which I had heard anything about Clover.

What did you go to see Lucy Rose about?—I went to see her in connection with the Donworth case. I was making inquiries generally among women in the district.

Were you specially engaged for that purpose in connection with this inquiry?—Yes. On 26th April I was told by her landlady, Mrs Robertson, 88 Lambeth Road, that she could give some information that would bear upon the inquiry. She told me that on the 26th, the interview with Rose was on the 27th, and the report to Inspector Harvey on the 28th. Until after the inquiry at Bow Street and the inquest I had never heard strychnine mentioned in connection with Clover. I first heard strychnine mentioned after Dr Stevenson's analysis of the body.

JOHN BENNETT TUNBRIDGE, examined by the ATTORNEY-GENERAL— I am an inspector in the Criminal Investigation Department, Scotland Yard. On 1st December I believe a letter reached the Criminal Investigation Department, Scotland Yard, from Dr Broadbent.

Was anything done in consequence of that letter?—Yes, an advertisement was inserted in the *Daily Chronicle* about 3rd December, with Dr Broadbent's sanction, and observation was kept on Dr Broadbent's house for two days, to see whether any person called in answer to the advertisement. It was thought that it was an attempt to extort money, and that some one would probably call

Evidence for Prosecution.

John Bennett Tunbridge

at Dr. Broadbent's house. No person called. Beyond that nothing was done and the letter remained in the department.

Did not Dr. Broadbent object to his name being used in the matter?—He did.

Was any inquiry made at 27 Lambeth Road?—No.

Was any communication made to the officer in charge of the L Division?—No.

Was any inquiry made about the girl Clover either at Lambeth Road or about Lambeth Road?—No, no inquiry was made.

By the Court—Do I understand that notwithstanding that this letter was received by the authorities at Scotland Yard on 1st December no inquiry was made about the girl Clover?—None whatever.

Not at 27 Lambeth Road?—No.

Nor as to the cause of her death?—No inquiries whatever were made except what I have said.

Can you account for that?—I may say that I myself had nothing to do with it. The letter was looked upon as a letter from an insane person. Other letters had been received of a similar character, and inquiries had been made and no one had turned up in relation to them.

Surely, surely, that does not account for it. Here is a real person who actually lived at 27 Lambeth Road, and it is said that this person was poisoned by strychnine. This information comes to Scotland Yard within a quarter of an hour's walk of the place. How comes it that no one took the trouble to make an inquiry at Lambeth Road?—Well, it was not done, my lord.

My surprise remains.

Examination continued—Nothing was done beyond watching Dr. Broadbent's house?—No.

The Court—But my surprise remains. (*To Witness*)—I cannot see why it should have been thought of more importance to watch Dr. Broadbent's house than to make this inquiry?—It was thought from the tone of the letter that it was an attempt to extort money without any ground such as that stated in the letter.

Suppose the man had been caught, would any inquiry of this kind have been made?—I presume so, my lord.

I should presume not, from what happened.

Examination continued—I first received instructions on 26th May to inquire into the South Lambeth poisoning cases, those were

Thomas Neill Cream.

John Bennett Tunbridge

the cases of Clover, Donworth, Marsh, and Shrivell, and into the attempt at extortion contained in the letter sent to Dr Harper In consequence, partly of a complaint by the prisoner that he was being watched, I went on 26th May to 103 Lambeth Palace Road and saw him there Miss Sabbatini was present I referred to the letter of complaint received from Messrs Waters & Bryan, and talked over the matter The prisoner alleged that the police having watched him had interfered with his business I then spoke to him about his business and his presence in this country He said he first came to this country in October last that was October, 1891, to consult an oculist that he was a doctor of medicine, and he had had a practice in America, that some time ago he had a serious illness, and that the night calls did not agree with him, and that in consequence he had given up his practice He showed me this medicine case I noticed this bottle labelled " 1-16th grain strychnine ' I said ' What are these pills composed of ?" and he replied ' 1-16th grain of strychnine, and the sugar coating only " I said, ' At that rate this bottle contains quite a large quantity of strychnine, and it would be highly dangerous that they should fall into the hands of the public in any quantity Neill said ' It is not intended to sell them to the public direct, but only to chemists and surgeons who will dispense them in their proper quantities " He did not say if he had sold any or if he had any customers He said he had taken up the agency in the previous February only, and that he had been travelling through Canada with them until he arrived in this country in April

On 26th May had you any knowledge that Clover had died from strychnine?—I had no such knowledge and no such suggestion had been made to me as that Clover had died from strychnine I had heard that her body had been exhumed

When did you first hear that her death was caused by strychnine? —About two days before the date of Dr Stevenson's report On 1st June I visited Barnstaple and saw Dr Harper and his son At that time I had received specimens of Neill's handwriting from Sergeant M'Intyre and Mr Priest, the chemist Upon that I applied on 3rd June for a warrant against Neill for sending a blackmailing letter I executed that warrant at 5 25 on 3rd June in the Lambeth Palace Road I told him I had a warrant for his arrest, and I read it to him He said, ' You have got the wrong man Fire away ! " I showed him the envelope in which the letter had been sent to Dr

Evidence for Prosecution.
John Bennett Tunbridge

Harper, and said, " This is what you are accused of sending." He looked at the writing on the envelope and said, " That is not my writing"; I took the letter from the envelope and said, " This is the letter." He made no reply. I took him to Bow Street where he was charged. He made no reply to the charge, but he afterwards said " Can I send to Messrs Waters & Bryan, my solicitors?" I said " You can wire them. I will get you a form." He said, " I write nothing. You do it for me," and I sent the telegram. He was searched, nothing was found on him relating to these matters. I afterwards went to his lodgings with Inspector Harvey and Sergeant M'Intyre, and Miss Sleaper pointed out the things she said belonged to the prisoner. Among them were this sample case produced, a dark blue overcoat, and a dark grey overcoat, a large portmanteau, a tin box, and other things full of clothing. I took possession of everything in the room that belonged to him. He was wearing a silk hat when he was arrested. I found two other silk hats and a soft felt hat.

Did you find a brown coat with a cape?—No. I found no brown coat.

Or a flat-topped felt hat, or light suits, or a gold watch?—No. The prisoner was wearing a silver or metal watch. I found in a chest of drawers in the room this envelope with certain initials and dates upon it. I found in the fob pocket of a pair of trousers belonging to the prisoner, a piece of paper with an address—but not in the handwriting of the prisoner. It was in the handwriting of the girl Marsh, and was ' Miss Alice Marsh and Miss Emma Shrivell, 118 Stamford Street, Waterloo Road." I also found two letters from the Harvey Drug Company of 26th February and 6th May, a certificate of baptism of Thomas Neill, father's name William Cream, dated 29th June 1850. The inquest on Clover began on 22nd June and the verdict was given on 13th July. On 18th July I re-charged the prisoner—then being in custody—with the wilful murder of Matilda Clover. I said to him ' You will be charged with murder," and he said ' What in the Clover case?" I said, ' Yes." The charge was taken and read over to him, and he said " All right." Later on he said "Is anything going to be done in the other cases?" I said, " Not at present I believe." He said " You will be sure to let me know if anything is to be done." I was present at the inquest, when a communication was made to the prisoner as to whether

Thomas Neill Cream.

John Bennett Tunbridge

he wished to be examined. He was then under arrest for sending the threatening letter. The Coroner told him he was at liberty to give evidence if he chose, and ordered the officer to hand him the book to be sworn. At first he refused to be sworn, but later on he took the oath and gave his name." What he said was taken down on the depositions.

Mr GEOGHEGAN objected to anything that took place at the Coroner's Court being given in evidence. Either it should come from the Coroner's depositions or the Coroner himself should be placed in the witness-box.

The ATTORNEY-GENERAL—If my learned friend desires to have the Coroner in the witness box I will see that he is called.

Mr GEOGHEGAN—I have a strong reason for asking that anything which took place at the Coroner's Court should come either from the Coroner or his depositions.

The COURT held that the point did not require a formal ruling, adding—I wish every Police Court had before them these depositions of the Coroner, as a sample of what depositions ought to be.

Examination continued—As a matter of fact the prisoner gave no evidence.

Cross-examined by Mr GEOGHEGAN—The Coroner's inquest took place in the Vestry Hall at Tooting. There was a large number of jurymen. I am not sure if it was twenty-three. Mr Gill appeared for the Treasury and examined the witnesses. The Coroner called formal witnesses, I believe, the witnesses were subpoenaed by the Coroner's officer. I believe I was the last witness that Mr Gill called before the Coroner. I mentioned before the Coroner that when I showed the prisoner the envelope, which I told him he was accused of writing, he said "That is not my writing."

At that time the prisoner was under remand at Bow Street on the charge of sending that letter?—Yes.

He could have been examined and cross-examined in the Coroner's Court, and the twenty-three jurymen and the Coroner and the Treasury counsel could have asked him questions?—Yes.

I think after your evidence Mr Gill said that that was all the evidence he had been able to get as to the inquiries that had been

---

* But see Introduction, page 27.

Evidence for Prosecution.

John Bennett Tunbridge

made, and then the Coroner proposed to call the prisoner, who was sitting between two warders as the last witness?—Yes

Did you hear Mr Waters as his solicitor, object to his client being called upon to give evidence while a criminal charge was hanging over him?—Yes, excited words passed between Mr Waters and the Coroner

The COURT—Excited or excitable?

Mr GEOGHEGAN—From what I know of Mr Waters I should say "excited"

Cross-examination continued—The prisoner said he was acting under legal advice and declined to give evidence, or words to that effect The Coroner said he had the right to administer the oath to any one in his Court, and exercising that right he called on the prisoner to be sworn

The COURT—After the advice given by his solicitor, the Attorney-General will hardly rely on this If a solicitor says, "Don't say anything" it would be rather stupid if the client did say anything

The ATTORNEY-GENERAL assented

Mr GEOGHEGAN—Then I will not press the point

Cross-examination continued—Is it the case that the police in addition to the ordinary telegraph wires have wires radiating from Scotland Yard to every part of London?—Yes

Is there a private wire to Kennington Lane and every other police station?—Yes

Did you receive the letter from Dr Broadbent?—No I first saw it on the day after the prisoner's arrest The post-mark on the envelope is " S E "

Was there a wire sent to Kennington Lane?—No

Although she had died within a quarter of an hour's walk of Scotland Yard, do you say that no wire was sent to Kennington Lane? —That is so

Whose fault was that?—The fault, if fault there be, rests with Scotland Yard

Is there any jealousy between Scotland Yard and the other police in London?—I know of no jealousy between the police of Scotland Yard and the other police in London

Were you present at Bow Street police station when Masters and May were called in to identify the prisoner?—Yes

I suppose for an identification you just catch hold of people and

Thomas Neill Cream.

John Bennett Tunbridge

bring them in from the street?—No, we cannot do that. We have to invite them to come in to assist at an identification.

Among how many persons was the prisoner placed?—About twenty.

Did they in any way resemble the prisoner?—Yes, we were some time trying to get in people from the street as near the prisoner's appearance as possible.

For how long would you be trying?—Perhaps a quarter of an hour. I took a statement from Masters and May on 11th June, and they described the man they had seen at Gatti's Music Hall.

Where did these twenty persons you speak of come from?—They were nearly all persons from the Court.

Had any of them silk hats on?—Many of them had.

Had any of them a squint?—No.

Had any of them moustaches?—Most of them had.

Brown moustaches?—No, not all, they were of all kinds. In a quarter of an hour I got twenty men all generally answering the description of the prisoner.

Were they all bald?—No.

Were they dressed similarly to him?—Yes.

Did the prisoner know that he was to be brought up for identification that day?—Yes, a little time before, probably half an hour before.

Was his solicitor present at the identification?—I think so, but I should not like to swear that he was.

Was the gaoler in the room?—Yes.

What happened when Masters failed to identify the prisoner with his hat on?—When she failed to identify him she went out, and May came in and May identified him.

Were May and Masters together in the room when the identification took place?—No.

Where was the prisoner placed?—He was placed with twenty persons in the charge-room.

And where were Masters and May and the other persons who came to identify him?—They were placed in a small room off the charge-room. That was the only time they were together, and that was before either was brought out to see if they could identify.

When Masters was brought in on the second occasion, and just before she identified the prisoner with his hat on, had not the gaoler

Evidence for Prosecution

John Bennett Tunbridge

touched him on the shoulder and said, "Come with me"?—I am perfectly sure that he did nothing of the kind.

Was the gaoler standing in front of the row of men?—Yes.

Was it not from an afterthought of yours that the men took their hats off?—No, it was from a communication made to me. They were about breaking up when Masters was brought back. I am sure the gaoler was not near the prisoner when Masters came in, and I am perfectly certain that he did not beckon to the prisoner or do anything of the kind.

May he not have done so?—He might have done so afterwards, but not when Masters was coming into the room.

Can you tell us about the prison regulations with regard to shaving?—No, I do not know these regulations.

Are all the bottles that you found at the prisoner's lodgings produced here?—Yes. I found several bottles empty and full, and they have been in my possession ever since. I find there is "opium" on the bottle now shown to me. There are very few pills indeed in it. I found no morphia. This bottle bears a label '500 pills opium 1 grain dose 1 or 2.' It is nearly empty.

Did you find any bottle containing opium in a liquid shape?—No. This bottle which is shown me is one-third full, and it is marked '500 pills *Cannabis Indica* extract, ½ grain, poison, dose, 1 to 3.'

Those have all been analysed by Dr. Stevenson?—Yes.

Re-examined by the ATTORNEY-GENERAL—The advertisement was inserted only once in the *Daily Chronicle*, and that was on Friday, 4th December 1891. It is as follows:—"Personal. M. Malone—Call or send this morning to arrange as in your letter of 28th ult. —B."

Inspector FREDERICK SMITH JARVIS, examined by the ATTORNEY-GENERAL—On 16th June of this year I was instructed to go to America in reference to this case. I left on the 18th. In consequence of a communication from the police authorities in Canada, I communicated with the witness M'Culloch, and it was at my instance that he came to London to attend this inquiry.

LAURA SABBATINI examined by the Hon. BERNARD COLERIDGE—I live in Chapel Street, Berkhamstead. In November last I made the acquaintance of the prisoner. I remember his leaving for America early in January. Prior to that date I became engaged to be

Thomas Neill Cream.

married to him. I received this letter from him, dated 3rd December, in reference to that engagement. Before leaving he made his will, he said it was a will that he could not revoke. He left it with me on his going to America. The document which is now shown to me is that will. It is in the handwriting of the prisoner, and it gives all his property to me. He gave me his address, if I was to write to him, as "c/o Daniel Cream, Quebec, Canada." I wrote to him there at Blanchard's Hotel, Quebec. I corresponded with him during his absence.

Did you receive letters or other documents from him?—Yes, but I have destroyed them. I had a number of letters but did not wish to keep them.

Cross-examined by Mr GEOGHEGAN.—I am not in the habit of keeping letters.

Did he not, whilst you and he have been walking out together, frequently go into chemists' shops and purchase opium for the relief of his head?—He did so.

WALTER DE GREY BIRCH, examined—I have been for twenty-seven years employed in the Manuscripts Department of the British Museum. I have had experience in the comparison of handwriting, and have frequently been consulted as an expert in these matters. I have examined the documents produced in this case as admittedly in the handwriting of the prisoner. Comparing them with the letter to Dr Broadbent and the envelope, the prescription written by Neill and other writings, I judge them all to be in the handwriting of the same person. (The documents with photographs of the same were put in and handed to the jury.)

The ATTORNEY-GENERAL stated that that was all the direct evidence in the Clover case, and that he now proposed to give evidence as to the deaths of three other women by strychnine, and the attempted administration of poison to a fourth, and to connect these acts with the prisoner.

Mr GEOGHEGAN observed that his learned friend (Mr Warburton), having addressed himself to this part of the case, would conduct the argument.

The ATTORNEY-GENERAL—The broad ground upon which he argued its admissibility was first, that the evidence would prove the prisoner's

Evidence for Prosecution.

Attorney General

possession of strychnine, then to show that the death of Matilda Clover was not, as the cross-examination seemed to suggest, a death from natural causes or from delirium tremens, but was a death by strychnine. The evidence it was proposed to give went to show that the prisoner had pursued the same course of action in other cases as it was alleged he had taken in the case of Clover. Next it was evidence to show a systematic and deliberate course of action. Lastly, he would ask his lordship to observe that in the Harper letter the prisoner had grouped the whole of the cases as a series of transactions, and had attributed them to one man—Harper. That, he contended, made the evidence admissible. He cited the following authorities:—R. v. Garney, 18 L.J. (M.C.) 215; R. v. Winslow, 8 Cox C.C. 347; R. v. Gates, 11 and 12, 316; R. v. Cotton, 12 Cox C.C. 100; R. v. Roden, 12 Cox C.C. 630; R. v. Hesson, 11 Cox C.C. 40; R. v. Heavens and Flannagan, 15 Cox C.C. 403.

Mr. WARBURTON—While accepting the general proposition admissible, because it was not relevant to the issue, and because it formed the subject matter of other indictments against the prisoner

The COURT—That would not of itself exclude the evidence.

Mr. WARBURTON—While accepting the general proposition as laid down by the Attorney General, contended that the facts in the present case were altogether different from those in the cases cited, in all of which cases the accused had lived under the same roof as the deceased persons and had admittedly prepared the food by which they were poisoned. In a case of this kind every case must be judged on the facts that arose in it. They started with the general principle that the evidence must be confined to the point in issue, and especially was that necessary in a criminal trial where the man ought to know exactly the charge he has to meet, otherwise they would practically be trying the prisoner on seven counts at one and the same time. He submitted that in this case there were none of the grounds upon which exception was made to the general principle he had laid down, and that it would be most unsafe to admit the evidence. If his lordship should determine to admit the evidence he would ask him to reserve a case for the consideration of Her Majesty's judges.

Mr. JUSTICE HAWKINS said it was expedient that he should give his opinion at once. He thought it would be more fair and satis-

Thomas Neill Cream.

Mr Justice Hawkins

factory that he should do no more than express his own judgment. If he were to explain all his reasons for giving his decision he should have to comment on the evidence, and that might be very unsatisfactory either to one side or the other. He was satisfied that the general proposition to admit the evidence was one that he ought not to refuse, and so the further evidence would be allowed. At the same time it must be remembered that admissibility was one thing and the weight of it quite another. In giving this decision he had to say that he entertained no doubt, and therefore he should not reserve a case.

LOUISA HARRIS examined by the ATTORNEY-GENERAL—I am known by the name of Lou Harvey. I am living now in Stamford Street. In October last year I was living at 44 Townshend Road, St John's Wood, with a young man Charles Harvey, under whose name I passed. I remember being at the Alhambra one night between 20th and 24th October, 1891. I fix the date because Harvey, who had been an omnibus man, left that employment on 13th October. The prisoner spoke to me at the Alhambra that night. After leaving the Alhambra I met him outside St James's Hall,* in Regent Street. He came up and touched my shoulder and asked me to go with him. We went to a hotel in Berwick Street, where we passed the night. He told me that he was a doctor at St Thomas's Hospital, and came from America. He said he was going back again, and would I accompany him back. He asked me my name and I told him it was Lou Harvey, and he asked my address, and I said 55 Townshend Road. I made a mistake in the number, the proper number was 44. I did it quite by mistake. I had lived just a week in St John's Wood.

How was the prisoner dressed that night?—He had a flat-topped hard felt hat, a black overcoat, and a black suit of clothes. He had an old-fashioned gold watch and wore spectacles. He had no beard, he had a moustache, the top of his head was bald. He was cross-eyed. Next morning he said that I had a few spots on my forehead, and he said he would bring me some pills to take them away. We parted, and he told me to meet him at half-past seven

---

* A famous concert hall, now departed, its site—between Piccadilly and Regent Street—being occupied by the Piccadilly Hotel. The Saint James's Bar and Restaurant was a well known haunt of men about town and ladies desirous of their company.

Evidence for Prosecution.

Louisa Harris

that same evening on the Embankment, near Charing Cross Station, and that he would give me the medicine and afterwards take me to a music hall. He asked me where I would like to go, I told him the Oxford Music Hall. I told him I was a servant, that was not correct.

Will you tell us what happened that evening?—I told Harvey about the pills or medicine. Accompanied by him I went to the Embankment, near the Charing Cross Station. I saw the prisoner waiting there for me. This would be about a quarter or ten minutes to eight. I left Harvey in Northumberland Avenue and walked on while he followed me on the other side of the way to the place of meeting. I said to the prisoner, 'Good evening, I am late.' I asked him if he had brought the pills, he said "Yes." He said he had them made in the Westminster Bridge Road. He invited me to have a glass of wine. I asked him if I should take the pills first, he said "No, not till afterwards." We then went together to the Northumberland public-house, which is close to the Embankment, and had a glass of wine. In the public house he bought me some roses from a woman who had come in. We then came out and walked back towards the Embankment. The prisoner then said that he could not go with me to the music hall that night because he had an appointment at St. Thomas's Hospital at nine o'clock, and he should be kept there till 10.30. He told me that I was to get into a cab and go myself and meet him at eleven o'clock outside the music hall, and we would go and spend the night at the same hotel. He gave me some figs, and told me to eat them after I had taken the pills. He took two pills out of his waistcoat pocket. They were wrapped up in a piece of tissue paper, they were long and rather narrower at one end than at the other. They were something like the capsule which is now shown to me, but they might have been a little larger. They were light coloured as near as I could tell, it was rather dark, they were a light colour. He gave them to me and said I was to take them, he said I was to put them in my mouth then and there one by one, and not bite them but swallow them. He put them into my right hand. I pretended to take them, putting my hand to my mouth and pretending to swallow them, but I passed them into my left hand. The prisoner asked me to show him my right hand, I showed it to him, it was empty, then he asked me to show him my left hand in which I had the pills. I threw the pills away behind

Thomas Neill Cream.

Louisa Harris

me and showed him my left hand. He questioned me no further, but gave me 5s. for my seat in the music hall and wanted to put me into a cab. I said, 'No, I can get a cab myself.' He then went away towards St. Thomas's Hospital, towards Westminster Bridge. As he was leaving he said, "Meet me at eleven." I met Harvey at the corner and told him what had happened, and then I went to the Oxford Music Hall. At eleven o'clock I went outside to look for the prisoner. I waited till 11.30; he did not come.

Did you ever see him again after that?—Yes, within a month afterwards I saw him standing at the corner of Piccadilly and Regent Street. I went up and spoke to him; he did not appear to recognise me. I did not stay long with him. He told me that he would meet me at eleven that night outside the St. James's, Piccadilly. Before making that appointment he asked me to have a glass of wine, and we went to a public-house in Air Street. As we were leaving the public-house I said, "Don't you know me?" as he did not seem to recognise me. He said, "No, who are you?" I said, "You promised to meet me outside the Oxford Music Hall." He said, "I don't remember. Who are you?" I said, "Lou Harvey," and upon that he did not speak again, but walked sharp away. That was the last occasion I ever spoke to him. I saw him again in the Strand about a fortnight or three weeks after going to Air Street with him. He was then walking with a young lady in the Strand; I don't think he saw me. I saw the report in the paper where my name was mentioned. I then wrote to the magistrate, Sir John Bridge, and Inspector Tunbridge came to see me and took a statement from me. I was afterwards examined at the inquest, and also at Bow Street.

Was the prisoner dressed always the same when you saw him?— No, he was not dressed in the same way when I met him the second time as he was the first.

Cross-examined by Mr. GEOGHEGAN—I think when you met the prisoner on the first occasion it was at night?—Yes.

And on the second occasion, in Regent Street, it was broad daylight?—Yes.

Are you in the habit of frequenting the Alhambra?—No, I am not.

Do you not go to a music hall in the evening as a rule?—No.

Evidence for Prosecution.

Louisa Harris

When were you last at the Alhambra?—I have not been to the Alhambra within the last month. It was an exceptional thing for me to go there.

Did you not say to the magistrate that it was on 20th October when you first met the prisoner?—No, it was between the 20th and 21th.

Have you and Harvey been living together since this matter?—Yes, sometimes, not all the time.

Have you talked to him about it?—Yes.

And has he shown you dates in a book?—Yes.

Before you saw the dates in that book did you not say that you thought it was the 20th?—No, I did not. When I met him in Regent Street I brought back to his recollection that I was alive and well. I said, "I was the woman you went with to such and such a hotel." I told him plainly, and he did not believe it. He did not look at me—he turned and walked away.

Before this you had had a glass of wine?—Yes.

What time would it be?—Between four and five.

When he gave you the capsules could you see them quite plainly?—No, I was standing under a lamp in the street. I could see that they were light ones.

Had you any spots on your forehead?—Yes, I had some.

Mr GEOGHEGAN—I desire to state at once in the most frank and free way that—reserving to myself the right to criticise any of the matters that may arise in this case—the Attorney-General went out of his way to afford me the opportunity of consultation, so that the prisoner should not be unfairly treated. I say this, reserving to myself the right to criticise even the Attorney-General severely if it should be necessary.

CHARLES HARVEY, examined by the ATTORNEY-GENERAL—I am by trade a painter, and I formerly lived in Brighton. In October, 1891, I and Lou Harvey lived together at 44 Townshend Road. One morning in that month Lou Harvey made a statement to me. She had passed the night before away from 44 Townshend Road. It was about the 20th or 21st October, I could not say for certain. I fix the date because it was a week after I had left work on the omnibuses, and I left about the 13th or 14th. I produced my book before, the last entry in my book is on 16th October, so that it was within

Thomas Neill Cream.

Charles Harvey

a week of that, I left the bus work on 16th October. In consequence of the statement Lou Harvey made to me in the morning I accompanied her the same evening to the Embankment. When we got near there I walked down one way and she up the other. We walked in opposite directions on the same side. I saw her meet some one on the Embankment—I had then turned back again, and when she met him I was within a few yards of them. I watched them. I saw them go to the Northumberland Arms, I followed them there and saw them go in. I did not address either of them. I saw them come out and walk towards the Embankment. I followed, and when they stopped on the Embankment I was on the opposite side, the width of the Embankment from them.

Have you seen that man since?—Yes, I saw him at Tooting and at Bow Street.

Can you recognise him?—Yes, he is the prisoner. They stood talking for a few minutes, and then I saw him hand something to Lou Harvey—I was not near enough to see what it was. Soon after he left her and walked towards the Westminster Bridge Road. She then joined me and made a statement as to what had taken place between her and the prisoner. She parted company from me at Charing Cross.

(Several witnesses were being called to speak to the case of the death of Ellen Donworth in order to give the defence the opportunity of cross-examining them if it was so desired. Mr. Geoghegan said it would be unnecessary. The Attorney-General was not certain that the cause of death had been sworn to, but would call a witness to prove that subsequently.)

Mrs. CHARLOTTE VOGT, examined by Mr. C. F. GILL—I live at 118 Stamford Street. On 22nd March of this year Alice Marsh and Emma Shrivell came to lodge at my house, occupying two rooms on the second floor. They let themselves in and out. There was a bell to the floor on which their rooms were. About 4 p.m. on Monday, 11th April, I saw Marsh, and about 6.30 I heard Shrivell speaking. I went to bed that night about eleven o'clock, the house was all quiet then. At half-past two I was awakened by a screaming and shrieking outside my door. In the passage I saw Marsh, who was screaming, and appeared to be in great agony. I sent my husband for a cab and a policeman. I then heard Shrivell screaming upstairs for "Alice!" Going up to her room I saw her on the floor at the foot

Evidence for Prosecution.

Charlotte Vogt

of the sofa, leaning against the sofa. She appeared to be in great agony. I spoke to her, and she answered me. I then heard Marsh screaming below again, and I went down to her and found her lying on her stomach in the passage and her body twitching as if in great pain.

Did that twitching continue?—It continued to come on and pass off and then come on again. I spoke to her, and when the twitching was not in operation she spoke to me. She was quite conscious. I asked her a question and she answered it. My husband came back with a cab and with the police, and the girls were carried after a little while and put into the cab and taken to the hospital. I first tried to give them an emetic, some mustard and water. They were carried out of the house and I never saw them alive again.

George Comley—I am a police constable, L Division. On the night of 11th April of this year my beat included the west side of Stamford Street. I should go off duty at six next morning on the 12th. 118 Stamford Street is on the west side, on which I was. I was passing along that west side on the early morning of the 12th about quarter to two, and I was about a dozen yards from No. 118, walking towards it when I saw a man being let out of No. 118. He was let out by a young woman. I saw her then and I saw her afterwards when I helped to take her to the hospital. It was Emma Shrivell.

How would you describe the man?—He was about 5 feet 9 inches or 5 feet 10 in height, and about forty-five to fifty years of age. He was dressed in a dark overcoat, with a silk high hat. As he turned by the street door I saw, by the reflection of the street lamp, that he had glasses. He had a moustache, no whiskers.

Where was the street lamp?—It was in front of the door, opposite No. 115, and on the same side of the street. The street is about as wide as this Court. He walked away rather sharply, but I was not surprised at that, as it was a cold morning. Later that same morning I was called in to 118 Stamford Street. About 2.30 I saw a four-wheel cab drive up to 118. I saw Constable Eversfield carry Shrivell into the cab. Eversfield spoke to me. I went into the passage. I found Marsh lying over the seat of a chair with her face downwards. I carried her into the same cab that Shrivell was in. Eversfield went with the two girls to the hospital in the cab, and I rode outside. We both put questions to Shrivell, who made a statement.

Thomas Neill Cream.

George Cumley

The ATTORNEY-GENERAL—We do not think the statements admissible in evidence, as we do not think the prospect of death was sufficiently present to the minds of the women, and moreover, we are not now inquiring into this particular case.

Examination continued—Marsh died on the way to the hospital. I made a report as to the man being let out. I was afterwards instructed to make a written report. I made it on the 14th. I knew nothing then of Neill's existence. After this occurrence I was on the look-out for a man such as I had seen coming out of 118 Stamford Street. On 12th May I was standing alone in the Westminster Bridge Road outside the Canterbury, between 7 and 8 p.m.

Was your attention attracted to anything?—Yes. I saw the prisoner walk up and down four times. I saw how like he was to the man I saw at 118 Stamford Street.

At that time did you know anything of the existence of Dr. Neill?—No.

Or of any suspicion attaching to him or any one else in connection with Matilda Clover?—No. I made a statement of it to Sergeant Ward. Ward made a report. I have no doubt it was the prisoner I saw in Westminster Bridge Road. The man who came out of 118 Stamford Street was like the prisoner in stature, height, and general appearance. He had glasses. He was not dressed the same. He was walking towards the Lambeth Palace Road, which is about a mile from Stamford Street, through York Road. There are many intermediate places he might have been walking to. He was dressed in a short coat in Westminster Bridge Road; in Stamford Street in a dark overcoat.

Cross-examined by Mr. GEOGHEGAN—I saw the man go from Stamford Street towards the Waterloo Road. I went down a turning. I lost sight of him.

You cannot say which way he went?—No, he might have gone down the Waterloo Road or along York Road and down the Westminster Bridge Road, or the Lambeth Palace Road. I have my report of the 14th.

Is it usual to see persons leave Stamford Street at an early hour in the morning?—Yes.

When you were outside the Canterbury Music Hall was the performance going on?—Yes.

Were women going into the music hall?—Yes.

Evidence for Prosecution.

George Cumley

And was this man looking at the women sharply?—Yes

Did that excite your suspicions?—Yes. Ward sent to me after that. I had seen Neill that night more than once. Ward was at the corner of the York Road and Westminster Bridge Road, that is, between 200 and 300 yards from the Canterbury. Ward and I had a conversation, that was about 11.30.

Re-examined by the ATTORNEY-GENERAL—This is the report I made. I first saw Neill between seven and eight. I did not see Ward then.

Did you speak to any one about the prisoner?—Yes, I spoke to the man outside the Canterbury, who calls the cabs, about the prisoner. I saw the prisoner that time for about half an hour and then he went away. I again saw him about 11.30 at the corner of Lambeth Palace Road and the Westminster Bridge Road. I saw Ward then. Neill was standing at the corner of a public-house on the other side of the road. In company with Ward I followed the prisoner home with a woman to 21 Elliott's Row, St. George's Road. We waited till they came out. They separated at the corner of the Lambeth Palace Road. Neill went to 103 Lambeth Palace Road.

By Mr. GEOGHEGAN—Do you know this woman's name?—No

Do you know where she walks?—No

Have you seen her lately?—No

How often have you seen her?—I have seen her once since.

WILLIAM EVERSFIELD—I am a police constable in the L Division. About 2.30 in the morning of 12th April I went to 118 Stamford Street. I saw Marsh and Shrivell as described. Marsh died in the cab. Shrivell made a statement at the hospital. Shrivell was up in the front room on the second floor, lying on a sofa on her face. I gave her an emetic and then took her to St. Thomas's Hospital. Marsh was lying on her face in the passage. She never spoke. They seemed to go into convulsions from time to time. Shrivell was sensible in the intervals, Marsh was not.

(Mr. Geoghegan objected to Shrivell's statement, and it was not read.)

Dr. CUTHBERT WYMAN—I am a medical practitioner. I was house surgeon at St. Thomas's Hospital in April of this year. On 12th April, about 3 a.m., I was at the hospital when Marsh and

Thomas Neill Cream.

Dr Cuthbert Wyman

Shrivell were brought in. Marsh was dead. Shrivell was suffering from tetanic convulsions, she showed all the symptoms of strychnine poisoning. I gave her an emetic, and afterwards chloroform. She died about eight the following morning. I made a post-mortem examination afterwards, I found no organic disease to account for death. The stomach and viscera of each girl were sealed up in jars and handed by me to George Hackett, to be conveyed to Dr Stevenson.

GEORGE HACKETT, examined—I am post-mortem assistant at St Thomas's Hospital. On 16th April Dr Wyman gave me three sealed jars to take to Dr Stevenson. I handed these jars to Dr Stevenson in the same condition as I received them.

The Court adjourned.

Fourth Day—Thursday, 20th October, 1892.

Dr THOMAS STEVENSON, recalled, further examined by the ATTORNEY-GENERAL—On 16th April of this year I received from the witness, Hackett, three jars properly secured and with unbroken seals.* Under instructions from the Home Office I carefully examined and analysed the contents. One jar was labelled " Alice Marsh " that contained a stomach kidney and liver. I proceeded in the ordinary way to test whether there was strychnine, firstly, by the colour test, secondly, by the alkaloid test, and thirdly, by taste. I also tried the same tests in the case of Matilda Clover. In all those tests I got the characteristic taste of strychnine.

By the COURT—There is one question. Is there any mode of testing for strychnine which is better than those you adopted?—No, my lord.

In testing for strychnine, did you adopt the methods which experienced and scientific knowledge suggested to you as best?—I did. I took extraordinary precautions in the Clover case, because the analysis was made so long after death.

Examination continued—The stomach in the first jar weighed 10½ ounces.

Mr GEOGHEGAN said he did not intend to cross-examine as to the weight of the contents of the jars, only as to the amount of poison which was found in the various organs.

Examination continued—I suppose I may say that your life has been spent in these studies and pursuits?—Yes. I am prepared to give the weights and quantities. In the contents of No 1 jar I found 6 39 grains of strychnine. There was nothing in the organs to suggest a cause of death except the strychnine. I arrived at the conclusion that death was so caused.

After hearing the symptoms, had you any doubt of that?—No. I should like to add that I found a further portion in the liver and kidney making altogether 6¾ grains. In the vomit of Emma Shrivell I found 1 16 grains, that would be nearly 1¼ grains. In the stomach and its contents 1 6 grains, and 0 2 grains in a small portion of the liver and one kidney. That quantity would represent much more than a fatal dose. There was nothing in that case to

---

* See Appendix VI

Thomas Neill Cream.

Dr Thomas Stevenson

account for death except the presence of the strychnine. After hearing the symptoms described I came to the conclusion that strychnine was the cause of death.

Cross-examined by Mr GEOGHEGAN.—I was present in Court and heard the evidence of M'Culloch. That the prisoner had shown him a bottle which he said contained crystals which he gave to women for a certain purpose. Sulphate of zinc is crystallised; its crystals are clear and glassy, while those of strychnine are opaque.

Is it not the case that they are very much alike?—To an ordinary observer they would look very much alike. But a very slight observation would distinguish the difference. One is a clear glassy crystal, the other is white and opaque.

(Mr Geoghegan handed to his lordship a question in writing in order to ascertain whether it was desirable that it should be put to Dr Stevenson.)

Mr Justice HAWKINS said that so far as the nature of the question went, they could not consider that, but in a Court of justice they were bound to ascertain anything that might bear on the case.

Mr GEOGHEGAN.—Quite so my lord. Those persons who come into a Court of justice must be prepared to hear things that may shock them. It is only for consideration of public morality that I have submitted the matter to your lordship.

(The question was then handed to the witness.)

Dr STEVENSON.—I have read it my lord. Yes.

Mr GEOGHEGAN.—But it is essential that the jury should know the question my lord as well as the answer.

Mr Justice HAWKINS (handing the question to the jury)—Read it gentlemen. You will see the obvious grounds on which I think it expedient that it should not be put in words.

Cross-examination continued.— Is with reference to the evidence of M'Culloch that the question is put. Is that an American theory?—It is a matter of common medical knowledge in this country. It is supposed to have come from America. It was mentioned in a notorious pamphlet.*

In the case of Marsh and Shrivell I received the articles on

---

* The question had reference to a use of strychnine medicinally but improper.

Evidence for Prosecution.

Dr Thomas Stevenson

the 16th, that was the day before Easter Sunday, within four weeks of the deaths. I commenced my post-mortem examination within three days of the death of Marsh and Shrivell, and I got a visible quantity of strychnine from the two bodies. There was a great difference between the post-mortem in those cases and in Clover's, both in colour and in the quantity obtained from the bodies. In the case of Clover I got in the portion extracted from the liver the characteristic taste of strychnine, which is extreme bitterness.

Other things besides strychnine have extreme bitterness?— Yes, but I do not think I could mistake the bitterness of anything except brucine for strychnine.

Science, like law, however, sometimes does make mistakes?— That is perfectly true.

Re-examined by the ATTORNEY-GENERAL—In strychnine there is a distinct, peculiar metallic bitterness which is a well known and distinctive character.

Mr JUSTICE HAWKINS (handing down a note to counsel)—I have received this. It does not seem to me that, in the present state of the case, it is at all important.

Mr GEOGHEGAN (to the Attorney-General)—Is it an anonymous letter? I have received four already. (Having read the letter.) I am much obliged to your lord-hip, but the matter has not been contested.

ALFRED WARD recalled, further examined by the ATTORNEY-GENERAL—In searching the room of Shrivell and Marsh I found the four pieces of paper which have been produced; these are they. They contain the names and addresses of men. I have had from Constables Cumley and Eversfield a description of the man said to have left 118 Stamford Street on the morning of 12th April; that description was given to me on the day following the event. At that time I had no suspicion, nor had my attention been drawn in any way to the prisoner. On the night of 12th May I was in Westminster Bridge Road, and my attention was drawn to a man whom I saw there walking up and down by his similarity to the description given to me by Cumley and Eversfield. I kept watch on him; he was watching women very closely as they passed him by, especially those having the appearance of prostitutes. I was

Thomas Neill Cream.

Alfred Ward

alone at the time my attention was first attracted to him. I sent for Cumley, and he made a statement to me and I to him, referring to the man, and we continued to keep watch upon him. I saw him go away with a woman to a particular place in Elliot's Road. I waited till he came out, and walked in the direction of Westminster Bridge Road, leading towards Lambeth Palace Road. After that date I was aware that the police kept observation of the prisoner. I was in charge of the observation. Up to 12th May I had never, directly or indirectly, any knowledge of who the prisoner was.

Cross-examined by Mr GEOGHEGAN—The prostitute whom he went away with had been seen alive up to the Wednesday following. There is no suggestion that any dose was given to her.

Mrs MARGARET ARMSTEAD, examined by the ATTORNEY-GENERAL —I am the wife of William Armstead, a photographer, of 129 Westminster Bridge Road. A person named Haynes came to lodge at our house in March last, about Easter. I think I made the prisoner's acquaintance through his coming to be photographed in my husband's studio. There he made the acquaintance of Haynes and they became intimate. In May when the prisoner was at our house, I became aware that some observation was being kept on our place and I called the attention of my husband and the prisoner to the fact. The prisoner said nothing then. I went to have some refreshment with him, and at the place we went to he pointed to a person and asked me if he was one of the men who was watching the house. I said that I could not see from the distance at which we were sitting.

Did he say anything about the Stamford Street case?—He said what a dreadful murder it was, and that whoever did it ought to be hanged.

Did you say anything further?—I asked him if he knew the girls Marsh and Shrivell. He said he knew them well, that they used to solicit up at the Bridge of an evening.

Did you ever see the prisoner in a square-topped hat?—I cannot remember.

The cases of Marsh and Shrivell were being talked about at that time?—Yes.

Cross-examined—Was it the common talk of the neighbourhood?—Yes.

Evidence for Prosecution.

Margaret Armstead

Was it through you that the prisoner first became acquainted with Haynes?—Yes

Did you tell the prisoner that Haynes had been a detective?—I may have done so, or else my husband may have done so. I do not know

Did Haynes say anything about having been a detective?—I believe he did. I believe my husband told the prisoner that Haynes had been a detective or engaged in detective work. I do not know whether the bridge he mentioned would be Westminster or Waterloo

John M Johnson examined—I am assistant to Dr Lowe, the medical officer of the South London Medical Institute. On the evening of 13th October I was sent for to 8 Duke Street, where I saw a woman described as Ellen Donworth, a woman of the "unfortunate" class. She was suffering from tetanic convulsions such as would be caused by the administration of strychnine. I considered her very bad. In fact she was in a dying state, and I ordered her to be taken to the hospital. I heard afterwards that she died on the way to the hospital to which I directed her to be sent

Dr Thomas Herbert Kelloch, examined—In October last I was house physician at St Thomas's Hospital. On the night of 13th October Ellen Donworth was brought to the hospital. She was dead when I saw her. There was nothing external to account for death. I afterwards examined her. I found nothing at all to account for death. I also analysed the contents of the stomach, and I was able to extract an appreciable quantity of strychnine. I estimated it was a quarter of a grain of strychnine in the contents of the stomach alone. I formed the opinion that the cause of death was poisoning by strychnine

Have you any doubt at all about that?—No

The Court—In looking over the depositions my eye is arrested by a matter to which I do not think attention has been drawn

The Attorney-General said his lordship was quite right, and it was only fair to say that a note had been handed to his learned friend (Mr Gill) after he had finished the examination of the witness to whose evidence the point referred, calling attention to the omission

Mr Geoghegan—Before the question is asked, I shall ask for proper evidence that the book is not forthcoming

Thomas Neill Cream.

Dr Thomas Herbert Kelloch

The COURT—I think it is right, if the Attorney-General desires to have that evidence put in, that it should be supplied, and it is desirable that it should be supplied at once. No one knows what it is that I have called attention to.

JOHN HAYNES, recalled, further examined by the ATTORNEY-GENERAL—On one occasion I was in the prisoner's room at 103 Lambeth Palace Road when he showed me an ordinary memorandum book, a quarter of an inch thick and about the size of a sheet of notepaper. I had it in my hand, but I cannot further describe it. The prisoner called my attention to some initials and dates in it.

By the COURT—Did you see where the book was taken from? No, my lord.

Examination continued—Did you ask him the meaning of the entries?—Yes, and he said they were the initials of the girls poisoned by Dr Harper and that the dates were those of their respective deaths. I never spoke to Tunbridge or any one about this fact. I called no attention to it.

LAURA SABBATINI recalled, further examined by Mr C F GILL—Neill visited me at Berkhemstead on three occasions. On the first occasion 8th April, I think, I introduced him to my mother. He went back to town on the 9th. He came again on the Wednesday after Easter Sunday 20th April, the occasion he went to church with me. He stayed one night, I think. The third time he came was on Saturday, 30th April when he stayed till Tuesday 3rd May. On the occasion of that third visit he asked me to write some letters for him. I asked him why he wanted me to write them. He refused to give me any reason. I do not recollect exactly what he said. I don't think I asked him more than once. He dictated some letters to me. Yes, this is one of the letters—

London 2nd May 1892

To Coroner Watt,
   St Thomas's Hospital,
      London

Dear Sir,

Will you please give the enclosed letter to the Foreman of the Coroner's jury, at the inquest on Alice Marsh and Emma Shrivell, and oblige,

Yours respectfully,

WM H MURRAY

Evidence for Prosecution.

Laura Sabbatini

I wrote the address on the envelope—I wrote this letter to the Foreman of the Coroner's jury:—

London, 2nd May, 1892

To the Foreman of the Coroner's Jury in the cases
of Alice Marsh and Emma Shrivell.

Dear Sir

I beg to inform you that one of my operators has positive proof that W. H. Harper a medical student of St Thomas's Hospital and a son of Dr Harper of Bear Street Barnstaple is responsible for the deaths of Alice Marsh and Emma Shrivell, he having poisoned those girls with strychnine. That proof you can have on paying my bill for services to George Clarke detective, 20 Cockspur Street Charing Cross, to whom I will give the proof on his paying my bill

Yours respectfully

WM H MURRAY

I also wrote this other letter at the prisoner's dictation and the envelope also—

To George Clarke, Esq, Detective,
20 Cockspur Street Charing Cross

London, 4th May, 1892

Dear Sir

If Mr Wyatt Coroner calls on you in regard to the murders of Alice Marsh and Emma Shrivell you can tell him that you will give proof positive to him that W H Harper, student, of St Thomas's Hospital, and son of Dr Harper, Bear Street Barnstaple poisoned those girls with strychnine provided the Coroner will pay you well for your services. Proof of this will be forthcoming. I will write you again in a few days.

Yours respectfully

WM H MURRAY

The prisoner took these letters and envelopes away with him returning to town that night. When I wrote the letters I asked him if he had that evidence he said that a friend of his, a detective, had it he did not mention his name. I asked him why I should sign the name of "Murray" he said that that was the name of his friend When I asked him what he knew of this or of Murray he said he would tell me all about it some day

By the Court—Tell you what?—Why that name was employed

Mr GEOGHEGAN—I have no question to ask the witness

WM FL DE GREY BIRCH recalled, further examined by Mr C F GILL—Among the letters is the one addressed to Dr Harper,

Thomas Neill Cream.

Walter de Grey Birch

of Barnstaple. This is it. It is, in my opinion, in the handwriting of the prisoner, and the envelope enclosing it. I also compared the memorandum, with initials and figures, produced by Inspector Tunbridge, with the handwriting of the prisoner, and in my opinion it is undoubtedly the same handwriting. Also the letter and envelope to Coroner Wyatt, relating to Donworth.

Inspector TUNBRIDGE, recalled, further examined by the ATTORNEY-GENERAL—I searched the prisoner's rooms on the day of his arrest. I took away everything belonging to him as told me by Miss Sleaper. It would be my duty carefully to examine the things and see whether they threw any light on the matter. I have all the things here, with the exception of certain things which I returned to the prisoner's solicitor. I see by my list I returned five books, medical works, one entitled "A Handbook of Therapeutics." There was one pocket-book, perfectly new, with no entries at all in it. If there had been any note-book with entries in it, it would have been my duty to examine it, and I should have retained it. There was no such book.

GEORGE RINDALL, examined—I am the secretary of St. Thomas's Hospital. In October 1891 and from that time down to April and May 1892, there was no person of the name of Dr. Neill or Neill Cream, connected with the hospital, so far as I know. It is usual for any gentlemen attending the hospital to register their names with me. There was no such person registered with me. I do not know the prisoner as in any way connected with the hospital, nor did I ever see him to my knowledge until I saw him here. I know the doctors and surgeons connected with the hospital and their names. There was a doctor of the name of Cream some years ago, but he has not registered with me.

Was there any person of that name connected with the hospital between October 1891, and June, 1892?—Not so far as I know. It sometimes occurs that old students may be attending without registering their names with me.

Inspector HARVEY, recalled, further examined—The verdict of the Coroner's jury in the case of Marsh and Shrivell was on 5th May, 1892. That inquest began on 13th April. The inquest on Matilda Clover, at Tooting, began on 22nd June and ended on 13th July. In the Donworth case I believe the inquest began on 15th October and ended on 22nd October.

Evidence for Prosecution.

Inspector Harvey

Cross-examined—In the case of Marsh and Shrivell it was thought at first that death was from tinned fish poisoning. There were two hearings. It was at the first hearing that strychnine was mentioned as the probable cause of death.

WALTER DE GREY BIRCH, recalled, further examined—This letter to Mr. Frederick Smith, which is now shown to me, is in the prisoner's handwriting, and the envelope also.

Evidence for the prosecution closed.

Mr. GEOGHEGAN intimated that he did not propose to call any evidence for the defence. But he wished to have a distinct understanding about certain facts. He asked the Attorney-General to agree with him that the Russell divorce case was heard on the 1st, 2nd, 3rd, and 4th December, and was reported in the daily papers on the 2nd, 3rd, 4th, and 5th.

The ATTORNEY-GENERAL—I do not at all doubt that.

Mr. GEOGHEGAN said that he also wished to fix the date of the prisoner's engagement to Miss Sabbatini.

The COURT—From a letter before me it might be imagined that the engagement was about the last of November.

Mr. GEOGHEGAN also desired to have any misunderstanding removed as to what M'Culloch said the prisoner told him he used the crystals for.

The COURT—My notes read—"He took a bottle. It contained whitish crystals. He asked 'Do you know what this is?' I said, 'No.' He said that it was poison. I said 'For God's sake what do you do with it?' He said he gave it to the women to get them out of trouble."

Speech for the Defence

Mr. GEOGHEGAN then addressed the jury for the defence. At the outset of his remarks he expressed his own and the prisoner's indebtedness to the counsel who were associated with him for the assistance they had rendered him. In a case with so great a mass of detail, number of dates, and number of witnesses it was difficult to know where to begin. If the prosecution had been conducted in the ordinary way the defence would have had this advantage—that,

Thomas Neill Cream.

Mr Geoghegan, no evidence being offered, the prosecution would have summed up and counsel for the defence would have known the facts relied on and the arguments used before rising to address the jury. He would then have been armed *cap-a-pie*, prepared at all points to rebut the evidence. But this case had not been conducted in the ordinary way. In saying that he should not be misunderstood. It was conducted by the Attorney-General in person, who had a right to reply. Counsel for the defence was at this disadvantage, that he could only judge of the strength of the case against the prisoner by hearing the evidence and listening to the opening. The Attorney-General had that inestimable advantage to an advocate, not of the last word to the jury, but of hearing the various points that would be submitted to them for the defence. He had noticed with appreciation that as much attention had been paid by the jury to the points for defence as to the points for the prosecution.

It was a difficult matter to know where to commence, but he did not think they could have a better starting point for making the defence clear than by asking the jury to accompany him over the rough ground that they had already traversed. He should not allow any mixed audience which might be in Court to deter him from doing his duty in speaking very plainly upon the points he thought necessary to urge for the defence. He described the situation of the various places referred to in the evidence, and pointed out the importance of having a clear conception of the locality. The case as to Matilda Clover was this. About 6th October, or before 9th October, Clover was living on the top floor of 27 Lambeth Road. She was a woman of about twenty-six, and she had a child aged two years. The landlady was a Mrs Vowles or Phillips, and there was a servant there named Lucy Rose. The father of that child was said to be a young man named Fred. Fred had been described as a young man of thirty, or thirty-two, with light hair, blue eyes, and a light moustache. There had been a quarrel between him and the woman Clover, whereupon Fred left the house, saying that he would never set foot in it again. Fred was said to be a commercial traveller, and for aught that was known to the contrary might have travelled in the drug trade. The reconciliation desired by Clover was never effected. On the night of 20th October it was stated that the woman Clover went out, having previously received a letter, in consequence of which she went out. The witness Rose saw the letter and read it, and remembered it so accurately that she

Speech for Defence.

Mr Geoghegan

could have told the Attorney-General its contents. At any rate he was justified in assuming he did not think it would be disputed that whoever wrote that letter was the person who lured Clover to her death. It was sought to fix the identity of the prisoner with the writer of the letter in several ways—first by evidence which raised the probability that he was the person said to have been present in the house on the night and morning of 20th-21st October. It was also sought to prove this by statements made by Neill and by the fact that he had in his possession at that time, if they were to accept the statement of certain witnesses as accurate, a deadly poison. Until inquiries were made by the police on the 28th April, and a communication was sent to Dr Broadbent, the secret of the poisoning of Matilda Clover was locked in the breast of the person who had administered the poison. The prosecution had put forward three propositions. The first was that Clover died from the effects of strychnine poisoning; the second, that the brain which had planned, and the hand that had administered the strychnine, and the heart that had actually conceived the devilish cruelty of such an internal murder, must have been the brain, and the hand and the heart of the prisoner at the bar. These were two of the propositions as to which the prosecution had to satisfy the jury beyond a shadow of a doubt. There was another proposition which was a deduction from the other two namely, that the strychnine must have been administered feloniously and with intent to murder. But unless the first two propositions were established, the prisoner was entitled to acquittal at the hands of the jury. If they entertained a reasonable doubt as to the first two premises of the argument the prisoner was entitled by the fact that he was being tried before an English jury, and an English judge and under the English law, to an acquittal. The evidence showed that Clover went out on the night of the 20th October and came back accompanied by a man, who was seen by Rose under the dim light of a paraffin lamp which was hanging in the passage. That man was described by Rose as a man of forty, having no whiskers, no beard, but as wearing a thick brown moustache, and as wearing dark clothes and a silk hat. That description conveyed nothing to his mind. There were 30,000 or 40,000 respectable people walking about the streets of London at the present moment to whom the description would apply. That man stayed in the house for an hour and went away. Clover afterwards went out and returned. About three o'clock the next morning

Thomas Neill Cream.

Mr Geoghegan

screams were heard in Clover's room. Rose's attention was aroused, and she went into Clover's room and found her in a state of agony, bathed in perspiration and convulsed with intermittent spasms. During an interregnum between the spasms she asked to see her child, as she thought she was about to die. The prosecution had to prove affirmatively that the death was caused by strychnine. Dr Stevenson, the analyst who had been called, had stated that the symptoms described were such as would lead him to suspect poisoning. A symptom of strychnine poisoning was that if a person died in convulsions the body became extremely rigid. Rigor mortis is more pronounced in a death like that than in a death arising from natural causes. Reference had been made to the well-known case of the Rugeley poisoning in 1856. Cooke was poisoned by Palmer and it was pointed out that in that case extreme rigidity might well have disappeared. The Attorney-General had suggested that the extreme rigidity and tension of the muscles might disappear in consequence of the length of time the body had been buried! Other evidence upon which Dr Stevenson based his opinion was that which had been discovered during the process of analysis. By the addition of a certain drug a beautiful violet colour was the result. That formed what was known as the colour test. In addition, there was the shape of the strychnine crystals. They were eight-sided, and they had also a peculiar bitter taste. There was also the physiological experiment with the frog. An injection was made into the back of a frog, it showed tetanic spasms and ultimately died. All this, it was said, showed that death had arisen from strychnine. He did not understand why the Attorney-General should reject the evidence which Dr Graham and Mr Coppin gave as persons not to be altogether relied on. Mr Coppin had shown that convulsions were present before the death of Clover. Clover's constitution was not that of a healthy woman. She was a woman of the town depending for her bread upon prostitution in the streets—one of that vast army, the legion of the lost that was to be seen in our midst. She was a woman who drowned her misery in drink. She was sodden with drink. She had been treated by Dr Graham for incipient delirium tremens. Was it not extraordinary that if this woman had received a dose of strychnine, with her nerves unstrung, she should have survived so long as she did, from three o'clock to half-past eight—five and three-quarter hours—and with nothing done to alleviate her sufferings? That showed on the very threshold of the

Speech for Defence.

Mr Geoghegan

case that medical science, great as it was, might have been mistaken. Dr Stevenson must have refreshed his memory when he spoke of Silas Barlow, and the length of time that the woman had existed after the fatal dose had been administered to her. The woman in that case was not a prostitute, her constitution had not been shattered, her nervous system was not deranged, as in the case of Clover. In that case medical aid was called in, chloroform was administered and morphia injected, and that might have prevented the too frequent recurrence of the spasms— those awful twitchings from the crown of the head to the soles of her feet which produced afterwards the distorted condition of the body to be seen in cases of death by strychnine. He could understand that a person of a firm constitution should live a longer time than one whose frame was shattered and health impaired. He contended that on the very threshold of the case doubt arose whether it was possible in any known circumstances that a woman of the constitution of this woman Clover could have existed for the time mentioned if her death was really due to strychnine. He had been astonished in the progress of the case—represented as the Crown was by four of the most highly trained intellects at the English bar—that such obvious slips had been made in the conduct of the prosecution. He said in the hearing of the judge and jury, that whoever wrote the letter seen by Lucy Rose, and read by her, was the person who lured Matilda Clover to her death. Was the handwriting of that letter so marked, so striking, that counsel for the prosecution had not dared to examine Lucy Rose on the handwriting? Other letters and documents were produced, admittedly in the handwriting of the prisoner. There was no cross-examination. If it was of vital importance to the prosecution that this letter should be admitted in evidence, there was a way to prove it as the prisoner's by showing the similarity of the handwriting to the other letters

This was not the first case of strychnine that had been inquired into. Who was the person more than any other who would remember the extreme rigidity of the body, would remember the appearances which the body presented? He could not expect Rose or Mrs Phillips or Measures to speak to it. Dr Graham might have spoken to it and above all the woman who laid out this unfortunate creature before she was wrapped in a pauper's shroud. It might be that she was an inexperienced witness and could not pronounce a definite opinion on

Thomas Neill Cream.

Mr Geoghegan

the subject! Dr Graham stated that he examined the body. If Dr Graham said in self-defence that he had examined the body, and if there had been what they would expect to find from a person dying from strychnine poisoning, it was a strange thing that Dr Graham had not mentioned that the appearance of the body led him to suspect other than natural causes, arising possibly from drink or convulsions caused by some disease of the spine, that could not have been discovered after the body had been in the earth for eight months. There was a *prima facie* improbability that a woman with a weakened constitution could have lived so long after the administration of strychnine. Dr Stevenson had told them that in the case of Marsh and Shrivell the quantity of strychnine found in their bodies was large and pronounced—six grains in one and three in the other, so that he was able to say from the appearance of the crystals he found that the death arose from strychnine. That assistance was not afforded to them in the case of Matilda Clover because in her case only a quarter of a grain was found and the crystals were so small as to be obscure. He pointed out that other matters besides strychnine were nauseous and bitter in the mouth and what might have occurred in the course of the decomposition of the body, which had been in the earth from 27th October to 5th May, was not for him to go into. Strychnine was a vegetable poison, and the test was infinitely more difficult than that for a mineral poison. Then as to the frog test—the injecting a frog which afterwards exhibited symptoms of tetanic spasms—he contended that no analogy could be drawn which would show that the woman died from strychnine poisoning. He was afraid that science, represented there by Dr Stevenson, did not assist them in this matter, and he denied that any true analogy or fair argument on which a man's life might depend, could be drawn from the experiment which had been conducted. If they took each one of the tests spoken to by Dr Stevenson none of them *per se* was reliable. They had to be twisted and mixed together before the inference could be drawn that death arose from strychnine. He said that Mr Coppin, who had an enormous experience in this part of London of drinking habits, of the degradation resulting from them and of the disease arising from them—who knew that the woman had been an alcoholised patient, had not been shaken by any scientific evidence when he described the death and the convulsions as arising from drink. Nothing had shaken

Speech for Defence.

Mr Geoghegan

the conclusion to which Mr Copson and Dr Graham came—that the death was due to drink.

At the time when he directed the attention of the jury to the evidence of poisoning he was discussing the evidence of identity. Lucy Rose had seen the prisoner in the most peculiar circumstances, which to all intents and purposes must have almost photographed his image on her brain. She saw him as he sat between two warders at the Coroner's inquest; she saw him also when he stood alone before Sir John Bridge in the dock at Bow Street. But neither before the Coroner, nor before Sir John Bridge, nor in the present court, had she been able to recognise the prisoner as the man whom she saw in the dimly-lighted hall of 27 Lambeth Road on the night of 20th October. Her emphatic answer was, 'I cannot recognise him.' On the identity of Neill rested the man point of this case. The prosecution, knowing this, had endeavoured to establish the identity of the person who went into the house on 20th October by the evidence of the women May and Masters. These two women were called to speak to the identity of Neill on two occasions—first to his identity with the man who was with them in Gatti's Music Hall on 6th October, and then with the man who passed by Orient Buildings on the afternoon of 9th October. Counsel admitted that Masters would be able to recognise the man who had gone with her to Gatti's Music Hall. He did not deny that Neill was that man. He would ask the jury—who and what was Neill? He was the agent of an American drug firm, and had come to London for the sake of his health. He had no friends here; he knew nobody; and, although a medical man, no patients ever visited him. He was thrown upon his own resources for amusement. Unfortunately for him he did not make the acquaintance at first of a modest woman, or his time might have been spent more to his advantage. He occupied a bedroom in one of the dreariest parts of London. His conduct was not that of a very happy man. But he was now not being tried for immorality—that was not the issue. Crime and crime alone was the question which they, the jury, had to determine. It was their duty to say whether he was guilty or not of this murder. There were people who could find amusement by constantly going to music halls—and he might envy them! There were others who chose to pass their evenings cramped up and half-suffocated in theatres, others who liked to walk about the streets and see what is called 'life' in London, and it might be that that was the course which

Thomas Neill Cream.

Mr Geoghegan

Neill adopted for his evening's amusement. As to what took place at Gatti's Music Hall, he did not deny that the prisoner was the man, but when they came to speak of Neill as the man who passed by Orient Buildings on the afternoon of 9th October he contended strongly that the evidence was not sufficient. The women did not see the person who passed their house in a favourable position. On that day May and Masters expected a visit from a man who had written a letter signed by two initials. He was to call between 3 and 5 o'clock. They were looking out of the window, and saw a man wearing a silk hat walking along in the street below. The man who they have said was the prisoner did not pass on the opposite side of the street, so that they had a clear view of him, but he followed the girl under their window, so that they did not see his face, but only had a glimpse of him from above, just as a man might be walking immediately beneath the jury box, supposing the jury to be looking down from a height. Counsel for the prosecution, he noticed, did not put one question to the women as to this point. They never asked either Masters or May whether or not they saw the face of the man who was following Clover. He watched nervously and anxiously for the putting of such a question, but not one word had he heard. The prisoner's was a remarkable face, so that if they had really seen him they could not very well have been mistaken. They put on their hats and followed him, but his back was now towards them. This alleged view of this man took place on 9th October. Eight months afterwards Masters and May were taken to Bow Street Police Court to identify the man who was in Gatti's Music Hall who was admitted to be Neill, but also to identify the man who passed by their place of abode on 9th October. The man who passed by Orient Buildings on 9th October had his hat on. The man who was with these women at Gatti's Music Hall had his hat off for a part of the time. Masters was called to identify first the men who had his hat off in the music hall, and, secondly, the man whom she saw with his hat on as he passed by Orient Buildings. She could not identify the man who had his hat on; it was not until she saw the persons with their hats off that she identified Neill as the man whom she saw at Gatti's Music Hall. When Masters was called to identify the man who passed by with his hat on she could not do so. As to his being the man who passed beneath their window they were clearly mistaken. Fearful mistakes had been made, as they well knew, in the past, and identification in police

Speech for Defence.

Mr Geoghegan

courts was nothing more than a mockery, a delusion and a snare Identification in such circumstances as obtained at Bow Street was a most dangerous identification

When they came to the question of the letter of 28th November the prosecution said, ' You, Neill, by the admission of your own counsel wrote on 28th November a blackmailing letter to Dr Broadbent You signed that letter 'M Malone', you demanded from Dr Broadbent £2500, you said that if that were not given to you, you would denounce him and say that he had assassinated Matilda Clover with strychnine at 27 Lambeth Road ' It was contended that no one at that time was acquainted with the facts From that the inference was drawn that it was the prisoner's hand that had administered the poison But who was Neill? It was known that he was a medical man who had practised in America It was essential to the case to remember the character of the locality It was certain that Lucy Rose, who had witnessed the terrible death scene, had seen the twitchings and spasms, made no secret of it and that it was freely talked about Neill with his peculiar habits and his taste for roaming about among the prostitutes of the south side of London might have heard the girl's death discussed and described Then from his medical knowledge he might have gathered from the symptoms that the death was due to strychnine and not to delirium tremens On the strength of this, he suggested Neill wrote the blackmailing letter to Dr Broadbent Ellen Donworth had fallen dead in the Waterloo Road within a short distance of this very spot, the fact that the result of the inquest upon her was known—all these things placed the prisoner in possession of the probable facts of Clover's death Dr Stevenson had said that from the account he had heard of Clover's death he was prepared to assert that there was *prima facie* ground to think that strychnine poisoning was the cause Was it too improbable to suppose that Neill, taking the same medical view of the symptoms described by these poor people as the " horrors " and remembering the death of Ellen Donworth from strychnine in this very neighbourhood, attributed Clover's death to the same admittedly unknown hand that murdered Donworth? He strongly condemned the system under which a letter giving real names and referring to the death of an individual from poison should have been pigeon-holed and so disregarded by the police authorities that it should have led to no inquiry on their part * With regard

---

* See Appendix I

Thomas Neill Cream.

Mr Geoghegan to the communication made to Dr Broadbent, it seemed singular that after the advertisement had been issued the prisoner, if he had really been attempting to procure blackmail, made no further effort to do so.

With regard to the evidence of the witness Haynes, the ex-detective, he did not know whether the prosecution solemnly asked the jury to accept his statements. Haynes, who had been connected with that remarkable man, Le Caron—one of the most remarkable men of modern times—and who had in knocking about the world acquired some little legal knowledge, had made the acquaintance of the prisoner. It could readily be imagined that as an ex-detective he would be anxious to take down and to utilise the statements made to him by the prisoner, and that in vulgar language he eagerly swallowed all that was told him, and asked for more. He suggested that the information given to Haynes by the prisoner was not seriously given, and that, Haynes having shown a credulous disposition, Neill "crammed" him to the top of his bent. As to the statement the prisoner was said to have made about Lou Harvey's death, it was abundantly shown that he had met that female weeks after it was alleged that he had offered her some pills as to the constitution of which there was no evidence at all. But it was admitted that the woman had an eruption on her forehead. The fact that he had turned upon his heel when he met the girl again was open to another inference besides that drawn by the prosecution who held that it tended to prove the guilt of the prisoner. It was in evidence that since he had first seen Harvey he had become engaged to Miss Sabbatini and naturally would not like to have been seen walking with Harvey in broad daylight. Although he had consented to slink into a public-house with her, that was a totally different thing to walking up and down two of the most fashionable thoroughfares on an October afternoon.

Turning to the deaths of Marsh and Shrivell, he reminded the jury that they occurred at 118 Stamford Street, on the morning of 12th April. The only evidence against the prisoner in their case was the piece of paper on which Marsh had written her address when she invited him to visit her at her rooms in Stamford Street. Identification in this case also had failed. Constable Cumley was on duty in the early morning in Stamford Street, and saw a man leave the house, No 118. He described him as being about forty years of age, broad, with a heavy moustache, and wearing glasses.

Speech for Defence.

Mr Geoghegan

But he had failed to prove that he was the prisoner at the bar. He afterward saw Neill outside the Canterbury Music Hall, and his suspicion was aroused by the fact that Neill was narrowly watching the loose women who were passing to and fro. But he did not identify Neill as the man who was in Stamford Street on the morning of the murder. Was it to be said that because in the pocket of a man admittedly addicted to the society of loose women was found the address of two women leading an immoral life it was conclusive proof that he was guilty of the death of those two women? Men of experience could speak to the manner in which women solicited them in the street, and there were two ways of dealing with them—either to order them away, or to deal with them gently and to get rid of them as best they could. It might be said that they would then write down their address, hoping that the person whom they were soliciting would give them a call. He suggested to the jury that, as Neill himself had said, the prisoner had met these two women, had passed the time in chaffing them, had given them a drink, and that that was the way in which the address came into the prisoner's possession.

He thought it was proved that Neill was a man who was addicted to the use of drugs. Miss Sabbatini, Haynes, M'Culloch, and Miss Sleaper all testified that Neill had been addicted to opium, morphia, and sometimes strychnine. It might be that under their influence he had made the most absurd statements, such as were to be found in the letters which he had written for the purpose of extorting money.

In conclusion Mr Geoghegan said—I have endeavoured to shorten your labours in this case, and I approach the conclusion of my speech with the utterance of a few remarks—solemn words they will be.

I remember the first time I ever heard sentence of death pronounced. It was in this Court. It was a long time ago, and it was before my lord the judge. I remember hearing four prisoners who were rightly convicted of murder sentenced to death. It was the case of some people who had tortured a poor woman to death by starvation.* I was a much younger man then than I am now. I remember going away and trying to picture to myself what those

---

* The Trial of the Stauntons, September, 1877. Included in the "Notable Trials Series."

Thomas Neill Cream.

Mr Geoghegan people must have felt as they lay under that sentence. I cannot help thinking that when you come to consider what a sentence of death means you will agree with me that it is the most awful position in which a fellow creature can be placed. That sentence means separation from one's fellow men; it means being immured in a prison cell; it means that the condemned is about to stand on the threshold of the most awful of all mysteries; and that, when that mystery is solved, his name shall be a hissing, a byword, and an abomination even to his nearest and dearest.

However, I have one consolation, and a strong one. In the days when I sat on the back benches unknown, eating away my heart, and considering if it would ever come to my lot that I, too, would have upon my shoulders the awful responsibility of the defence of a man's life, I was accompanied by an illusion of which I could not rid myself. Though God knows the sins and tragedies which we who practise in these Courts see take place under our eyes are enough to conquer any illusion or romantic ideals of youth we may have had, I say between you and the prisoner at the bar, between the Crown and the prisoner, there stands a figure, and that figure is the Genius of the Law of England. It is the best protector an accused man can have in his hour of need. It demands that the guilt of the accused shall be brought home to him as clear and as bright as the light of heaven now streaming into this Court, and it is under the protection of that figure that I leave my client, Thomas Neill.

Closing Speech for the Crown

The ATTORNEY-GENERAL said that his right of reply was an almost immemorial right vested in the office he had for the time being the honour to occupy, and they might rest assured he would make no attempt to abuse his privilege. His duty was simple. It was to lay before the jury without passion honestly and fully the whole of the facts touching the matter they were inquiring into, leaving the responsibility of judgment upon the facts to them. He agreed that the onus lay on the prosecution to establish to their satisfaction two propositions—first, that Matilda Clover died of poison; secondly, that that poison was murderously administered to her by the prisoner. If either of these propositions was not

The Attorney General (Sir Charles Russell, QC, MP, afterwards Lord Russell of Killowen)

Closing Speech for the Crown.

Attorney General

made out to their reasonable satisfaction the prisoner must be acquitted. They ought not to let their minds be influenced in their decision on those two very important points by suspicions which might have crept in in relation to other parts of the case. The crime with which alone the prisoner was charged was that of the murder of Matilda Clover, and the other incidents in the case which had been necessarily gone into were to be looked at only in so far as they afforded corroborative proof of the charge. The evidence against the prisoner in the case of Clover depended upon the testimony of Masters and May and Lucy Rose, and on the stronger evidence of the statements admittedly in the prisoner's handwriting. Counsel for the defence had admitted the identity of the prisoner with the person who was with Masters and May at Gatti's Music Hall, and he urged that, not only was that identification complete, but that the fact of the prisoner going to 27 Lambeth Road with Matilda Clover had been proved by the women who were waiting for him, and, seeing him pass their window with Clover, had followed and seen him go with her into the house in which she lived. As to what had happened on the 20th October, it was known that the man "Fred," who was said to be the father of Clover's child, had had a difference with her, and had gone away, there being nothing to suggest that their intimacy was subsequently renewed. The suggestion of prisoner's counsel that "Fred," the father of Clover's child, might have been a traveller in the drug trade—meaning thereby strychnine—was entirely unsupported by evidence, and was one which could hardly be expected to be accepted by the jury. Apart from this, it had been sworn that the man admitted by Lucy Rose on the night of 20th October answered in all the main characteristics the description of the prisoner. The young woman Clover went out again that night, and returned at a late hour. Later on the household was aroused by her screams, and ultimately she expired. The theory was advanced that the death then became talked about—but by whom, how and where did not appear—that it reached the ears of the prisoner somehow or other, and that then he applied his medical knowledge and put down her death to strychnine. Three witnesses had given an account of her death-bed agony, and even Mr. Coppin himself came to the conclusion that she died, not of poison, but from the effects of her drinking habits, delirium tremens. According to Coppin's statement, he was in the poor

Thomas Neill Cream.

Attorney General

woman's room when she was shrieking from agony of a mortal kind, yet he only remained with her for ten or twelve minutes, and in that respect he thought there seemed a want of humanity in his conduct. He was not suggesting that he had attempted to deceive, for it was apparent that he, like the others, came to the conclusion that the woman was suffering from excessive drinking, and that she had died from its effects accordingly. None of these persons knew at that time that the unfortunate woman had died of strychnine, so that they could not have communicated a fact of that kind to the accused. The conduct of Dr. Graham, he must confess, showed a state of things that called for reform. He had gathered from the landlady the particulars of the woman's death, and yet he gave a certificate that he had attended her during her last sickness and that she died from alcohol and syncope. The certificate was not true, for he had not seen the woman in her death agony and therefore could not have known the real cause of her death. During the month that followed, till May (1892), there was only one person who could know that Clover had died of strychnine poisoning. Yet, on 28th November (1891), they had it under the admitted hand of the prisoner that she died a poisoned woman, and poisoned by strychnine. They had further the evidence that the prisoner asked Miss Sleaper to go to Lambeth Road to make inquiry about the young woman. How could he, at this time, have learned that Clover was poisoned by strychnine? His learned friend had suggested that the prisoner had become suspicious from what he had heard of the symptoms that Clover had died of strychnine poisoning. Was it conceivable that an innocent man, becoming suspicious of such a murder, should have written a blackmailing letter to Dr. Broadbent instead of communicating with the police? Why the demand for money? Why the assumed name? He was undoubtedly brought into association with Clover on 9th October and again on the 20th, and the fact that he was so brought into association with her was proved to demonstration by the fact that on 28th November he wrote to a stranger of the cause of her death. The story of Lou Harvey deserved an ampler consideration than his learned friend had given it. It was a remarkable story, and one which he thought the jury would be of opinion threw a strong light on the case. If the prisoner's object in promising to give her medicine was a kindly and not murderous act, surely he would simply have written a prescription

Closing Speech for the Crown.

Attorney General

instead of appointing a special meeting in the streets at night and showing such extraordinary anxiety to become assured that she had taken the capsules. The story of Lou Harvey threw a strong light on the case. As to the Donworth case, it was one on which the prosecution in no sense relied as against the prisoner in this case. But the Marsh and Shrivell case was an extraordinary one, and the prisoner's knowledge of these women was abundantly shown. It was remarkable that Police-Constable Cumley had recognised the prisoner as he had sworn he did in Stamford Street at an early hour on the morning of 12th May, and that within two hours he should have been called back to the house the prisoner had been seen leaving, to assist in the removal to the hospital of the two women who so soon afterwards succumbed to the effects of strychnine. With regard to the statements made by the prisoner to the witness Haynes, he thought the criticism of his learned friend was hardly justifiable. The jury would see how that evidence was corroborated by the surrounding facts as placed before them. That Haynes spoke confidentially to Neill and Neill to him did not appear to be questioned or questionable, and it was right, in justice to him, to say that, except in one or two things, there was nothing in the statements he had attributed to the prisoner that was not thoroughly consistent with the statements the prisoner had admittedly made. Then came the evidence of the destruction of the note-book. Why was that note-book destroyed, and why was it destroyed at the time chosen for that act? It had been shown that at that time the prisoner was being watched, and it was a significant fact also that the capsule box, which had been seen by Miss Sleaper, was not forthcoming when the prisoner's room was searched. All these matters, coupled with the finding in the trousers pocket of the prisoner the piece of paper on which the woman Marsh had written her name and that of Shrivell, and their address, served to support in a remarkable degree the case against the prisoner.

Addressing himself to the question whether or not strychnine was the cause of death, he referred to the scientific attainments of Dr. Stevenson and the definite conclusions at which he had arrived. Dr. Stevenson had no interest to serve except the interest of truth, and it might be assumed that he had used the best-known modes of analysis.

In conclusion, addressing the jury, he said—You have been

Thomas Neill Cream.

Attorney General

told in words of warning eloquent and solemn that you have a grave duty to perform. That duty you ought to perform in accordance with the spirit of law as it prevails and is administered in this land. I join my learned friend in his appeal to you. The law of England deems every man to be innocent until the constituted tribunal of fact —the jury—has pronounced otherwise. That jury is composed of a number large enough to prevent the views of one prevailing over the good sense of all, although to each member of the jury is the individual sense of responsibility to be preserved, large enough therefore, for the good sense of all to operate on the minds of all, small enough, therefore, to preserve to each man among you a sense of individual responsibility for the verdict, as if it were his alone. If, after you have heard my lord, there remains in your mind a doubt— not a doubt to be conjured up, but a real doubt, such as would operate on your minds in any important affair of daily life—by all means let the prisoner have the benefit of that doubt. But if the course of this evidence has driven into your minds and left resting there a solemn conviction that this man is guilty, why, then, you will discharge your duty conscientiously, you will discharge your duty with fortitude.

The Court adjourned.

Sir Henry Hawkins and his dog Jack

Fifth Day—Friday, 21st October, 1892.

Charge to the Jury.

Mr. Justice HAWKINS said he hoped that the jury would bear in mind that the responsibility of the verdict, whatever it might be, was with them and not with him; that it was their duty to investigate the facts, and their duty to pass judgment upon them according to their honest belief. With that he had nothing to do. He had to assist them to the best of his ability in pointing out to them such parts of the evidence as in his judgment bore upon the case. Having done that, his duty was at an end and their's began, and with their verdict the matter would terminate.

He could not begin the observations he had to make without expressing sincerely to the learned counsel who appeared before them, both on the part of the Crown and the prisoner, his great obligations for the assistance they had given him and the jury. While on the one hand no case was ever put before a jury on the part of the Crown with more temperate comment than the present case had been placed before them by the Attorney-General. Every word of his had been in a spirit of fairness. A very difficult task was thrown on the learned counsel for the defence in consequence of the mass of evidence which had to be dealt with. He had to say that the counsel had conducted that defence with a zeal and ability which had been rarely equalled and never excelled in his recollection.

The case which they had to inquire into was as to the death of Matilda Clover, who died on the morning of 21st October last year. It was alleged that she had been poisoned—wilfully poisoned—murdered by the administration of strychnine, and that that poison was administered wilfully by the prisoner. That involved two or three important questions, two of which, however, would give them more difficulty—if they had any difficulty in determining them—than the third. The first would be, did Matilda Clover meet with her death in consequence of poison in the shape of strychnine administered to her? If they decided that poison was wilfully administered to her the next question would be, was that done with the intent to kill or to do her grievous bodily harm? As to that question the learned counsel for the defence had most wisely and prudently offered to

Thomas Neill Cream.

Mr Justice Hawkins

them no observations, because it almost stood to reason—although it remained a question of fact for them to determine—it almost stood to reason that if one administered to another deliberately a fatal dose of poison there could be but one intent and that must be either to kill or to do grievous bodily harm. Then the third and the all-important question would be, did the evidence which was before them bring them to the conclusion that that poison was administered by the prisoner at the bar? If it was not administered by him, they were not inquiring as to who else could have done it. The question was, did the evidence reasonably satisfy them with the same reasonable satisfaction which they would desire before acting in any important matter of their own private affairs?

It was not to be expected in every case that there should be mathematical proof of the commission of the crime. It often happened as in that particular case that there could be no eye-witness called to prove the commission. In such a case it was almost impossible that anything like mathematical proof could be given.

In the course of the case a legal discussion arose as to whether or not in the circumstances which were now before them evidence of the three or four other deaths could be offered to the jury as to the circumstances in which these deaths occurred. After a very long and a very able argument he came to the conclusion, and he had seen no reason to doubt the justice or the good sense or the legality of that conclusion—that it was impossible on the present occasion to keep seperate and distinct the various cases, or rather that it was impossible to exclude the evidence offered on the subject. He thought that as they proceeded with the investigation of the evidence they would find that it would be impossible to come to anything like a satisfactory conclusion, unless they had had that evidence which had been offered and which had been listened to so patiently by them. They could not prove, in order to convict a man of robbery from John Jones, that he had a month before committed a robbery on somebody else unless they could show that those two cases had a bearing one on the other. If the circumstances of one case legally and legitimately threw light on the other evidence of two crimes might be given. It would be the height of absurdity to say that they should never in any circumstances allow two crimes to be investigated at the same time because, if so, they would very often fail to offer to the jury that which was essential to the case and which was material to put before them for their discussion. But as the Attorney-

Charge to the Jury.

Mr Justice Hawkins

General had told them there was no issue raised as to any death except that of the girl Clover, and the evidence offered in the other cases was simply as corroboration, and that was the ground on which they were to take it into their consideration.

The direct evidence on this part of the case was exceedingly simple, assuming that the jury gave credit to the witnesses. Matilda Clover, who was an unfortunate, seemed to have been a quiet, well-conducted girl following her calling, but had given way to habits of drink. She had a little boy, the son of a man called Fred, about whom there was no reason to believe he had appeared on the scene since a month before the date of the murder, an estrangement having occurred between Matilda Clover and himself. On the question whether the prisoner ever met or was associated with the girl, the jury had to go back a week before the murder, to 9th October, on which date two witnesses, Masters and May, swore they saw the two pass their house and enter the house in which Clover was poisoned, 27 Lambeth Road. So far as he could see, these women gave their evidence in an honest manner, and seemed to have no interest to serve. They desired only to tell what in their honest belief was the truth.

The prisoner, who came to England from America, landed in Liverpool early in the month of October. He had made his way to London, and on 5th October had taken a room at Anderton's Hotel, in Fleet Street. He did so with the intention of living there until he had found suitable lodgings. On 6th October he went to 103 Lambeth Palace Road and engaged a room. He met Masters at Ludgate Circus on the same day, and, according to her account, she had an appointment on that evening to meet a girl named May at Gatti's Music Hall. She had a glass of wine with him. There was no question but that he was the person—that was not disputed. They went on to Gatti's Music Hall, where Masters met her friend May. They had some drink at the bar, and they went back to Ludgate Hill—the man and the two girls—in a hansom cab. In Gatti's Music Hall Masters had given him her address, and he promised that as soon as he was away from the hotel and had a room of his own he would communicate with her. They parted at Ludgate Hill. On the morning of 9th October Masters received a letter stating that the person to whom she had given her address at Gatti's Music Hall would call on her that same afternoon between three and five o'clock, and expressing the hope that she would not be so cross as she

Thomas Neill Cream.

Mr Justice Hawkins

was when they were at Gatti's. He had mentioned the visit to Gatti's Music Hall for the purpose of showing the opportunities the girls had of knowing the features and the general appearance of the man. Having received that letter on the morning of the 9th it was not unnatural to suppose that the girl to whom he was going to pay the visit would be on the lookout for him. Masters was sitting with her friend May at the window for the purpose of watching the arrival of the man. Masters and May first of all saw coming along the pavement a girl whom they both knew by sight. It was Clover. Clover was in the habit of going to market with her basket, and generally wore a white apron with shoulder straps. The girls saw a man following behind her. She was going in the direction of Lambeth Road, and she turned round and smiled at the man. Masters and May swore that the man they saw following the girl was the prisoner. They were both ably cross examined, with the view of shaking their testimony, but each of them declared that the prisoner was the man they saw. The jury had to ask themselves whether these girls were speaking correctly. The girls had an opportunity of knowing the man and of seeing his general appearance, which, he took it, was what a great many people judged by. Unless they were abandoned, perjured prostitutes they spoke to the same fact. Each of them swore both to Clover and to the prisoner whom, it must be borne in mind, they were expecting and looking for. So satisfied were they that he was the man who had made the appointment to come between three and five in the afternoon that they both put their hats on and went downstairs for the purpose of following to see where he went. They followed him to the corner of the street which commanded a view of the Lambeth Road, and they saw the girl and the man go to No 27, and enter the house and stay for a considerable time. That was the evidence which the jury had before them on the point whether the prisoner had met and knew Matilda Clover at the time of the murder. Afterwards, when the prisoner was arrested, the two women were called to see him in company with sixteen or more others, and there was no doubt that at first Masters failed to recognise him. But there was no reason to suppose that any unfairness was practised on the occasion, if there had been, Masters would have recognised him at once. When she had failed to recognise him with his hat on she left the room, and May was called in and recognised him. Masters was then recalled, and recognised him with his hat off. If

Charge to the Jury.

Mr Justice Hawkins

that evidence was accepted it showed that the prisoner was the man who was seen walking behind the girl Clover on 9th October and who entered the house in Lambeth Road with her.

Passing on to the night of the 20th, Lucy Rose, who spoke to admitting Clover and a man into the house, honestly said that she could not recognise the prisoner as that man, though he answered to some extent, to the description she gave of him. Her evidence was that the girl went in with a man who was tall and broad, and wore a heavy moustache. That description, as far as it went, corresponded with the description of the prisoner. In the passage was a dim light from a small paraffin lamp, and though Rose was able to give a description to some extent, she did not recognise the prisoner. During the time the man was in the house Clover seemed to have gone for some beer. Afterwards Rose heard them go to the door and Clover said 'Good night.' The man went out. Clover returned to her room, and subsequently she went out again. She returned, and at three o'clock in the morning the witness Rose was awakened by dreadful screams. She called Mrs Phillips, and they went into Clover's room and found the unhappy girl rolling in agony, with her head wedged between the bedstead and the wall. Lucy Rose, not being medically educated, could only describe things in her own simple way, but it was clear that Clover had intermittent spasms or fits, during the intervals of which she was bathed in perspiration and complained that she was suffocated, but during these intervals she was perfectly sensible and rational. These points were of importance when they came to the evidence of Dr Stevenson. There was another feature, when she was free from pain, on one occasion she said that she thought she should die, and that she wished to see her baby.

As Clover got worse, Mrs Phillips went for a doctor, and Mr Coppin saw the girl about seven o'clock. She was bathed in perspiration. He put some questions to her, saw her in one of her fits, and then left, saying he would send some medicine which was accordingly sent or brought. The moment she took the medicine the girl turned black in the face. It was not said that Coppin was present at that time, and he hoped he was not. He was sent for again, but this time he did not come. Although he had left the poor girl, as he said, in a dying condition, and was urged to go and see her again at eight o'clock, neither he nor Dr Graham, who was sent for, came near her, and at 8.45 she succumbed and died. For the sake of their own feel-

Thomas Neill Cream.

Mr Justice Hawkins

ings he hoped that each of these gentlemen had something like a legitimate excuse for not attending that unfortunate girl in her last moments.*

In the course of the day it was necessary that her death should be registered, and the woman Phillips did so register it, stating, untruthfully, that she was present at the death. Dr Graham, who had been sent for, and according to his own account, had attended her for alcoholism eight or nine times, had not seen her till the breath was out of the body, but made inquiry of Mrs Phillips, of whose reliability the jury must judge from what he had already said. Dr Graham also asked questions of Coppin, and then gave a certificate of the cause of death, stating that he had attended her in her last illness, and that he had seen her on the 21st, and that the cause of death was delirium tremens and syncope. He did not know what the people of the house thought. He attached no blame to the servant girl Lucy Rose, because she had no control over anything. That poor girl never left the bedside and remained with Clover till the end. But he rather marvelled that those who knew how the night had been passed by the poor thing did not think it necessary to have some investigation as to what was the real cause of death. But inquiry was not made, the girl had died, the doctor had certified from delirium tremens and syncope. She was buried in a pauper's grave on 27th October, and in that grave she rested till 5th May. All who knew of her death—so far as was known—believed that she had left this world in a state of intoxication, and that nothing worse had happened to her. Her name was almost forgotten. They were truly told by the Attorney-General that if the poor girl did die from the effects of poison administered to her by some one or other, nobody but the person who had administered the poison could have known of the fact, and inasmuch as they had no particle of evidence to show that even a shadow of a shade of suspicion that she had died of poison was breathed until the latter end of the month of April, it was difficult to see how one could find fault with the conclusion which the Attorney-General asked them to draw, namely, that the one person who alone knew by whom the strychnine was administered was the person who administered it.

He would not discuss the evidence of Dr Stevenson, because he

---

* Dr Graham was attending a childbirth, and Mr Coppin was convinced that all had been done that could be done.

Charge to the Jury.

Mr Justice Hawkins

could not pretend to have acquired one-twentieth part of the scientific knowledge possessed by that learned gentleman, but that the unfortunate girl had come to her death by strychnine there could be no manner of doubt whatever. Dr Graham and Mr Coppin had expressed their opinion that she had died from excessive drinking, but in that opinion they were altogether mistaken. Dr Stevenson came to the conclusion that she had died from the administration of strychnine. The woman's death occurred on 21st October. She was buried on the 27th. On 28th November, just a day more than a month later, a letter purporting to be signed "M. Malone" and proved to have come from the prisoner and to be in his writing, was addressed to Dr W. H. Broadbent, accusing him of having been hired to poison and of having poisoned by strychnine Miss Clover at 27 Lambeth Road, on 20th October. (Mr Justice Hawkins read the letter.*)

The Attorney-General had asked, how came the prisoner, when every one else believed that death had come through intemperance, and when Dr Graham had so certified and when no suggestion had been made that any poison had been taken into her body, to write on 28th November to Dr Broadbent and say that death was by strychnine? Why make that assertion? The Attorney-General said it was because the prisoner having administered the poison, knew about it. He himself would point out the great significance of that letter. It was written with a view to intimidate and get money from Dr Broadbent, but fortunately Dr Broadbent was not intimidated. He handed over the letter to the authorities at Scotland Yard, where it was put by. There was a faint endeavour to find out the writer by inserting an advertisement such as was invited in the letter, but nobody answered it, and so the matter rested.† But the fact was beyond the possibility of doubt—if the jury believed this to be the prisoner's letter, and it was not disputed by his counsel—that on 28th November when—according to all the evidence—no suspicion of poisoning had been breathed, the prisoner wrote to Dr Broadbent to say that Clover had died on 20th October poisoned by strychnine.

One other point in the direct evidence bearing on the case remained to be noticed, and that was the statement by Miss Sleaper

---

* See page 49
† See Appendix J

Thomas Neill Cream.

Mr Justice Hawkins

that she was asked by the prisoner to go to the house in Lambeth Road, where a lady who had a child had been poisoned. After she had declined to do so, he told her that the inquiry had been made by Haynes. He asked the jury to remember that point when he came to discuss the credit which should be attached to the evidence of Haynes in dealing with the remarkable conversations he had had with the prisoner, because one of these conversations related to his being sent by the prisoner to make the inquiry. If that were so, the fact that the prisoner afterwards told Miss Sleaper that he had sent Haynes would go to corroborate Haynes in the story he told.

On the question of poison, it might naturally be asked—but does anybody suggest that the prisoner had poison? Yes, that was suggested, and the evidence given by M'Culloch went to show that when the prisoner was staying in the same hotel as he in Quebec he showed M'Culloch a bottle of crystals which he said was poison, and which he used to get young women out of trouble.*

As to the cause of death, Dr Stevenson, a gentleman of great scientific attainments, of vast experience, and of untiring perseverance in discovering the truth in all matters entrusted to him—no one in the world would doubt this—had for many years been employed by the Government of the day in making all the most important inquiries which in the public interest they had thought right should be made. No one could gainsay, or say one word in disparagement of his qualities of learning and experience in dealing with matters of this description. He was cross-examined with the view of ascertaining whether the theory of Dr Graham and Mr Coppin could be supported, and looking to the facts that there had been in Clover's case the symptoms of a feeling of suffocation, of being bathed in perspiration, or suffering from tetanic spasms, and of being perfectly sensible and rational in the intervals between the fits, he had said in his evidence that they were the symptoms of poisoning by strychnine. The body of the poor girl was exhumed on 5th May, and Dr Stevenson took from the body on 6th May such portions of it as enabled him to form his judgment by analysis as to what was the cause of death. He examined the body with a view to see whether there was anything at all to account for her death. Other than that charged in the indictment there was no disorder to account for death. Dr Stevenson

---

* Apparently Mr Justice Hawkins did not remind the jury that it had been proved that Cream had purchased nux vomica and capsules in London.

Charge to the Jury.

Mr Justice Hawkins had told them that he had applied every test that could be applied in the analysis he made, and that every one of the tests and every one of the symptoms of the illness pointed to the presence of strychnine and that he had come to the conclusion that the poor woman had died from strychnine poisoning. The prosecution relied upon that evidence to prove the death of Clover by poison.

As to the corroborative evidence, four other deaths had taken place.

The first was that of Ellen Donworth, who, in the early part of October,* fell suddenly down in the in Waterloo Road and died while being taken to hospital. It was discovered that she died by strychnine, but the murder was not now being attributed to the prisoner. One feature of these murders was that they were each followed by threatening letters for on 5th November the prisoner wrote to Mr F. W. D. Smith of W. H. Smith & Son threatening to incriminate him with the murder of Ellen Donworth by strychnine poisoning. He directed their attention also to the letters admittedly sent by the prisoner to Dr Harper and to Deputy-Coroner Wyatt, and to other documents in the case.

As to the Lou Harvey incident, when the prisoner met Harvey on the Embankment and gave her two pills, which he said would remove the spots on her face, Harvey, who was followed at a distance by the man with whom she was living, appeared to have been suspicious and while pretending to take the pills did not, in fact, do so but threw them away, and there could therefore be no evidence as to what they contained. She parted with the prisoner with an appointment to meet later on the same night which the prisoner did not keep. Some weeks afterwards Harvey met the prisoner, and he treated her to a glass of wine but did not appear to recognise her, and on her recalling her name to his recollection he turned on his heel and left her. That had a significance in view of a statement which the prisoner was said to have made when he spoke of another person having poisoned some girls "and Lou Harvey." In connection with that incident he reminded the jury that the prisoner had received from Harvey a wrong number as her address in Townshend Road, and that this wrong house was pointed out by him to the witness Haynes as the house in which Lou Harvey had lived.

---

* 1891

Thomas Neill Cream.

Mr Justice Hawkins

They came now to a part of the case which was of a very serious nature. On 6th January the prisoner left this country to go to Canada for some time, and they had the evidence of M'Culloch that, while they were together in Quebec, the prisoner showed him, in addition to a box of samples similar to those that had been produced, a bottle of crystals which he said were poison. Further than that, in his conversations with M'Culloch, the prisoner described himself as having been living a very low kind of life among the unhappy prostitutes who were to be met with in the locality included in and by the Waterloo Road, the Westminster Bridge Road, Lambeth Road, and Victoria Road.

With the return of the prisoner to this country they reached the history of the wretched girls Marsh and Shrivell. On 10th April —a Monday—the prisoner dined at home, contrary to his custom, and, announcing that he had a late engagement, he left the house at ten o'clock at night, and nobody saw him return. That same night Police Constable Cumley, on duty in Stamford Street, saw a man leave the house in which Marsh and Shrivell lived, and saw enough of him to be able to give a description of him. Within three-quarters of an hour of the man coming out the landlady was roused by screams, and found Marsh lying in the passage in fearful agony, suffering from the tetanic spasms of which the jury had heard so much. Upstairs Shrivell was lying in the same condition, and they were removed in a cab to the hospital, Marsh dying on the way, and Shrivell after some hours. An inquest was opened upon their bodies, and at the inquest Dr Stevenson gave evidence that the one had had administered to her six times, and the other three times, as much poison as would constitute a fatal dose. On 5th May a verdict was returned of wilful murder. But pending the verdict, and during the adjournment of the inquest, on 17th April the prisoner expressed a desire to see a report of the evidence which had already been given, and on the following day took advantage of the absence of Mr Harper, who lived in the same house, to go into his (Harper's) room. There had not been in the course of the trial the slightest imputation of any kind cast, nor, he dared say, could any be cast, on young Mr Harper. He was as innocent of the murder of any of these women as the gentlemen of the jury or as himself. During the absence of Mr Harper the prisoner went into his room, looked at his books and papers, put a number of questions about him to Miss Sleaper, and, as Haynes said, stole a photograph of Mr Harper

Charge to the Jury.

Mr Justice Hawkins

Then he went to Berkhamstead, and got Miss Sabbatini, to whom he had become engaged, to write the letters to Colonel Wyatt, to the foreman of the Coroner's jury, and to Mr Clark, private detective, which had been put in evidence, and in which Mr Harper was accused of the murder of the two girls by poison. It was—as he had already pointed out—a curious part of the case that these murders, as were the previous ones, were followed by the prisoner sending out threatening letters.

The next question to be put was—was the prisoner acquainted with Marsh and Shrivell, and in relation to that he referred them to the evidence of Police-Constable Cumley and of Police-Constable Eversfield and Sergeant Ward, who recognised the prisoner from the description which Cumley had given of the man whom he had seen leave the house in Stamford Street. Further, they had the evidence of Haynes. Some reflections had been cast upon the value of his evidence, and the jury must judge for themselves. Haynes had been employed by the Government as a secret agent very often in important affairs, requiring, one would think, great care, and he should say requiring also great truth. A man who was to be employed as secret agent and who was not a trusty or truthful man would be worthless. However, the jury must judge for themselves the credit they ought to attach to the evidence given by Haynes. It was also part of the evidence connecting the prisoner with these two girls that on his arrest their address was found on a piece of paper in his possession.

Haynes stated that he had seen entries of initials and dates in a note-book belonging to the prisoner, and further there was the evidence of M'Intyre as to the prisoner having said, 'I am going out of town for a few days, do you think I shall be arrested before I go?' And the further statement that when asked to accompany M'Intyre to Scotland Yard, the prisoner, after going a part of the way, stopped and said, 'Oh, you sent a "rip" to ask questions about me the other day. I suspect you of doing the double, and I won't go.' Furthermore, there was the fact that the box of capsules known to have been kept in the prisoner's cupboard could not be found when looked for.

The direct facts as regarded the case with which they were now dealing were the fact of the prisoner having been seen in company of the woman and going into her house with her; the fact that the man who was let in by the servant girl to some extent answered his description, the fact that the girl had died of poison, that she was buried with no suspicion of poison attaching to her death, that no man or woman knew that the poor creature had had strychnine administered to her except the person who administered it, if it was administered, and that the prisoner wrote to Dr Broadbent boldly accusing him of poisoning the girl by strychnine. They could only deal with this case—or with any other case—by taking the evidence as a whole, looking at it solely with a desire to determine the truth, and the questions they had to answer were: did they believe that the girl died by strychnine poisoning? Did they think the poison was administered—if administered at all—with intent to kill? Now the all-important question was, looking at the whole of the circumstances which were before them, had they the conviction borne into their minds that the prisoner was the person who committed this diabolical crime of poisoning Clover—for a diabolical crime it was by whomsoever committed. If they were not so convinced, the prisoner was entitled to be acquitted. But if they were satisfied that he was the man who did commit the crime, then it was their duty to say so, fearlessly and firmly. The question was in their hands to determine the innocence or guilt of the prisoner.

[The jury retired at 1.45 p.m., returning to the Court at 1.55 p.m.]

Their names having been called over,

The CLERK OF ARRAIGNS—Have you agreed upon your verdict?

FOREMAN—We have.

The CLERK OF ARRAIGNS—Do you find the prisoner guilty or not guilty of the murder of Matilda Clover?

FOREMAN—Guilty.

The CLERK OF ARRAIGNS—Prisoner at the bar, you stand convicted of the crime of wilful murder. Have you anything to say why the Court should not give you judgment to die according to law?

The prisoner did not make any reply.

Sentence.

Sentence

Mr. Justice HAWKINS—Thomas Neill, the jury, after having listened with the most patient attention to the evidence which has been offered against you in respect of this most terrible crime, and having paid all attention to the most able arguments and the very eloquent speech which your learned counsel addressed to them on your behalf, have felt it their bounden duty to find you guilty of the crime of wilful murder, of a murder so diabolical in its character, fraught with so much cold blooded cruelty, that one dare hardly trust oneself to speak of the details of your wickedness. What motive could have actuated you to take the life of that girl away, and with so much torture to that poor creature, who could not have offended you, I know not. But I do know that your cruelty towards her, and the crime that you have committed, are to my mind of unparalleled atrocity. For the crime of which you have been convicted our law knows but one penalty—the penalty of death. That sentence I must pronounce upon you in accordance with my duty. I would add one word, to beseech you, during the short time that life remains to you,—for remember that when you descend the steps from the spot where you now stand this world will be no more to you—to endeavour to seek your peace with Almighty God. Pray Him to pardon you for your great sin. He alone can grant you pardon. The crime which you have committed I have already said can be expiated only by your death. I proceed, therefore, to pass upon you the dread sentence of the law, which is that you be taken from hence to the place whence you came, and thence to a lawful place of execution, and that there you be hanged by your neck until you be dead, and that when you are dead your body be buried within the precincts of that prison within the walls of which you shall have been confined last before the execution of this judgment upon you. And may the Lord have mercy upon your soul.

The CHAPLAIN—Amen.

APPENDICES

APPENDIX I

CENTRAL CRIMINAL COURT, Saturday, 22nd October, 1892

Before Mr Justice Hawkins

THE QUEEN v. THOMAS NEILL,

FOR MURDER

Mr Justice Hawkins—Before I commence the business of the day, I am very desirous indeed of removing any unfavourable impression that may have been entertained by anybody with reference to the incident about the letter to Dr Broadbent. I mean the letter which it was said was sent to Scotland Yard, and that no inquiries were made about it. I have received the most satisfactory explanation, of not only what was not done, but of what was done, and I must say that I think it removes the slightest possible ground of complaint against the authorities of Scotland Yard. And with regard to the impression that I am afraid that was conveyed also in the language which I used, that I expressed some complaint and criticised the action of the police generally, concerned in the case I can only say that, so far from wishing to cast anything like a censure on them, I think that the conduct of the police from the commencement to the end of the case is admirable. It was only the one little incident with reference to Dr Broadbent's letter which made me think that more might have been done, but I am satisfied now that all was done that I should myself have desired to be done in the matter.

The Attorney General—I have no doubt that your lordship's public statement to that effect will be received with satisfaction, and, so far as it rests, or it is proper for me to say anything, I certainly would like to take the opportunity of endorsing what your lordship has said as to the most creditable conduct of Inspector Tunbridge, who is connected with Scotland Yard, and that of Inspectors Harvey and McIntyre, and of Constables Comley and Eversfield.

Mr Justice Hawkins—And Sergeant Ward also.

The Attorney General—Yes, and Ward also.

The Clerk of the Court—My lord the Grand Jury wished to commend Inspector Tunbridge and all the officers concerned in the case.

[Note.—As is usual many willing persons volunteered information, most of which was entirely useless, some stated that they knew Neill and much about him but wild-goose chases were the only outcome. Indeed, this whole case is a striking example of the ceaseless care and vigilance which characterises Scotland Yard, but for which it is too seldom given credit.—W. T. S.]

Thomas Neill Cream.

APPENDIX II

The following is an extract from the *Chicago Tribune* of 19th June, 1881:—

'DR. CREAM

IN THE TOILS FOR SENDING SCURRILOUS POSTAL CARDS

Dr. Cream, who was tried once in the Criminal Court on an indictment charging him with abortion and acquitted, is in the toils again, with a prospect of being rewarded according to his deserts. His offense consists in the sending of the vilest sort of postal cards through the mails—an offense for which the revised Statutes prescribe a fine of from $100 to $500, with imprisonment from one to ten years. The recipient of his foul abuse is a man by the name of Joseph Martin, living at 129 West Thirteenth Street, engaged in the business of preparing furs for some of the wholesale and retail fur houses in this city. Cream had attended his family as a physician, and appears to have had some difficulty in regard to a bill. Martin claims that he paid the doctor all he owed him, while the latter, claiming that Martin was in his debt to the amount of $20.00, resorted to the despicable scheme of sending him scurrilous postal cards, in order, perhaps, to hasten matters and bring about a settlement of the alleged debt. The postals were preceded by a couple of letters written in the same hand as the cards, signed 'Thomas N. Cream,' and valuable in the case as a means of identifying the writing on the postal card. In the first letter, the doctor very plainly informed Martin that his (Martin's) wife and children were suffering from diseases which he said they had contracted through Martin himself. He then proceeded to threaten him with an exposure of the matter unless his bill were paid, and, to be more circumstantial, added that the proofs of his allegation consisted of certain prescriptions on file at one Knos's drug store. The second letter was similar in its tone but wound up with the threat ' I will learn that damned vixen of a low wife of yours to speak ill of me '—from which it might be inferred that Mrs. Martin had perhaps been somewhat free in the use of her tongue.

The postal cards are three in number, and were all sent day before yesterday. The postmarks show that they were mailed from the West Side station, one at 9 a.m. and the other two at 6 p.m. The first is signed " Dr. Cream," and the second and third with the doctor's initials, ' T N C.'

The second runs as follows:—

'You had better learn that low, vulgar wife of yours to keep her foul mouth shut, with her second hand silk dolimans and second-hand silk dresses, and not talk about others. Two can play at that game. I heard on very good authority that you had to leave England on account of a bastard child you left behind. T N C'

The third and last was evidently intended as a clincher. It reads as follows:—

Appendix II.

"You had better learn that low vulgar woman of yours to keep a civil tongue in her head and not talk about others. Two can play that game. Remember the bastard child you left in England.

"T. N. C."

Such abuse as this would have been bad enough even if it had been based on facts. It was all the worse, therefore, because as Martin claims infamously false. Whether true or false, however, the sender of such stuff committed an offense in the eyes of the law, and Mr. Martin is determined to get justice. A warrant for Cream's arrest was accordingly sworn out, and he was brought in quite late in the afternoon, naturally very wroth at the turn which the affair had taken, and held in $1,200 bail to await the preliminary examination Monday.

This thing of sending scurrilous postal cards through the mails, and thereby attempting to blacken the reputation of people, has gone far enough. Cream has added the crowning infamy of attempting to blast that which every man holds dearest—the fair name of his wife and children—and the average husband and father will be pretty apt to conclude that even hanging would be too good for him should he be proved guilty.

171

Thomas Neill Cream.

APPENDIX III

Extracts from the *Chicago Tribune*, 22nd September, 1881

Belvidere, Ill. 20th September, 1881.—The case of Dr. Thomas N. Cream for the murder of one Daniel Stott of Garden Prairie last June commenced in the Circuit Court of this county yesterday. The Hon. D. W. Munn of Chicago is defending Dr. Cream. State's Attorney B. W. Coon, Senator Chase Fuller, and the Hon. A. B. Coon appear for the people. A jury was obtained in the case at three o'clock to-day. Thus commenced the most noted case that has ever occurred in the history of this county. State's Attorney B. W. Coon opened the case in a very lengthy and able manner, stating to the jury what the prosecution expected to prove: that Dr. Cream had been doctoring Daniel Stott, that Mrs. Julia A. Stott was the wife of the deceased, that she visited the office of Dr. Cream in Chicago for the purpose of obtaining medicine for her husband, it was expected to prove that Dr. Cream had illicit intercourse with Mrs. Stott, that said Mrs. Stott visited Dr. Cream's office on the 14th of June the last for the purpose of obtaining medicine for her husband, that Dr. Cream gave her a prescription, and told her to go to Buck & Rayner's, druggists, and get it filled, that she did so, that after getting the prescription she returned to Dr. Cream's office, that he took the medicine and put something in it, that they were in company there in his office together until the 10.15 train started, that he went to the depot with her, that she came home to Garden Prairie and gave the medicine as prescribed to her husband, and that in a short time he was cold, that Dr. Cream telegraphed to the coroner of Boone County, after the burial that he thought Daniel Stott was poisoned, that a dose of the medicine was given to a dog and in fifteen minutes he was dead, that the stomach and medicine were analysed by Professor Haines of Rush Medical College of Chicago, and that he perceived the medicine to have enough strychnine in to kill a person, and that the stomach contained enough strychnine to poison three men; that Dr. Thomas Cream had said that he was in need of some money, and getting one to the medical profession Mrs. Stott's power of attorney to prosecute Buck & Rayner, the druggists who put up the prescription.... State's Attorney Coon made a very fine statement of the case. He was followed by the Hon. D. W. Munn on behalf of the prisoner. Mr. Munn made a very able and eloquent speech to the jury telling them how he proposed to show on behalf of they were in the medical profession were circumstantial. Two witnesses were examined but stated nothing important. The Court adjourned till eight o'clock to-morrow morning.

21st September 1881.—The case of Dr. T. N. Cream for the murder of Daniel Stott of Garden Prairie, last June was resumed in the Circuit Court of this county to-day. The first witness called was Dr. S. Whiteman, M.D., Coroner of Boone County. He heard of the death of Daniel Stott 14th June, the day he was buried. He received telegrams and letters from Dr. Cream stating that he thought Stott was poisoned. He disinterred the body, cut the stomach out and sent it to Chicago to Professor Walter S. Haines, and that upon analysis it was found to contain 3.394/1000 grains

Appendix III.

of strychnine, and that there were 2 622-1000 grains of strychnine in the medicine that was given to Stott that caused his death. The next witness called was Dr. Charles Minoprio of Belvidere. He testified that he carried the stomach into Chicago and delivered it to Professor Haines. The next witness called was A. S. M'Clellan, prescription clerk of Buck & Rayner's drug store in Chicago. He put up the prescriptions that were presented by Dr. Cream for Daniel Stott. There was not enough strychnine in the prescription to cause death. James B. Rayner was the next witness called. He belongs to the firm of Buck & Rayner. He personally knew that the prescriptions were put up by A. S. M'Clellan their prescription clerk just as the prescriptions read. The firm had never put up any prescriptions for Dr. Cream before. A. T. Ames, Sheriff of Boone County, was the next witness called. He arrested Dr. Cream at Belle River, Canada, on 27th July last. He brought him to Belvidere without extradition papers, according to Cream's own wishes, on the following Monday, and has had Dr. Cream in his charge ever since. He testified very strongly against Dr. Cream. The next witness sworn was Mrs. Julia A. Stott, wife of the late Daniel Stott, the person indicted with Dr. Cream for murder. She is thirty-five years of age, very delicate looking and very plain-spoken, and although the attorneys tried to mix her up on her examination they did not succeed. She testified that she got the prescription from Dr. Cream, and got it filled at Buck & Rayner's, that she came home and gave the medicine to her husband, and that he died about twenty minutes after she gave the medicine to him. She said that Dr. Cream took the medicine after it was put up by the druggist in his office, and she thought he put something in it. She also testified that Dr. Cream had been on criminal terms with her since she first went to see him. On the whole, she turned State's evidence, and tried to convict Dr. Cream to save her own neck. Mrs. Virgo, No. 275 West Madison Street, Chicago, was the next witness called. She is in the millinery business. Saw Dr. Cream and Julia A. Stott come into her store together in the month of June last. Cream outfitted her about getting a corset and trimmings. Amy Revell Stott, daughter of Julia A. Stott, was the next witness called. She is only ten years old, but testified very straight for a child of her age. She said, "Dr. Cream told me he loved my mother and would like her as his own." She also testified as to the death of her father Daniel Stott. She said he took medicine that was prescribed by Dr. Cream, and immediately after died. She is a very brilliant girl for one of her age. Mrs. Mary M'Clellan, of No. 163 Larrabee Street, Chicago, was the next witness sworn. She is the strongest witness against Dr. Cream that has yet been produced. She testified that on the night of the death of Daniel Stott Cream was at her house in Chicago, and he told her he expected to hear of Daniel Stott's death at any time as he knew he had been poisoned. The lady is quite elderly, English born, and impressed the audience quite favourably with her testimony. They did not finish cross-examining her. The Court adjourned till eight o'clock to-morrow morning. The Courtroom was filled to its utmost capacity.

22nd September, 1881.—The third day of the trial of Dr. Thomas N. Cream for the murder of Daniel Stott was resumed in our Circuit Court to-day. They finished cross-examining Mrs. M'Clellan. She testified that

Thomas Neill Cream.

she had hard feelings towards Dr. Cream, that she went his bail on a postal card scrape, and that he skipped out.

Dr. Charles Scott was the next witness called. "Have been a physician in Belvidere for six years. It is not customary to put sugar and calomel in capsules."

Frank Nordstrand, a brakeman on the Galena Division of the Chicago & North-Western Railway, was called next. "Have seen Dr. Cream with Mrs. Julia A. Stott at the Wells Street depot in Chicago about half a dozen times."

Charles Warren was sworn next. He had roomed in the same cell with Dr. Cream since he had been in jail. Cream admitted to him that he had slept with Julia A. Stott several times. He said he never had been convicted of any crime.

The people here rested the case.

The first witness sworn for the defense was Dr. Thomas N. Cream, the defendant. He is about 5½ feet and very thick-set, very good and intelligent-looking, and thirty-five years of age. He says he never has been convicted of any crime in his life. "I was arrested 18th June for threatening to expose a man in a postal card, and was put under a $1,200 bail. Mrs. M'Clellan, of No. 105 Thirteenth Street, went my bail. I left for Canada before my case came off. I knew Daniel Stott of Garden Prairie. I doctored him about five or six months for epileptic fits. I gave Mrs. Stott in my office a prescription on 11th June for Mr. Stott. She got the prescription filled at Buel & Rayner's drug store. She came home and gave him the medicine as I directed. From the effects of it he died. In my prescription there was nothing to cause death. I did not direct which drug store Mrs. Stott should go to to get the prescription filled. I did not have the medicine in my hands after she got it at the drug store. After I heard of Mr. Stott's death I suspicioned foul play, as he was improving under my treatment, and I understood he died quite suddenly. I suspected Mrs. Stott had poisoned him. I had several reasons for so thinking. The first one was that some time ago she wanted to get a prescription from me for str[y]chnine. She said she wanted to give it to her husband to fix him. The second reason was that I was not notified of Mr. Stott's death until after he was buried, and they asked me for no certificate of death. The third reason I suspicioned Mrs. Stott was I had heard her make several threats against her husband. For these reasons I thought there had been foul play, and I telegraphed to the Coroner of Boone County to have the body disinterred. I never made love to Mrs. Stott and never had a criminal connection with her. I have been a practising physician in Chicago for two years." The doctor told a very straightforward story and talked very intelligently.

Mary Dunlap was the next witness sworn. She lives in Garden Prairie. "Have doctored with Dr. Cream. Have been to Chicago to see Dr. Cream with Mrs. Stott. I never heard him make any improper proposals to Mrs. Stott or myself."

Mrs. Adell Gridley, of No. 434 West Madison Street, was the next witness called. "Dr. Cream's office is on the same floor that I live. He has the front rooms. I live in the back rooms. I rent him the rooms. I know Mrs. Stott. She never lodged with Dr. Cream in his office. Dr. Cream was at home all day Sunday, 12th June."

Mr. Frank Gridley, husband of the last witness, was sworn next.

Appendix III.

"Dr. Cream was in his office all day Sunday, 12th June to my certain knowledge. I remember it because I lent him twenty-five cents.' The witness is very small and wants to verify his statements by betting on them.

The defense here rested their case.

R. W. Coon, State's Attorney, commenced to argue the case to the jury at quarter past three o'clock. He was followed by the Hon. A. B. Coon who made a very intelligent and able speech. Col. D. W. Munn will argue the case tomorrow forenoon in behalf of the prisoner, and Senator Fuller will close the case in the afternoon for the State. Court adjourned until nine o'clock tomorrow morning.

22nd September 1881.—The case of Thomas N. Cream for the murder of Daniel Stott was resumed in the Circuit Court of this county today. Col. D. W. Munn argued the case to the jury on behalf of the defense this forenoon, and a portion of the afternoon. He made a very brilliant, able and eloquent argument, and if his client, Dr. Cream, is convicted of murder, it is not the fault of Col. Munn as he has defended his client faithfully and ably all through his trial. Col. Munn was followed by Senator Fuller of this city who closed the case for the people. He made a very intelligent and oratorical argument to the jury, taking the stand that both Thomas N. Cream and Julia A. Stott were equally guilty of the crime of murder. After the Court gave fourteen instructions for the people and twenty-one for the defendant, the jury retired at 4:50 p.m. The general impression of the people of this county is that the jury will not agree on a verdict. Should they agree it will probably convict the defendant. The Court took a recess till tomorrow morning.

23rd September 1881.—The jury in the Cream murder case came in at nine o'clock with a verdict of guilty, fixing the punishment at imprisonment for life in the penitentiary. Col. Munn, in behalf of the prisoner, made a motion for a new trial. Judge Kellum set a special term for the 17th October next to consider the motion. Col. Munn says he expects to get a new trial. Cream, the prisoner, took the verdict very coolly.

17th October 1881.—The Circuit Court of Boone County convened in adjourned session at two o'clock p.m. today. Judge Charles Kellum presiding. After disposing of several minor matters the motion for a new trial in the case of Dr. Thomas N. Cream, convicted of the murder of Daniel Stott of Garden Prairie, was taken up. Col. D. W. Munn of Chicago, again appeared for the defendant Cream. Some eight or ten points were named in the written motion filed in the case, but Col. Munn relied on but two in his argument. The first of these was that the Court erred in giving the eighth instruction given on behalf of the people. The instruction simply informed the jury that if they believed from the evidence that criminal relations had existed between Dr. Cream and Mrs. Julia A. Stott, the wife of the murdered man, the fact of such relations existing constituted a material circumstance in the case, and that if the defendant Cream had sworn falsely in regard to such material circumstance, then they were at liberty to disregard all of his testimony except where it was corroborated by other evidence or circumstances proven in the case

Thomas Neill Cream.

The second point relied on was that of newly discovered evidence. This was shown by the affidavit of Mr and Mrs John Johns, of 436 West Madison Street, Chicago, who claimed that they knew of the whereabouts of Cream on Sunday, the 19th June and that he could not have been at the residence of Mrs Mary McClellan, as she had testified. Col Munn made an able appeal to the Court on behalf of his client, whom he professed to believe entirely innocent of the crime of which he has been convicted. He was followed in the argument by R W Coon Esq, State's Attorney, and Senator Charles E Fuller, on the part of the people. These gentlemen claimed that the instructions complained of correctly stated the law, and that the newly discovered evidence claimed must have been known to the defendant when Mrs McClellan gave her testimony as well as now, and that the defendant then had ample time to procure the attendance of those witnesses if he desired to do so. Also, that the alleged new evidence was only impeaching testimony, and that evidence of such nature was not sufficient in law to grant a new trial upon. The Court promptly overruled the motion, and plainly indicated that he was of the opinion that Cream had had a fair trial and he was not disposed to interfere with the verdict of the jury. Judge Kellum then sentenced the notorious doctor to be taken to the penitentiary at Joliet there to be confined for the term of his natural life, one day of each year to be spent in solitary confinement. Defendant's counsel intimates that the case will be taken to the Supreme Court and sixty days were given in which to prepare a bill of exceptions, but the general opinion is that the case is at an end, and that even if a new trial could be obtained, it would do Cream no good, but that if another jury were to pass on the case the death penalty might be inflicted

---

18th October, 1881.—Sheriff Ames will start for Joliet to-morrow with "Dr" Thomas N. Cream, yesterday sentenced by Judge Kellum to confinement in the penitentiary for life for the murder of Daniel Stott at Garden Prairie in June last. Mrs Julia A Stott paramour of Dr Cream and widow of the murdered man remains in the county jail, her trial as an accomplice in the murder having been postponed until the next term of Court which does not convene until the second Monday of February next. Your reporter this morning interviewed Senator Fuller one of the counsels for the people in regard to this case and his views in regard to the probability of the Supreme Court granting a new trial in case the matter comes before it. The Senator says that he believes there is as little error in the record of this case as in any criminal case he was ever connected with, and he does not believe it possible for the Supreme Court to find anything that can reverse the case. It is a case he says where there can be no possible doubt of the guilt of the defendant and the crime is one that stands almost without a parallel in the annals of crime. Mr Stott was deliberately poisoned by his physician and his ruthless wife simply for the purpose of putting up a blackmailing job on a reputable drug firm of Chicago. The jury which found the doctor guilty was composed of some of the best citizens of the county, men of sound judgment, conscientious and honest and if ever a man had a fair trial and an able defense, Mr Cream is that man. The people of the county are well pleased and satisfied with the result of the trial and the conviction of Mrs Stott in February next is confidently predicted.

Dr. Neill of 102 Lambeth Palace Road London S.W. desires to acknowledge the receipt of Two Guineas from Henry Stear Esq M.D. of Saffron Walden Essex and a similar amount from W. No. B. on behalf of the Widow and Children of the late Dr. Wm. H. P. Stanbury.

Dr. Neill desires also to say that these kind donations are really the means of keeping this poor Woman and her Children out of the Workhouse

Handwriting of Thomas Neill Cream.

This letter was used by the police to compare with the handwriting of the blackmailing letters. The widow mentioned in it was the daughter of Mrs Sleaper, Cream's landlady.

Appendix IV.

APPENDIX IV

CREAM'S HANDWRITING

The letter from Cream, of which a facsimile faces this page, was reproduced by the police authorities and used by them for purposes of comparison with writings of which Cream denied the authenticity. He seems to have been collecting money for the widow of Dr. Wm. H. R. Smiley, being a sister of Miss Sleaper and daughter of Mrs. Mary Sleaper, his landlady at Lambeth Palace Road. Dr. Stead to whom this is addressed died in 1917. I have been unable to obtain any further information about this matter which was mentioned at the inquest on Matilda Clover.—W. T. S.

Thomas Neill Cream.

APPENDIX V.

EXCERPTS FROM THE REPORT OF THE PROCEEDINGS WITH REFERENCE TO THE DEATH OF MATILDA CLOVER

On Wednesday, 22nd June 1892, Mr A Braxton Hicks, the Mid Surrey Coroner opened an inquiry at the Tooting Vestry Hall, with reference to the death of Matilda Clover, aged twenty seven a single woman which occurred at 27 Lambeth Road, on 21st October, 1891 from the effects of strychnine poisoning The exhumation of the body took place on 5th May, in consequence of certain facts which came to the knowledge of the police during their investigation of the charges against Thomas Neill, who was under remand at the Bow Street Police Court accused of sending letters attempting to blackmail Dr Harper of Barnstaple and others One letter, which mentioned that Matilda Clover died through being poisoned by strychnine, was dated 28th November 1891 five weeks after the death of the deceased, and was addressed to Dr W H Broadbent

Mr C F Gill and Mr Stevenson, instructed by Mr Williamson, appeared on behalf of the Treasury, Inspector Tunbridge of Scotland Yard, and Inspector Harvey and Sergeant M'Intyre of the L Division, represented the Chief Commissioner of Police, and Mr Bryan watched the proceedings on behalf of Neill Cream, who was brought into Court in the custody of two warders from Holloway Prison

Neill asked whether he might be furnished with paper and pencil as his solicitor had not yet arrived The Coroner having replied in the affirmative, Neill said that he presumed he might retain possession of the notes he made and that the officers would not take possession of them Mr Gill said that he would not take advantage of any notes which the prisoner might take

The Coroner then gave instructions that the prisoner should be allowed to tear up his notes or give them to his solicitor He reminded Neill that by English law no prisoner was accused in a Coroner's Court until a formal verdict had been returned He did not wish to take any unfair advantage of the prisoner, in fact, that was his reason for having him present in Court, and he would allow him to give evidence if he thought fit

ROBERT TAYLOR a brass finisher of 10 London Road Southwark, identified the body as that of his niece, whom he saw for the last time on the day of her death She was a domestic servant She had spoken to him about a man named Fred, and the witness met her with him at the Mason's Arms, Lambeth Road, about a month before her death She told him he might form his own opinion as to how she was earning her living About a month before she died the witness was introduced to the man Fred He considered Neill to be very much like the man, but was not absolutely positive He was sent for on the night of the death by the landlady, whom he saw He told her he thought it was very strange for a young girl like that to go off so suddenly He noticed that her body was drawn up in the bed, and he thought she died in great

Appendix V.

agony. Her legs were drawn up. He could not remember what the landlady said, but she satisfied him as to the circumstances under which the girl died. He had his suspicions, however, that everything was not right. He did not know who the doctor was. The landlady said the doctor had given a certificate to the effect that death was due to delirium. Witness was not aware that his niece drank. He did not know whether Fred visited his niece on the night of her death. The witness went on to say he knew that his niece had a child two years old, but he did not know whose it was. He believed his niece's papers and things were still at the house. An application had been made for them by Mrs Swift, a sister of Clover. He was not told by his niece who Fred was. In answer to Neill, the witness said that he was sure the man Fred did not wear a silk hat. He had a moustache, but no side whiskers, and he was not then wearing glasses.

Lucy Rose, a domestic servant, residing at 90 Merton Street, Walworth Road, said that in September last she took a situation with Mrs Phillips at 27 Lambeth Road. The young woman, Matilda Clover, occupied two rooms on the second floor with her little child. She used to bring men to the house. On the night before she died she remembered letting her into the house with a man. It was early in the evening. There was a lamp in the hall, but it did not show a very good light. The man was very tall and broad and was about forty years of age. He had a very heavy moustache but no whiskers. He was wearing a silk hat, but was not wearing glasses. He was in the house about an hour. While the man was in the house Clover went out for something, and later on he went out. The witness went to bed about ten o'clock, and was wakened by hearing Clover screaming loudly as if she were in pain. She got up and called the landlady and they went to Clover's room. Clover was lying across the foot of the bed with her head fixed between the bed and the wall. Her head was bent backward and she was lying on her back. Clover said "That wretch Fred has given me some pills and they have made me ill." She also said that she was not in pain but that she trembled so much that she was taken with convulsions. She said Fred had poisoned her. The witness lifted her up and put her on the pillows, when she said something seemed to be sticking in her throat. She vomited a great deal and witness gave her some tea. She asked for drink several times. She told the witness that while she had gone Fred had made the pills and told her to take them before she went to bed. He gave her four pills.

In answer to the Coroner the witness said that the landlady knew that Clover had said she had been poisoned. Witness went on to say that during the time she was speaking to the deceased she did not appear to have attacks of pain, and was quite conscious. She had convulsive fits, which left her quite exhausted. She trembled all over and stretched out. While a fit was on she groaned: these occurred every two minutes, and while the attacks lasted she seemed in great agony. She said she thought she was going to die, and would like to see her baby. At that time the landlady had gone for the doctor. Clover asked that Dr Graham should be sent for. Mrs Phillips came back and said Dr Graham was not in, and she went for Dr Coppin who came. Witness asked Mrs Phillips if she had told the doctor about Clover having taken pills, and

Thomas Neill Cream.

she replied that Dr Coppin had asked Clover what pills they were Clover told him, whereupon the doctor said that the man, meaning Fred, must either have been drunk or mad to have given them to her. Witness had never seen Dr Coppin before. She remained with Clover from the time the doctor came until she died. Some medicine came, and when the deceased took a teaspoonful she turned black in the face and her eyes rolled about. Mrs Phillips had gone for the doctor again when Clover died. That was about 9.15 a.m. In the afternoon Dr Graham came, and Mrs Phillips told him what had taken place. Witness told him what the deceased had said about being poisoned, and that pills had been given her. Upon hearing that he told her that he should not want her again. The deceased's box was still at Mrs Phillips, so far as the witness knew. Witness had seen a letter addressed to Clover, which was as near as she could remember as follows:—"Dear Miss Clover,—Will you meet me outside the Canterbury at 7.30 to-night? Do you remember the night I bought your boots? You were too drunk to speak to me. Please bring this paper and envelope with you.—Yours, Fred." Witness added that the deceased went out to keep the appointment, but did not take the letter with her. Witness could not find it after her death, however. Mrs Phillips never told her not to say anything about the circumstances of the death. She had never seen any other man with the deceased, but Mrs Phillips generally opened the door. She did not know Dr Graham by sight. She did not know the character of the house before she went to it.

EMMA PHILLIPS said her real name was Vowles, and she was the landlady of 27 Lambeth Road. Clover had lodged with her for three months. She came as a married woman, but afterwards said that a gentleman named Fred kept her. Witness had seen him on many occasions. He was of slight build fair and wore a light suit. She had never seen Neill until that day. He was not in the least like Fred, who was a much smaller man. The witness emphatically denied having heard the deceased say she had been poisoned nor did she hear her say that a man had given her some pills, or that she thought she was dying. What she said was that she was very ill, and that if she got over it she would never drink again. On the evening before she died witness had been out, and when she returned Rose told her that a gentleman had been there with Clover. The witness had not seen Fred at the house for at least a month before that. Witness thought Clover was suffering from delirium tremens. She did not tell the doctor that Clover had taken pills, because she was not aware of it. She could not remember whether she told Sergeant Ward that she heard Rose tell the doctor that Clover had taken pills. She did not remember Rose telling the doctor that Clover had been poisoned. The witness registered the death. She did not know what was the cause of death except that it was through drink. Dr Graham gave her the certificate the next morning. Dr Coppin had referred her to Dr Graham for the certificate. She did not represent that Dr Graham last saw the deceased on 21st October. She did sign her name as being at the death, when was untrue. Clover left no papers. The witness pledged Clover's boots after she was dead. She put the deceased's baby into the workhouse and it had since been adopted by a respectable family.

WILLIAM THURSBY, of 29 Lambeth Palace Road, deputy registrar for

Appendix V.

births, marriages, and deaths, of Lambeth, stated that he registered the death of Matilda Clover. The death was stated to be due to delirium tremens and syncope, and was certified by Robert Graham, L.S.A. and the original was signed by Emma Phillips, of 27 Lambeth Road, as being present at death.

FRANCIS COPPIN stated that he lived at 138 Westminster Bridge Road and was assistant to Dr. M'Carthy, who also resided at that address. He remembered in October last being called to No. 27 Lambeth Road to see Clover. He could not fix the date, but the time was about 7.30 in the morning. He went because Dr. M'Carthy was out. He found the woman in a state of tremor, cold skin, hands and feet and a rather quick pulse. She did not complain of pain. She said she had been drinking brandy on the previous night. When he was leaving the room Lucy Rose the servant told him that Clover had informed her that a man had given her some pills on the night before. The witness did not question Clover on the subject and she did not mention it. Mrs. Phillips, the landlady, was not there when the pills were mentioned. Witness was in the house about ten minutes altogether, during which time Clover had a convulsive fit. He considered it an epileptic convulsion due to drink. Her face was not drawn. He could not remember the appearance of her eyes. The fit he saw lasted two or three minutes and she was conscious both before and after it. The only question he put to her was as to how much she had had to drink. He did not remember her complaining of pain. The servant certainly did not tell him that she had complained of being poisoned. He did not speak to the landlady about the pills, nor she to him. Before he went upstairs Mrs. Phillips said that the woman had been drinking for more than a week and that only on the previous day she had drunk a bottle of brandy in less than two hours. Not suspecting anything about poison, he naturally attributed her illness to drink. He saw the vomit and was shown something in a newspaper which he was told the deceased had been taking the night before. They wanted to know whether it was poison. He could not remember who showed it to him, but it was either the landlady or the servant. He told them it was sulphate of magnesia. He prescribed medicine consisting of a solution of bicarbonate of soda and hydrocyanic acid. He did not hear what was the effect of the medicine that Rose gave evidence at the inquest. After sending the medicine the witness sent to Dr. Graham to tell him that he ought to see the woman. At a little before nine o'clock Mrs. Phillips came again to say that Clover was worse. He gave her a draught and afterwards heard that the patient was dead. He did not go to the house again. He had no qualification whatever, and therefore could not give a certificate as to the cause of death. He told Mrs. Phillips that as Dr. Graham had been attending the deceased for a week, he would grant a certificate. He had no authority from Dr. Graham to make that statement. He informed Dr. Graham of the circumstances of the death. Dr. Graham had never given a certificate in any other case that the witness had attended. In Clover's case he detected what he considered were symptoms of incipient delirium tremens. He had passed the Arts examination. Dr. M'Carthy's practice formerly belonged to the witness's father.

ROBERT GRAHAM, a Licentiate of the Society of Apothecaries, of 56 Upper Kennington Lane, said he first saw the deceased about twelve days

Thomas Neill Cream.

before her death. He had no previous knowledge of her nor of Mrs. Phillips. The first time he was at 27 Lambeth Road was on the day of the death. Clover visited his surgery eight or nine times during the twelve days. The last time he saw her was either on 19th or 20th October. When she came on 9th October he examined her and found her suffering from alcoholism, for which he treated her. He remembered Mrs. Phillips coming for him on the night of 20th October or morning of the 21st. He was unable to go, and recommended her to call in Dr. M'Carthy. He went to 27 Lambeth Road about two o'clock, and found that Clover was dead. He made a superficial examination of the body. Rose told him about her having heard Clover screaming in the night and of finding her "trembling and shaking." He was not informed about the pills nor about Clover having expressed a belief that she was poisoned. He had no conversation with Rose. He knew that no qualified medical man had seen the woman, and was aware that if he had not given a certificate an inquest would have been held. Mrs. Phillips asked him for a certificate, and he told her that she had better come to his office in the morning. As Clover had suffered from alcoholism, he thought she might have died from syncope. He was aware that Mr. Coppin was with the deceased only ten minutes.

Dr. THOMAS STEVENSON, Lecturer on Medical Jurisprudence at Guy's Hospital and one of the analysts of the Home Office, stated that on May last he examined the body at the Lambeth Cemetery, Tooting, assisted by Mr. L. A. Dunn, Senior Demonstrator of Anatomy at Guy's Hospital. The body was for the most part in an extremely good state of preservation. He examined all the great cavities, those of the head, chest and abdomen minutely. The brain was free from tumour or hæmorrhage. The lungs, heart, stomach, liver, and spleen were normal. No diseased appearance was met with. By chemical analysis he detected strychnine in the stomach, in the liver, and in the brain. The amount of strychnine he obtained was small—too small to permit of its weight being accurately ascertained. He extracted about one-sixteenth of a grain of strychnine, that quantity, a full medicinal dose, pointed to the administration of a fatal dose of that poison. The Coroner having read to Dr. Stevenson the evidence given on the previous day by the witness Rose as to the symptoms displayed by the deceased during her last moments, Dr. Stevenson said those symptoms were not only consistent with but actually pointed to poisoning by strychnine. The symptoms were not those of delirium tremens.

ALBERT G. KIRKBY, assistant to Mr. Benjamin W. Priest, a chemist, of 21 Parliament Street, Westminster, was called and examined by Mr. Gill. He stated that, about the beginning of last October, he made the acquaintance of Dr. Neill, who came to his employer's shop to make some purchases. He said he was Dr. Neill, adding that he was a medical student at St. Thomas's Hospital. About ten days after his first visit he came and asked for some nux vomica. As the drug is a poison scheduled under the Pharmacy Act, witness considered it a proper thing to ask for a written order, and he asked Dr. Neill to write his name and address in his presence, handing him a piece of paper for that purpose. He identified the paper produced. It read as follows:—"Tinc. nucis vom., one ounce, 10 to 20 drops in water. Quin. sulph., two ounces.—T. Neill M.D., 103

Appendix V.

Palace Road." That was written in his presence by Neill, whom he now saw in Court. He served Neill with one ounce of nux vomica. He did not take any quinine. Having received the nux vomica, Neill asked for some gelatine capsules, and said he wanted them empty. Witness had none in stock and told him so, whereupon Neill asked him to obtain some for him. On the same day witness went to Messrs. Maw, Son, & Thompson, wholesale chemists, of Aldersgate Street and procured a box of 100 empty capsules. On the following day Neill came to the shop, and witness gave him the capsules. He looked at them and said they were too large, explaining that he wanted them about half that size. Witness took them back to Messrs. Maw's and changed them for smaller ones. Two days afterwards Neill called and asked for them. He used to come to the shop about two or three times a week, and he bought nux vomica on three or four occasions to the best of witness's recollection. The quantity varied from one to four ounces at a time. Witness got a written order from him on each occasion. He had searched for the orders but the only other one he had been able to find was the one produced. He used to see Neill occasionally from October until January, and then he lost sight of him until April. When he described himself as "Dr. Neill M.D.," he said he was attending a course of lectures on the eyes at St. Thomas's Hospital. He gave no further information about himself and did not say what he wanted the nux vomica for. Witness believed he had a medical qualification, and when he looked in the medical register and was unable to find his name, he thought he had an American diploma.

Dr. WILLIAM HENRY BROADBENT, M.D., of 34 Seymour Street, Portman Square W., stated that he was physician to St. Mary's Hospital. On 30th November 1891 he received by post a letter (produced). He had never heard of the Miss Clover mentioned in the letter, and he had never been at 27 Lambeth Road. He knew nothing whatever of the writer of the letter. Having read it, he immediately handed it to the police authorities. The handwriting was not that of any person he was acquainted with.

The Coroner read the letter which was signed "M. Malone" and demanded £2500 for information relating to Dr. Broadbent's connection with the death of Clover.

ELIZABETH MASTERS, of 121 Lambeth Road S.E., stated that about the middle of October a gentleman met her in Ludgate Circus and took her one evening to Gatti's Music Hall. They were joined by a friend of hers named Elizabeth May. He told them that he had come from abroad to claim some property, his brother having just died. He explained that when a young man he was a student at St. Thomas's Hospital. He took off his hat and she noticed that his head was bald. Neill was the man who met her. The gentleman told her that he was staying at a hotel in Fleet Street, and after the music hall performance the all three drove to Ludgate Circus. He said he was going to remove from the hotel and was going to live at Chelsea. He said he had been three weeks in England. Before they parted he promised to write to her soon. On the following Friday she received a letter which she kept for about three months, afterwards destroying it, because she was changing her lodgings. In the letter the writer asked her to look out for him between three and five o'clock,

Thomas Neill Cream.

and to keep the letter. She did not remember the signature, but the postmark was Lambeth. That afternoon Elizabeth May was with her sitting at their window when she saw Neill on the road. He was following a young woman. She was wearing a white apron with straps across the shoulders and she was carrying a basket. The witness and Miss May went downstairs, and walked in the same direction. She saw the young woman enter 27 Lambeth Road. She beat at the door with the handle in her hand and watched Dr Neill come up to her. He also entered the house. Witness and her friend watched there more than half an hour, but he did not come out.

(A photograph of Clover was here shown to the witness who said it was very much like the women so seen, but she should think it was seen a very long time ago.)

The witness continued, saying she knew Clover by sight, but not to speak to. On the 17th inst. she was shown some men at Bow Street police station. She did not recognise Neill at first, but she did when she saw him with his hat off. She had no doubt he was the man she had an appointment at Ludgate Hill with some one else — whom she met Dr Neill for the first time. He was particular in his dress. She could swear he was the man who went with her and after, with her to the music hall. When he was at Ludgate Hill he was wearing a hard bowler hat with a flat top and a black dull cape or coat. She noticed he had been quite some time on the watch. On Friday last before Sessions She picked the defendant out from ten men.

Lizzie May stated that she lived at 15 Paris she Buildings, Charles Street Blackmore Road until recently returned. In October last she was residing at Orient Buildings, Lambeth, in the same house and was acquainted with Elizabeth Masters who had lived there some time. She went before she left there on November. She remembered some Masters in the company of a gentleman (Charles MacHill) this gentleman was introduced to Dr Neill. She went out this evening with them, and they went to perform to a hall, and drove in a cab to Ludgate Cross. They went into a public house and Neill then came up to meet them and went on the drive to Old Street. He was wearing a hard felt hat with a flat crown and a light overcoat. He was wearing glasses. She was positive Neill was the man. A few days afterwards she was sitting at the window with Masters when she saw Neill go by. Previous to this she had seen him, coming up behind at 27 Lambeth Road, pass. She was wearing a white apron with straps across the shoulders and carrying a basket. Dr Neill, who was dressed in much the same clothes and a black hat was following her, and witness saw them both enter 27 Lambeth Road. The next time witness saw Neill was when he picked him out Bow Street. At the music hall she noticed that Neill's eyes looked very strange. The witness identified a photograph of Clover. When Neill passed the house Masters remarked to her how different he looked to last but

By the Warders — After they had been to Bow Street Masters asked her whether she thought Neill was the same man. She replied in the affirmative saying she was positive about it. She was done when she identified him.

Miss Laura Sabbatini stated that she resided at Chapel Street, Berkhamstead Herts. She made the acquaintance of Dr Neill in November

154

Appendix V.

last when she was in London. He was introduced to her as Dr. Thomas Neill Cream, and he told her he was a doctor in America. She saw him frequently, but he was not at that time introduced to her relations. Shortly after she became known to him he proposed marriage to her and she accepted him. The letter produced contained his proposal of marriage. On 6th January Neill went to America for the purpose, as he said, of seeing about his father's estate. Previous to this, on 23rd December, he made a will in her favour, in which he described himself as "Thomas Neill Cream, physician, late of the city of Quebec," and left her the whole of his property. (Will produced.) Her age was sixteen years to-day old. He gave her the will of witness's home in Berkhamstead. While he was in England he wrote her several letters, and when he went away he gave her the following address to write to — "Care of Daniel Cream, Quebec, Canada," and he told her he would be staying at Blanchard's Hotel, Quebec. The letter proposing marriage and the will were both in his own handwriting. He came back from America at the end of April, and he came immediately on his return. After he had been some days in England he went again to live at 103 Lambeth Palace Road.

Mr. GILL said he did not wish to ask witness any further questions, but was it not a fact that she never had letters up to the end of his days. (See page 134.)

She did not remember his saying anything about expecting to be apprehended. He said the drug case contained samples of pills that he was going to sell, and that they had been supplied to him by his people in America. The case she spoke of him being in danger was when it was released. She never saw him in police custody but he asked to call one. She was with him when he made a private statement to her husband. That was at 103 Lambeth Palace Road on 20th May. He did not call on her. He said nothing about expecting to be arrested. She told him of her speaking to Inspector Tunbridge about being followed by a detective. She thought he said he would not answer questions put to him relating to his complaint about the police watching him.

Emily SLEAPER, landlady, 103 Lambeth Palace Road, said she resided there with her mother and took lodgers. Dr. Neill came to reside there on 7th October, having taken the second floor front room on the previous day. He said that he had been some time at Anderton's Hotel. He did not mention the name, but she saw Anderton's Hotel on his luggage. He said he was Dr. Neill of Quebec. He stayed there until 6th January, occupying his time with reading and writing. He had no business occupation as far as she knew. A week after he came there he began to wear spectacles, and he bought prescription spectacles. When he went out he was wearing a hard felt hat. She understood that he came to England for the benefit of his health. In October she remembered him asking her to take a letter round to Lambeth Road. She asked him what it was for, and he replied, "I know a girl there, and think she has been poisoned. I want to find out if she is dead or not." Witness said, "No, you had better go yourself, as I do not like to go under the circumstances." He did not say what the girl was. After she had declined to go he said he would enquire himself, adding, "I think I know who poisoned her." Witness asked him who he thought it was, and he replied, "Lord Russell." That was about the time the Russell matrimonial suit was on. He did not state where he

Thomas Neill Cream.

got his information from, and nothing more was said about it. In January he went to America, returning to England on 7th April, when he engaged the second floor back room. When he came back he told her he was agent for the Harvey Drug Company, and showed her the case of pills produced. He remained in her house until he was arrested. He always seemed to have money, but never saw any one on business. Witness did not hear anything about the death of Clover until recently. She had another gentleman stopping as a lodger in her house, named Harper. One day when Mr Harper was away Neill came into his room, where witness was, and spoke about him. He asked what kind of gentleman he was and where he lived. Witness answered all his questions. She remembered hearing about two girls, named Marsh and Shrivell, being murdered by strychnine poisoning, and Neill told her he wanted to see the inquest in a Sunday paper, remarking that it was a cold blooded murder. About three weeks after the newspaper incident Neill came in in a very excited state and spoke about the deaths of Marsh and Shrivell. He said, "Do you know who poisoned these two girls in Stamford Street?" Witness said "No" and he said, "If I tell you, you are not to tell any one, it was Mr Harper." Witness said "What a fearful accusation to make against any one. How do you know it was he?" He replied "The police have proofs of it," adding that he had a detective friend. Witness told him she thought Mr Harper would be the last man in the world to do such a thing. After that he said the girls had received a letter warning them that Mr Harper was poisoning them and not to take the stuff he would give them. He went on to say that the police had the letters. When the detectives were watching Neill the latter remarked to witness that it was a very good thing she did not go to the house in Lambeth Road, as they were going to exhume the body. He came in one morning and said the house was being watched. He did not say why, but witness said, "They are watching you." He replied "They have made a mistake, but as I am an American they are suspicious of me." He afterwards said they were watching the house for Mr Harper. When she asked him why he took such an interest in the inquest of Marsh and Shrivell he said he thought the scoundrel ought to be brought to justice. He never said he had seen the girls or what they were. She asked him whether he knew them and he said, "No." Once he went away for a week, and witness minded his cash box, some letters and a note book. The latter contained some figures which he said, related to his estates in Quebec. When he returned she gave him his things and he tore the note book up in her presence and threw it into the fireplace. That was while the police were watching the house. Witness saw the capsule box (produced) in his cupboard. He had said nothing to her about being afraid of being arrested or as to leaving the house. On 25th May he said he was ill, and unable to write, and he asked her to write out a statement which he dictated. While he was in bed he dictated the document, and she wrote it all, including the signature. She asked him whether he would sign it, and he said, "No," so she signed it for him.

He said he wanted this statement of his movements to give to Sergeant M'Intyre, who came while witness was in his room. She saw Neill give it to the sergeant. She never heard him mention the name of Donworth. When he stayed out all night he never told her where he had been.

LOUISA HARRIS, of Upper North Street, Brighton, stated that in

Appendix V.

October last she was living in Townshend Road, St. John's Wood, with a young man named Charles Harvey, whose name she took, going as Lou Harvey. Between the 20th and 25th October she was spoken to by a gentleman she now recognised as Neill outside the St. James's Restaurant. He told her that he was a doctor at St. Thomas's Hospital, and that he had come from America. When she first saw him he was wearing a black felt hat with a flat top, and he had a gold watch and a hair or silk chain. He was also wearing gold-rimmed spectacles. He remarked upon the fact that she had some spots upon her forehead and said she wanted some medicine. He promised to meet her the same evening on the Embankment, near Charing Cross. She had told him she was a servant. When he spoke about giving her medicine she was afraid and told Harvey all that had occurred. She took the latter with her to the Embankment and left him near Charing Cross Station. She met Neill, as arranged, and he told her that he could not take her to a music hall, as he had promised, having an engagement at St. Thomas's Hospital. He then said, "I have brought your pills. I have had them made up in the Westminster Bridge Road." He showed her the pills and she asked him whether she should take them then. He replied, "Not till you have had a glass of wine." They went to the Northumberland Arms and had some wine. Harvey meanwhile watching them, and while they were in the house a woman came in selling roses. Witness said she would like some. Neill replied, "Yes certainly, you shall have your wish," and bought her some. They then walked towards the Embankment where he gave her some figs in a bag to take after the pills. He also gave her two long pills similar to those produced. He said, "Don't bite them, swallow them as they are." Witness was afraid to take them. She received them in her right hand, passed them to her left hand and threw them away behind her. She then put her hand to her mouth pretended to swallow the pills, and made a noise with her throat. He then asked her to show him her hands which she did.

Mr. GILL remarked that the pills the witness selected from those produced were two grain capsules.

The witness continuing said that after she had, as he thought, taken the pills Neill gave her 5s. to pay her cab fare and entrance to a music hall. He then bade her "good bye for the present," and walked away. After he had gone, witness joined Harvey and told him what had occurred. Neill promised to meet her at eleven o'clock the same night outside the Oxford Music Hall but he did not put in an appearance. Some three weeks later she saw him in Piccadilly Circus and spoke to him. He did not recognise her. They went into a public house in A— Street, and he promised to meet her again the same night outside the St. James's Restaurant. Witness said "Don't you remember me?" and he said, "No." Witness then said "Not when you promised to meet me outside the Oxford Music Hall?" He said, "What is your name?" and upon witness replying "Lou Harvey," he turned round and walked sharply away. That was the last time she spoke to him, but she saw him about a month afterwards in Piccadilly Circus walking with a short, dark, young woman. He did not see her. Before she saw her name in the papers she had read a description of Neill. She subsequently read an account of the inquest and communicated with Sir John Bridge and the Coroner.

By the CORONER—When she saw him with the young woman Neill

Thomas Neill Cream.

was wearing a silk hat and a gold chain. She had noticed a peculiarity about his eyes, which were a little crossed.

The COUNTESS RUSSELL stated that in December last she was staying at the Savoy Hotel. While there she received a letter addressed to herself, which she showed to several persons, including Mr. George Lewis. In that letter her husband was accused of the murder of a woman named Clover. It was addressed from the Lambeth Road. She could not remember whether strychnine was mentioned, but it certainly said "by poison." Witness was positive the name mentioned was Clover, and fancied the Christian name was Matilda, but could not swear as to that.

By the CORONER—There was a suit pending about that time in which Mr. George Lewis was acting for her. She had endeavoured to find the letter, but without success. She did not remember what the writing was like. If she should come across the letter she would send it to the Coroner at once.

ANNIE CLEMENTS, a charwoman, of 18 Jowers Street, Westminster Bridge Road, said that she knew a young woman named Ellen Donworth who died on 13th October. She lived at 8 Duke Street, Westminster Bridge Road. Witness used frequently to see her living in the same house. She also knew a young man named Ernest Linnell. On the Saturday before her death Donworth received a letter by the first post which she said was from a gentleman. She also received a letter on the Tuesday morning by the same post, which, she said, was from the same gentleman whom she was to see outside the York Hotel, Waterloo Road. She was to take back the letter to the gentleman to prove that she had received it. She said she expected to hear from him every other day. The gentleman, she told witness, was bald headed and cross eyed. When Donworth went out she was quite well, but an hour and a half afterwards she was brought back very ill by a gentleman. Dr. Lowe's assistant saw her. She said the tall man had given her something to drink out of a bottle—some white stuff. She did not say where he said was given her, but said it was the same man who had written the letter.

CONSTANCE LINFIELD, of 43 Little Surrey Street, said that she knew the girl Nellie Donworth who died on 13th October. Witness saw her at about seven o'clock on the evening of that day. Donworth told witness he was going to meet a gentleman at the York Hotel, and she subsequently saw her talking with a tall man. A few minutes afterwards she saw her come out of a court with the man, who had rather a strange look. She could not identify the man.

JAMES STAITS, a costermonger, of 43 East Street, Lambeth, stated that on the evening of 13th October he was in Waterloo Road when he saw Donworth, who was leaning against a wall suddenly fall forward on her face. She was shivering and trembling, and told witness that some one had given her a drink. Witness with the assistance of a man named Adams took her home.

JOHN JOHNSTONE, assistant to Dr. Lowe, of the South London Medical Institute, who was called in to see Donworth said she was being held

Appendix V.

down in bed by several persons. In answer to witness's questions, she said that she had drunk some white stuff out of a bottle in the street. She was quite sensible, and complained of pain all over the body. Her words were that "a tall, dark cross-eyed fellow" had given her a bottle to drink from, and that she believed she was dying. Her symptoms were consistent with strychnine poisoning.

Mr GILL intimated that he now proposed going into the cases of Marsh and Shrivell, who died in Stamford Street.

CHARLOTTE VOGT, the landlady of 118 Stamford Street, stated that Alice Marsh and Emma Shrivell lodged at her house, occupying the front and back room on the second floor. On 11th April witness saw them both during the day. She retired to rest between eleven and twelve and was awakened about half past two by her husband. In consequence of what he said she went downstairs and found Marsh lying on her face in the passage. As she seemed very ill witness sent for the police and a cab. She afterwards heard Shrivell screaming, and upon going upstairs to her room she found her on the bed calling for "Alice". Marsh was only partially dressed.

Police Constable GEORGE COMLEY 211L said that on the night in question he was about ten yards from 118 Stamford Street when he saw a gentleman leave the house and walk away. There was a lamp opposite the door and witness saw his profile. He was wearing gold rimmed spectacles, and was between forty-five and fifty years of age. He was about 5 feet 10 inches in height, and was wearing a dark overcoat and a silk hat. Shortly afterwards witness was called into the house and saw Marsh in the passage in great agony. Having administered emetics to the two girls, he placed Marsh in a cab and conveyed her to the hospital, but she was dead when she arrived there. He had asked her what she had eaten and she replied, "I have had some supper, and a gentleman gave us three pills each." Witness said, "Was it the gentleman you let out at a quarter to two with glasses on" and she replied "Yes" adding that they called him "Fred". She described the pills as being long thin ones. On the night of 12th May witness again saw the gentleman in Westminster Bridge Road, but he was then wearing a short coat. He believed Neill was the man, as he had seen him several times. The man went in the direction of York Road.

Police Constable EVERSFIELD, 194L, stated that he found Shrivell in the second floor room also in great agony. He questioned her, and she said that she had been three weeks in London from Brighton. She explained that she and Marsh made the acquaintance of a man named Fred, who was very bald on the top of his head and wore spectacles and a silk hat. She said he gave her three long pills. Witness made a note of the description she gave to him.

Mr WALTER JOSEPH HARPER MRCS, LRCP, of The Terrace, Braunton, North Devon, said that until April last he was a student at St Thomas's Hospital. For two and a half years he had lodged at 103 Lambeth Palace Road. During the latter part of the time he knew there was such a person as Neill lodging in the house. He saw letters lying in

Thomas Neill Cream.

the hall addressed to him. There were other lodgers in the house, and he did not know which of the lodgers was Dr Neill. He never knew or heard of Alice Marsh, Emma Shrivell, Ellen Donworth, or Matilda Clover. The first he heard of the names was when they came out at the inquiry. He had never heard of the name of Lou Harvey. He had never spoken to any one about the poisoning of these girls. He never had anything to do with a Mr W H Murray.

By the CORONER—He was not aware that the girls Marsh and Clover lived at 118 Stamford Street or elsewhere, he had no knowledge of them whatever. He knew Neill by sight, and he was now able to identify him.

EDWARD LEVY, a licensed victualler, of 20 New Street, Houndsditch, stated that in the years 1880 and 1881 he was in business with his brother-in-law in Chicago——

Mr WATERS asked whether evidence of Neill's doings prior to his first coming to England, which was admittedly on October last——

The CORONER interrupted, and said he was not going back to that. He had spoken to Mr Gill on the subject.

Mr GILL said he was going to prove that Neill was practising as a medical man in the name of Thomas Neill Cream, and, of course, it was important to ascertain that in order to show whether he had certain knowledge.

The WITNESS went on to say that he recognised Neill as Dr Thomas Neill Cream who practised as a medical man in West Madison Street, Chicago. Cream attended witness's brother-in-law, and during the greater part of the time he was on very intimate terms with him. His attention was directed to this case by seeing a picture of Neill in a newspaper. Witness had been to Cream's surgery on many occasions.

At this point the Coroner announced that he had received the following letter, addressed to Mr Hicks, Vestry Hall Tooting:—"Dear Sir,—The man that you have in your power, Dr Neill, is as innocent as you are. Knowing him by sight, I disguised myself like him, and made the acquaintance of the girls that have been poisoned. I gave them the pills to cure them of all their earthly miseries, and they died. Miss L Harris has got more sense than I thought she had, but I shall have her yet. Mr P Harvey might also follow Lou Harvey out of this world of care and woe. Lady Russell is quite right about the letter, and so am I. Lord Russell had a hand in the poisoning of Clover. Nellie Donworth must have stayed out all night, or else she would not have been complaining of pains and cold when Annie Clements saw her. If I were you, I would release Dr T Neill, or you might get into trouble. His innocence will be declared sooner or later, and when he is free he might sue you for damages.—Yours respectfully, JUAN POTTEN, *alias* JACK THE RIPPER. Beware all. I warn but once."

Inspector JOHN TUNBRIDGE, of the Criminal Investigation Department, New Scotland Yard, said on 26th May he was instructed to take up the inquiry into the South London poisoning cases. On 29th May he asked or

Appendix V.

Neill what was the business in which he was engaged in this country. Neill replied that he represented the Harvey Drug Company, and showed witness the case or wallet produced. On looking through it witness noticed that one of the bottles contained pills with one sixteenth of a grain of strychnine, and he spoke to Neill as to the size of the pills, remarking, "They are very small, what are they composed of?" Neill replied "One-sixteenth grain of strychnine and sugar coating only." After Neill's arrest he went to 103 Lambeth Palace Road and stripped Neill's room of everything belonging to him. Amongst the articles he found were two overcoats, three silk hats, and a felt hat. Of the 56 bottles in the drug case 54 contained pills. In a chest of drawers in Neill's bedroom witness found an envelope (produced) bearing the following dates and initials :— "Oct. 13, M C, Oct. 19, Oct. 13, Ap 11, E S, Apr 11, Oct 23, L H, Oct 23."

By the CORONER—19th October would refer to the date on which Matilda Clover was poisoned, and 13th October was the date of Lieut. Donworth's death, while 23rd October was the night on which Lou Harvey received the capsules on the Embankment. 11th April would fully with the date of Emma Shrivell's death.

Mr. GILL said that was all the evidence he had been able to get as the result of the inquiries that had been made.

Mr. WATERS, in answer to the Coroner, said that he did not wish to call any witnesses.

The CORONER then asked Neill to take the oath. Neill refused and said that he was instructed not to testify. (See pages 27 and 114.)

The CORONER proceeded to sum up, remarking that the object of the inquiry was *primâ facie* to ascertain the cause of the death of Matilda Clover. He would ask the jury if they had any reasonable doubt that the letter written to Dr. Broadbent was penned by Neill. He could not guide their opinions, but he had no doubt in his mind that the handwriting was the same as that contained in the will and other documents. If that person were Neill, he was the man who knew that the deceased died from strychnine poisoning, that her name was Matilda Clover, and she lived at 27 Lambeth Road, and that she died in October. It was impossible to deal with the case of Clover without bringing in the others, but it must be borne in mind that Neill was the only person that assumed to have a knowledge of the death of Clover from strychnine poisoning, for he mentioned it, not only in his letter to Dr. Broadbent, but also to the witnesses M'Intyre, Haynes, and Sleaper. Could they, then, have any doubt, on the face of it, that Clover died from the effects of strychnine administered to her by Neill, who in that event ought to be charged with her murder?

The jury retired, and, after twenty minutes deliberation, returned into Court with a verdict, "That Matilda Clover died from the effects of strychnine poisoning and that the poison was administered by Thomas Neill with intent to destroy life."

The CORONER said that was a verdict of "Wilful murder" against Neill.

Thomas Neill Cream.

APPENDIX VI.

REG. v. NEILL CREAM

Cases of Alice Marsh, Emma Shrivell & Matilda Clover

(Copy of the late Sir Thomas Stevenson's notes in the above cases.)

1892

Cases of Alice Marsh & Emma Stivel (Shrivell) for Home Office in April

In Ap 14 recd at Sandhurst Lodge telegram from I. G. Hopkins. Wired Dr Wynan H P at St Thos Hospital & wrote to him (Cuthbert W., M B)

Sat Ap 16 recd Home Office order No X 3790/2 & 2 enclos
At 11.40 a.m recd in person from hands of Geo Hackett P M porter St Thos Hospital, 3 sealed jars & gave recpt. Wrote Home Office

1. A glass jar marked "Alice Marsh" & covered with white mackintosh sheeting tied & sealed in red wax with motto seal & labelled on sheeting "Alice Marsh" Stomach Kidney, Liver "Sealed by C Wynan M B St Thomas's Hospital"

2. A similar jar labelled "Emma Stivel" covered with pink calico, tied & sealed like No 1 & marked on calico "Sealed by C Wynan M B, St Thomas's Hosp. Vomit of Emma Stivel"

3. A similar jar labelled "Emma Stivel," covered & sealed just like No 1 & marked on sheeting "Sealed by C Wynan M B St Thomas's Hosp. Stomach, Kidneys Liver of Emma Stivel"

Placed in cupboard & opened at 10.30 a m Ap 19th (Tuesday)

Shrivell's viscera hyperæmic but nothing else abnormal. Hypostasis & decomposition but not putrid. Stomach tied at each end. Contents black as if from charcoal & semi fluid.

Alice Marsh

The contents of the glass jar (1) :—

1 Kidney	4 ounces
Liver	5¾ ,,
Bloody fluid	7 ,,
Stomach	10½ ,,
Stomach contents	19¼ ,,

Appendix VI.

The contents were very acid & had gastric odour. Stomach normal & all other viscera, but some hypostasis & decomposition, though not actually putrid. The stomach contents, almost as consistant as thin jelly, & scarcely fluid. They contained much mucus, some dried currants, potatoes, flesh of fish, starch.

Took 15 c.c. of fluid acidified with acetic acid, extracted with ether, alkalised with potassium hydroxide & extracted with chloroform ether. The ether evaporated was bitter & gave with sulphuric acid – manganese dioxide doubtful purple, but later distinct Strychnine red colour.

Stomach Contents. Took 6 ounces, & digested with methylated spirit.

20th Poured off, squeezed through muslin, raised to the boil, cooled, filtered & evaporated. Digested residue with fresh methylated spirit.
21st Poured off, squeezed through muslin, added spirit in which stomach had been digesting, raised to the boil, cooled, filtered & evaporated. Digested residue with fresh methylated spirit.
22nd Poured off, squeezed through muslin, raised to the boil after adding spirit in which stomach had been digesting, cooled, filtered & evaporated.
23rd Rubbed up with absolute alcohol & digested.
25th Filtered, washed & evaporated.
26th Took up residue with water & filtered into stoppered cylinder.

Extracted with ether in acid condition, then made alkaline with sodium carbonate, & extracted with chloroform ether, once. Refer below.

1st extract evaporated to dryness —

    Dish — residue 23.8430 grams
    Dish 23.8050 ,,

    Residue 0.0380 = 0.59 grain

The residue was a little coloured, crystalline, almost pure, intensely bitter. Dissolved gave copious precipitate with Mayer's solution. It gave fine Strychnine colours with sulphuric acid – potassium dichromate & with sulphuric acid – manganese dioxide. No colour with nitric acid.

The remaining extractions were first shaken with acid water, then made alkaline with sodium carbonate, shaken with chloroform ether & evaporated.

    Dish — residue 18.2415 grams

    Residue 0.0910 = 1.40 grain

(38 milligrams × 1¼ = 122 milligrams for whole stomach contents or 38 mgms = 0.59 grain or 1.88 grain for whole stomach contents. Add to this 91 mgms gives 129 mgms = 1.99 grain or 6.39 grains for the whole stomach contents.)

The alkaloidal residues of the stomach contents of Marsh gave no Morphine reactions with sulpho molybdic acid, or with iodic acid & chloroform.

Thomas Neill Cream.

The stomach contents did not liberate Iodine from iodic acid in the presence of chloroform

Extracted some stomach contents with amyl alcohol + ammonia washed out amyl alcohol with dilute acetic acid. The acetic acid solution did not react for morphine with iodic acid + chloroform, and evaporated gave no Morphine reaction with sulpho molybdic acid, the amyl alcohol after washing with acetic acid was evaporated, taken up with dilute sulphuric acid, the solution gave no Morphine reaction with iodic acid + chloroform

---

Kidney & Liver. Took 2 ounces of Kidney & 3 ounces of Liver, & digested with methylated spirit made acid with tartaric acid

20th Poured off, squeezed through muslin raised to the boil cooled, filtered & evaporated
21st Poured off squeezed through muslin, raised to the boil cooled filtered & evaporated
22nd Poured off, squeezed through muslin, raised to the boil, cooled filtered & evaporated
23rd Rubbed up residue with absolute alcohol & digested
25th Filtered, washed & evaporated
26th Took up residue with water & filtered into stoppered cylinder
27th Extracted with ether in acid condition, then made alkaline with sodium carbonate & extracted with chloroform-ether, evaporated chloroform-ether in tared dish —

$$\begin{array}{rl} \text{Dish + residue,} & 27.6840 \text{ grams} \\ \text{Dish} & 27.6720 \text{ ,,} \\ \hline \text{Residue} & 0.0120 \quad = 0.185 \text{ grain} \end{array}$$

Crystalline very bitter almost colourless

Gave copious precipitate when dissolved in dilute sulphuric acid with Mayer's solution. Gave fine Strychnine colours with sulphuric acid + potassium di-chromate and with sulphuric acid + manganese di-oxide. No colour with nitric acid

Injected into a frog, its solution killed the animal with strong tetanic convulsions

---

Re *Emma Shrivel*

The contents of the glass jar (5) —

Stomach,	8¾ ounces
Stomach contents	4 ,,
1 Kidney,	4½ ,,
Liver	2 ,,
Bloody fluid	½ ,,

Jar (2) Syphoned from this jar 21 ounces of clear fluid. The remaining
(Vomit) clear fluid measured 3½ ounces, & the semi solid mass 10 ounces,

Appendix VI.

the whole measuring 34½ ounces. Some filtered gave white precipitate with ammonium sulphide and with barium chloride + hydrochloric acid

(2) Vomit Syphoned off 21 ounces clear liquid and evaporated over water bath
20th Ground up residue with absolute alcohol, & digested, poured off & evaporated
21st Gave a third digestion with absolute alcohol filtered and evaporated
   Took up residue with water & filtered into a 50 c.c. cylinder
22nd Extracted with ether in the acid condition, made alkaline with sodium carbonate, & extracted with chloroform ether. Evaporated chloroformic ether in tared dish —

$$\text{Dish + residue, } 24.0313 \text{ grams}$$
$$\text{Dish, } 23.9735$$
$$\text{Residue, } 0.0578 \text{ ,,}$$

(= 0.0949 grain on the 34½ ounces, or 1.46 gram)

The residue intensely bitter crystalline nearly colourless, dissolved, gave intense precipitate with Mayer's solution and beautiful Strychnine colour reactions with sulphuric acid and manganese dioxide, and with sulphuric acid + potassium dichromate.

A little conveyed into rectum & injected beneath skin of back of frog on April 23rd set up most intense opisthotonos and rigidity, which persisted in limbs after decapitation

The residue did not colour with nitric acid gave no Morphine reaction with sulpho-molybdic acid and no Morphine reaction with iodic acid + chloroform

The Vomit gave no Morphine reaction with iodic acid + chloroform. Extracted vomit with amyl alcohol + acetic acid. Evaporated amyl alcohol gave no Morphine reaction with iodic acid + chloroform.

Acetic acid solution gave no Morphine reaction with iodic acid + chloroform and evaporated gave no Morphine reaction with sulpho-molybdic acid

---

Stomach Content

In (3) Took 2 ounces of Stomach, chopped together with scrapings of stomach and digested with methylated spirit
20th Poured off, squeezed through muslin, raised to boiling, cooled, filtered and evaporated
   Digested residue with fresh methylated spirit
21st Poured off, squeezed through muslin, added spirit in which stomach had digested, boiled, cooled, filtered and evaporated. Digested residue with fresh methylated spirit
22nd Poured off squeezed through muslin, added spirit in which stomach had digested, boiled, cooled, filtered and evaporated
23rd Ground up residue with absolute alcohol and digested

Thomas Neill Cream.

25th Filtered washed and evaporated

26th Took up with water & filtered into stoppered cylinder Extracted with ether in acid condition, then made alkaline with sodium carbonate, and extracted with chloroform ether Evaporated chloroform ether in tared dish —

$$\begin{aligned}\text{Dish + residue,} &\quad 21.2262 \text{ grams} \\ \text{Dish,} &\quad 21.1742 \quad\text{,} \\ \hline \text{Residue,} &\quad 0.0520 \quad\text{, } = 0.80 \text{ grain}\end{aligned}$$

($= 0.104$ gram for whole stomach contents, or 1.60 grain.)

The residue was partly white and crystalline partly brown but mostly pure. Intensely bitter. Dissolved gave abundant precipitate with Mayer's solution. Gave good Strychnine reactions with sulphuric acid + manganese dioxide & with sulphuric acid + potassium dichromate. No red colour with nitric acid.

Kidney & Liver

Jan (3) Took 2½ ounces of Kidney and the whole of the Liver submitted (2 ounces), shredded up and digested with methylated spirit, made acid with tartaric acid

20th Poured off squeezed through muslin raised to the boil cooled, filtered and evaporated
Digested residue with fresh methylated spirit

21st Poured off, squeezed through muslin boiled cooled filtered, evaporated and digested residue with fresh methylated spirit

22nd Poured off, squeezed through muslin raised to boil cooled filtered and evaporated

25th Rubbed up with absolute alcohol and digested, filtered washed and evaporated

26th Took up residue with water and filtered into stoppered cylinder Extracted with ether in acid condition then made alkaline with sodium carbonate and extracted with chloroform ether. Evaporated chloroform ether in tared dish —

$$\begin{aligned}\text{Dish + residue} &\quad 24.1716 \text{ grams} \\ \text{Dish} &\quad 24.1624 \\ \hline \text{Residue} &\quad 0.0092 \quad\text{,}\end{aligned}$$

(This amount, 0.0092 gram = approximately 0.013 gram in the whole of the Kidney & liver submitted for analysis = 0.20 grain.)

This residue was brown. Dissolved in dilute sulphuric acid very bitter, gave copious precipitate with Mayer's solution and fine reaction on evaporation of a drop and then sulphuric acid + manganese dioxide.

A little injected into frog produced intense Strychnine convulsions (tetanus & opisthotonos)

Appendix VI.

Re *Matilda Clover*

Aet 27 Died Oct 21 1891 Buried in Lambeth Cemetery Oct 27, 1891 grave 22154 as a pauper A prostitute

Home Office order for exhumation April 30th 1892, No A53887
Treasury order for analysis 3/5/92

Visited grave in Lambeth Cemetery with Dann & Harvey 11 35 am and saw grave in presence of PC George Steers John Measure undertaker, 75 Waterloo Road identified coffin and stamp on plate which he made was present at interment

It was an elm and deal coffin with plate "M Clover 27 yrs" John Measure identified body from dress when coffin opened

William Robert Taylor 10 London Road Southwark identified body by projecting front teeth

---

Length of body 5ft 1in right forefinger nail ridged, deformed and different from left darkish brown hair on head, thick abundant and long mouth large, and upper teeth good but irregular An adult female by external genitals

Abdominal wall fairly thick with fat, muscles fairly fresh, intestines well preserved, mamme collapsed, features swollen and skin rough but pock marks could not be made out

Removed womb and appendages, calcareous deposits in front of womb, Fallopian tubes on both sides adherent to womb no corpus luteum womb empty, no visible ovum, extreme length $3\frac{1}{2}$ inches (womb), large open elongated os uteri Bloody thin fluid in both pleural cavities, much more in right than left, got $7\frac{1}{2}$ fl ounces out of it into a bottle Fat omentum

Ligatured stomach at each end, and removed it into bottle Spleen pulpy Stomach dryish and normal to eye Ligatured duodenum at each end and placed in same bottle as stomach

Removed Liver which was dry, smooth and palish, cut up and placed all in a bottle Usual size

Kidneys normal and stripped well, placed both in bottle Adhesion at base of left lung Removed 1 fl ounce of fluid from chest cavity and added to previous $7\frac{1}{2}$ fl ounces

Nothing unusual in lungs

Bladder empty Heart flaccid and empty, placed it in a bottle Right ear pierced, left softened and nothing made out as to its being pierced

Right incisor carious

Removed all Brain, which in membranes was in fairly good state and put in a bottle

Post mortem examination began 11 45 am and finished at 1 25 p m May 6th, 1892

(Initialled) T S
L A D

Thomas Neill Cream.

Weights of the Viscera:—

Stomach	4¼ ounces
Duodenum	2
Heart	6¾
Brain,	33
Liver,	50¼
Kidney (1)	3½
Kidney (2)	3
Spleen,	2½
Bloody fluid	6½
	111¼ ounces

The Brain & fluid were alkaline to litmus, the Liver & Stomach were slightly acid

The fluid on May 10th still showed characters of fresh blood solution and gave its Oxyhæmoglobin bands easily reduced to Hæmoglobin band, and no bands in red of spectrum

Stomach & Duodenum

7th May Peinsched 3 ounces of the Stomach result negative after 2 hours Digested remainder of Stomach & Duodenum with methylated spirit & tartaric acid

9th May Poured off squeezed added to the bulk cooled and filtered Evaporated 3/4ths of the filtrate Reserved 1/4th for assay Added more spirit to residue for second digestion

10th May Poured off squeezed and treated as before Added more spirit to residue

11th May Poured off treating as before Digested a fourth time

12th May Poured off as before Evaporated all filtrates together reserving however 1/4th of each

13th May Ground up residue with absolute alcohol, & digested several times Evaporated extracts Took up with little water and transferred to stoppered cylinder Extracted with ether in acid condition made alkaline with sodium carbonate and extracted three times with washed chloroform ether Evaporated ethers in dish —

Dish + residue, 44 120 grams
Dish 44 061 ,,
Residue, 0 059

Residue much coloured Re-assayed —

Dish + residue 22 592 grams
Dish 22 579
Residue 0 013 , = 0 2 gram

The residue in the cylinder was acidified, re-precipitated with sodium carbonate, and extracted with amyl alcohol The extractions were passed

Appendix VI.

through successive quantities of acid water, and the acid waters were afterwards mixed and evaporated

The 0.013 gram of alkaloidal residue above gave with sulphuric acid + manganese dioxide no clear Strychnine reaction

---

Brain

6th May Took 2 ounces, and digested with methylated spirit and a little tartaric acid
7th May Poured off & squeezed through muslin, raised to the boil, cooled & filtered. Evaporated filtrate in oven. Added more spirit to residue in jar for second digestion
9th May Poured off second digestion & squeezed through muslin. Raised to the boil, cooled & filtered. Evaporated filtrate. Added more spirit to residue
10th May Poured off & treated as before. Evaporated all filtrates together
11th May Ground up residue with absolute alcohol & digested
12th May Poured off absolute alcohol extract & filtered. Digested four times altogether with absolute alcohol. Evaporated filtrates
14th May Took up residue with ice & filtered into stoppered cylinder. Extracted with ether three times in acid condition, made alkaline with sodium carbonate and extracted three times with chloroform-ether

Evaporated ethers in tared dish —

   Dish   residue   21.3450 grams
           Dish   21.3325

           Residue   0.0125   , = 0.19 grain

Acidified residue in cylinder, made alkaline again with sodium carbonate & extracted twice with amyl alcohol. Evaporated alcohol. The residue obtained was not weighed, as it was brown and viscous. Dissolved & filtered from oily matter, and tested with iodic acid — starch & also with iodic acid — chloroform—no blue of free iodine, and the chloroform, though coloured brown, was not red, and its colour not discharged by ammonia

The 0.0125 gram residue above, tested for Strychnine with sulphuric acid – manganese dioxide gave obscure red reaction of Strychnine

---

Liver

6th May Took 16 ounces shredded up & digested over night with methylated spirit & a little tartaric acid
7th May Poured off & squeezed through muslin. Raised liquid to the boil, cooled & filtered. Evaporated the filtrate in oven
9th May Poured off second digestion & squeezed through muslin. Raised to the boil, cooled & filtered. Added more methylated spirit to residue for third digestion. Evaporated filtrate

Thomas Neill Cream.

10th May Poured off & treated as before   Digested a fourth time
11th May Poured off & treated as before   Digested a fifth time
12th May Poured off & treated as before   Evaporated all filtrates together
Ground up residue with absolute alcohol & digested about 6 times
Evaporated extracts in two portions   Took up each with a little water & transferred to two cylinders   Extracted four times with ether in acid condition, made alkaline with sodium carbonate, & extracted with washed chloroform ether —

$$\begin{aligned}\text{Dish} + \text{residue,} &\quad 21.030 \text{ grams}\\ \text{Dish,} &\quad 20.950\\ \hline \text{Residue} &\quad 0.020\end{aligned}$$

(1st portion)

$$\begin{aligned}\text{Dish} + \text{residue,} &\quad 48.487 \text{ grams}\\ \text{Dish,} &\quad 48.405\\ \hline \text{Residue,} &\quad 0.082\end{aligned}$$

(2nd portion)
These residues which were highly coloured were mixed and restressed —

$$\begin{aligned}\text{Dish} + \text{residue,} &\quad 20.970 \text{ grams}\\ \text{Dish,} &\quad 20.950\\ \hline \text{Residue} &\quad 0.020 \quad = 0.31 \text{ grain}\end{aligned}$$

This 0.020 gram residue gave no purple with sulphuric acid + potassium dichromate but red with sulphuric acid + manganese dioxide   Repeated, and got with sulphuric acid + manganese dioxide a Strychnine purple to red reaction, but not very clear from colour   Very bitter taste

The aqueous residue in cylinder was acidified re precipitated with sodium carbonate, & extracted with amyl alcohol   The extractions were passed through successive quantities of acid water, & the acid waters were afterwards mixed and evaporated

This residue gave no coloration with nitric acid & no Strychnine colour with sulphuric acid + manganese dioxide

---

The residue from absolute alcohol was extracted several times with absolute alcohol, & the extracts evaporated   The residue was taken up with water extracted with ether in acid condition, made alkaline with sodium carbonate, & extracted with chloroform ether   The chloroform ether was evaporated in tared dish —

$$\begin{aligned}\text{Dish} + \text{residue,} &\quad 22.598 \text{ grams}\\ \text{Dish} &\quad 22.578\\ \hline \text{Residue,} &\quad 0.020 \quad = 0.31 \text{ grain}\end{aligned}$$

Appendix VI.

Took up with one drop of sulphuric acid & absolute alcohol evaporated to dryness   Taken up with water the solution had no marked bitterness

Liver (repeat) —

20th May Took a fresh 16 ounces shredded up, & digested with methylated spirit but without acid
21st May Poured off squeezed through muslin raised to the boil cooled & filtered   Added more spirit to residue
23rd May Poured off & treated as before
24th May Poured off & treated as before
25th May Poured off & treated as before, this being the 4th digestion without acid   The filtrates were evaporated together   Added more spirit to residue, & a little tartaric acid
26th May Poured off 1st acid digestion & treated as before
  Added more spirit to residue
27th May Poured off 2nd acid digestion   Added more spirit and tartaric acid
28th May Poured off 3rd acid digestion, & treated as before   Evaporated acid digestions together but separately from the non acidified extracts.

Ground up the residues with absolute alcohol & digested separately Each was digested six or seven times with absolute alcohol, and the last extractions were practically colourless   Evaporated extracts

Took up with water and transferred to two stoppered cylinders   Extracted with ether in acid condition made alkaline with sodium carbonate, and extracted with washed chloroform ether Evaporated ethers of acidified & non acidified portions together

The residue was highly coloured, & was not weighed
Re stassed —

```
Dish + residue   21 366 grams
Dish             21 332   „
                 ─────────
Residue          0 034    = 0 32 grain
```

This 34 milligrams taken up with sulphuric acid + alcohol, and evaporated to dryness   A little of this gave faint Strychnine reactions with sulphuric acid + manganese dioxide & with sulphuric acid + potassium ferrocyanide   It gave a very copious brown precipitate with iodine in potassium iodide, and was very bitter

About 1/2 was precipitated with iodine in potassium iodide, the precipitate washed & dissolved in sulphurous acid water and evaporated

Residue gave faint Strychnine reactions with sulphuric acid + manganese dioxide & with sulphuric acid + potassium dichromate, and was bitter

---

Bloody Fluid

6th May Took 5 fluid ounces, added an equal volume of methylated spirit & some tartaric acid, & digested
7th May Poured off & squeezed the half-solidified mass raised to the boil, cooled & filtered Evaporated filtrate in oven   Digested residue with more methylated spirit

Thomas Neill Cream.

9th May Poured off liquid raised to boil, cooled & filtered Added more
spirit to residue for third digestion
10th May Poured off & treated as before Evaporated all filtrates together
11th May Ground up residue with absolute alcohol & digested
12th May Filtered off & digested 3 times more Evaporated filtrates
13th May Took up residue with water & filtered into stoppered cylinder
Extracted three times with ether in acid condition, made alkaline
with sodium carbonate & extracted three times with chloroform
ether Evaporated ethers in dish —

    Dish + residue, 23 737 grams
      Dish 23 666 ,,
    Residue 0 071 .

Residue highly coloured Re stassed with chloroform ether —

    Dish + residue, 23 676 grams
      Dish 23 666 ,,
    Residue 0 010 , = 0 15 grain

Acidified residue in cylinder, made alkaline again with sodium carbonate,
& extracted twice with amyl alcohol
Residue was not weighed as it was brown & syrupy Dissolved in
water & filtered off from oily matter, & tested it with iodic acid + starch
and also with chloroform No blueing of starch, and the chloroform, though
brown, was not red and colour was not discharged by ammonia

The 0 010 gram residue (see above) gave with sulphuric acid + manganese dioxide no clear Strychnine reaction red brown

---

Took mixed alkaloidal residues 0 010 gram of Fluid 0 0125 gram of
Brain, 0 013 of Stomach, and 0 020 of Liver acidified took up with alcohol
& water, & filtered Still a little turbid Filtered extracted with ether
twice, then alkalised with sodium hydroxide, & extracted three times with
ether chloroform and washed alkalised ether twice with dilute sulphuric
acid Then alkalised acid liquid with sodium hydroxide extracted
with ether-chloroform several times filtered ether & evaporated Residue
nearly colourless —

    Dish + residue, 23 6695 grams
      Dish, 23 6655 ,
    Residue 0 0040 ,,

Dissolved residue in dilute hydrochloric acid & evaporated, took up
with water Solution very bitter, gave dense precipitate with Mayer's

Appendix VI.

solution. A little evaporated, gave purple with sulphuric acid + manganese dioxide, passing into mahogany colour, and also with sulphuric acid — potassium di-chromate purple (goodish) passing into mahogany.

Repetition with both experiments with less success. A little (1/4th or so) injected into a frog, in 30 minutes produced intense & prolonged tetanic rigours, & death on May 23rd, /92

Microscopical Examination

Marsh — In Stomach contents —

    Dried currants
    Salmon
    Bacon
    Apple
    Cheese
    Wheaten starch

Stroll — In Stomach contents —

    Charcoal
    Starch
    Muscular fibre

In Vomit —

    Dried currants
    Mustard
    Muscular fibre
    Wheaten starch

Summary

Marsh —   Strychnine

Stomach and contents,	6.39 grains
Liver and Kidney,	0.40 ,,
	6.79

Stroll —

Vomit,	1.46 grains
Stomach and contents	1.60 ,,
Liver and Kidney,	0.20 ,,
	3.26

Clover —

The amount of Strychnine extracted from the Stomach, 1/3rd of the Liver 1/4th of the Brain, and half the Chest fluid, was approximately 1/16th grain

Thomas Neill Cream.

REPORT (by MARSH AND SHRIVEL)

On the 16th April 1892 I received in person from George Hackett three jars, all duly secured and sealed with unbroken seals, and by the instructions of the Home Secretary I have carefully examined and analysed the contents of these vessels.

(1) Was a glass jar marked "Alice Marsh Stomach, Kidney, Liver Sealed by C Wyman M B St Thomas's Hospital"
(2) Was a similar jar marked " Sealed by C Wyman M B St Thomas's Hospital Vomit of Emma Shrivel"
(3) Was a similar jar, marked ' Sealed by C Wyman M B St Thomas's Hospital Stomach Kidneys, Liver of Emma Shrivel '

On April 23rd I received in person from Wm F— shield P C No 191, L Division an open & empty preserved salmon tin

---

The contents of No 1 jar were the following viz, in etc, of an adult.— One kidney 4 ounces, 5¾ ounces of Liver, a Stomach and appendages, 10½ ounces, its contents 19¼ ounces, and a little fluid

The stomach was the normal stomach of a person that had died during digestion of a meal, the contents were partly digested food, viz fish (salmon) bacon, cheese, apple, dried currants, and wheaten starch. The Kidney and Liver were normal

There was also Strychnine present 6 59 grains in the stomach and its contents and 0 4 grain in the piece of liver and kidney, or about 6¾ grains in the viscera in this jar

A fatal dose of strychnine for an adult is less than one grain. I found no pigment or any indication of the form in which the poison had been given or taken

The jar No 2 contained 34½ fluid ounces or about 1¾ pints of turbid liquid—fluid from a stomach. It contained fish (salmon) dried currants, and wheaten starch, also mustard and sulphate of zinc which are emetics. The contents of this jar also contained Strychnine 1 65 grain

The jar No 3 contained the following viscera of an adult.—a Stomach 8¾ ounces, its contents, 6 ounces, a Kidney 4½ ounces 2 ounces of Liver, and a little fluid

The Stomach was hyperemic or congested, but otherwise was normal, the Liver & Kidney were normal

The contents of the stomach consisted of fish (salmon) starchy matter and charcoal (which is an antidote to some poisons)

There was also Strychnine present—1 6 grain in the stomach and its contents and 0 2 grain in the portion of liver and the kidney—altogether 1 8 grain in the contents of this jar

The quantity of Strychnine in the viscera and stomach fluid or vomit of Shrivel was about 3¼ grains

Neither in the stomach contents nor in the vomit could I detect any pigment or indication of the form in which the Strychnine had been taken or administered

Appendix VI.

The salmon tin was open, and practically empty, and was scarcely corroded. The small pieces of preserved salmon adhering to the inside of the tin were fairly fresh, and were free from strychnine or other poison.

Report (re Matilda Clover)

On May 6th, 1892, acting on the instructions of the Solicitor to the Treasury, I examined (exhumed) the remains of a woman, Matilda Clover, at Lambeth Cemetery, Tooting. I was assisted by Louis Albert Dunn, M.B. Lond., L.R.C.S. Eng., Senior Demonstrator of Anatomy at Guy's Hospital. I reached the grave at 11.35 a.m., and inspected it in the presence of Elijah George Steers, Assistant Superintendent of the Cemetery, who was present at the interment on October 27th, 1891, and I saw the impress of an adult's coffin in the grave. The grave was a very dry one. I found the coffin deposited in a mortuary shed. It was of elm & deal & had been in dry earth. The coffin was identified by John Measure, undertaker, 75 Waterloo Rd., S.E., who conducted & had been present at the funeral & made the coffin plate which was inscribed "M. Clover, 27 years."

On opening the coffin Measure identified the body as that of the M. Clover he had buried by the grave clothes. The features were bloated and not clearly recognisable. The police informed me that the deceased could be identified by (a) being marked with smallpox, (b) having a deformity of one finger nail, (c) the presence in abundance of long, dark brown hair.

The decomposed state of the skin of the head does not permit me to state with certainty that the body was pitted with smallpox, though it was very rough suggestive of pitting. There was a marked deformity of the fore finger nail of the right hand. The hair was long, dark brown and abundant.

William Robert Taylor, uncle of the deceased, also identified the body by the upper front teeth which were prominent, sound & irregular.

The body was that of a well developed female, about 5ft. 1in. in height. It was dry and for the most part in an extremely good state of preservation. Age probably between 25 & 30 years.

I examined all the great cavities, those of the head, chest and abdomen, minutely. The brain was semi-fluid from decomposition and was free from tumour or hæmorrhage. The lungs, heart, stomach, bowels, liver, spleen, kidneys and other appendages were normal. The bladder was empty. No diseased appearances were met with, and nothing to account for death. The womb was unimpregnated and that of a woman who had borne a child or children. Both the uterine appendages known as the Fallopian tubes were adherent to the womb (a condition common in prostitutes). The stomach was empty of food. I removed the following viscera:—

The Stomach 4½ ounces, a portion of the bowels 2 ounces, the Liver 50¾ ounces, the Spleen 2½ ounces, each Kidney 6½ ounces, the Heart 6¾ ounces, the Brain 33 ounces, and 8½ fluid ounces of fluid from the chest cavity.

By chemical analysis I detected a poison, Strychnine, in the stomach, in the liver, in the fluid from the chest & in the brain. A frog was killed

Thomas Neill Cream.

by the poison thus obtained, after the usual symptoms of poisoning by Strychnine.

The amount of Strychnine obtained was small—too small to permit of its weight being accurately ascertained after purification. Approximately I extracted from the Stomach, one third of the Liver, one fourth of the Brain, and half of the Chest fluid 1/16th grain of Strychnine.

This quantity (a full medicinal dose) points to the administration of a vital dose of Strychnine.

(signed) THOS. STEVENSON

June 10th 1892.

(Copy of Report on examination of Pills, &c. in the case of Matilda Clover.)

On the 4th July, 1892 I received in person from John B. Tonbridge, Inspector of Police, a case of pills, a box containing several kinds of coated pills and other medicaments, and a single separate pill in paper. I have carefully examined and analysed all these pills and medicaments with the following results:—

The case contained 54 bottles of pills, all in bottles to which I assign numbers. Of these 7 kinds contained Strychnine, viz.—

No. 2   1/22nd grain strychnine in each pill (marked as containing 1/16th grain in each pill). Of these pills 9 would form a minimum fatal dose and 22 an ordinary fatal dose, for an adult.
No. 8   1/16th grain strychnine in each pill
No. 20   1/130th grain strychnine in each pill
No. 25   1/60th grain strychnine in each pill
No. 32   1/100th grain strychnine in each pill
No. 48   1/60th grain strychnine in each pill
No. 51   1/60th grain strychnine in each pill

Five of the kinds of pills contained Nux Vomica, which is a substance containing the alkaloids Strychnine and Brucine. The quantities of alkaloids in these pills were—

No. 6   1/27th grain in each pill
No. 10   1/13th grain in each pill
No. 16   1/67th grain in each pill
No. 19   1/13th grain in each pill
No. 35   1/20th grain in each pill

Of these alkaloids rather less than one half was Strychnine and rather more than one half was Brucine, which is a much less potent poison than strychnine. It thus appears that No. 2 pills were the only pills which when taken in anything short of immoderate quantities would be likely to kill from strychnine poisoning.

The other pills in the case were ordinary pills containing various poisons in non-poisonous doses—such as Conium, Henbane, Opium, Morphine, Aconite and Digitalis, whilst others contained no poison.

Appendix VI.

The box contained 14 bottles & packages mostly of coloured pills. One of these kinds of pills only an aperient pill No 59 contained Nux Vomica yielding 1/4th grain of alkaloids or so, or at least than 1/40th grain of strychnine per pill

---

The other pills were similar to those in the case, such as pills of Opium Content etc in non poisonous doses.

The box also contained a box of ordinary hypodermic injection tablets and also a preparation of Corrosive sublimate for external use.

The single pill in paper weighed 2 grains or either it its coming about 1 grain. Its exact composition could not be made out owing to lack of material but it was free from Strychnine and other mineral poisons.

(signed) Thos STEVENSON

May 11th 1892

To/

Sir A. K. Stephenson KCB

Thomas Neill Cream.

by the poison thus obtained, after the usual symptoms of poisoning by Strychnine.

The amount of Strychnine obtained was small—too small to permit of its weight being accurately ascertained after purification. Approximately I extracted from the Stomach, one-third of the Liver, one-fourth of the Brain, and half of the Chest fluid 1/16th grain of Strychnine.

This quantity (a full medicinal dose) points to the administration of a fatal dose of Strychnine.

(signed) THOS. STEVENSON.

June 10th 1892.

(Copy of Report on examination of Pills, &c. in the case of Matilda Clover.)

On the 4th July, 1892, I received in person from John B. Tonbridge, Inspector of Police, a case of pills, a box containing several kinds of coated pills and other medicaments, and a single separate pill in paper. I have carefully examined and analysed all these pills and medicaments with the following results:—

The case contained 54 bottles of pills, all in bottles to which I assign numbers. Of these 7 kinds contained Strychnine, viz.:—

No. 2 1/22nd grain strychnine in each pill (marked as containing 1/16th grain in each pill). Of these pills 9 would form a minimum fatal dose and 22 an ordinary fatal dose, for an adult.
No. 8 1/16th grain strychnine in each pill
No. 20 1/130th grain strychnine in each pill
No. 25 1/60th grain strychnine in each pill
No. 32 1/100th grain strychnine in each pill
No. 48 1/60th grain strychnine in each pill
No. 51 1/60th grain strychnine in each pill

Five of the kinds of pills contained Nux Vomica, which is a substance containing the alkaloids Strychnine and Brucine. The quantities of alkaloids in these pills were—

No. 6 1/27th grain in each pill
No. 10 1/13th grain in each pill
No. 16 1/67th grain in each pill
No. 19 1/13th grain in each pill
No. 35 1/20th grain in each pill

Of these alkaloids rather less than one-half was Strychnine and rather more than one-half was Brucine, which is a much less potent poison than strychnine. It thus appears that No. 2 pills were the only pills which when taken in anything short of immoderate quantities would be likely to kill from strychnine poisoning.

The other pills in the case were ordinary pills containing various poisons in non-poisonous doses—such as Conium, Henbane, Opium, Morphine, Aconite and Digitalis; whilst others contained no poison.

Appendix VI.

The box contained 14 bottles & packages mostly of coated pills. One of these kinds of pills only, an aperient pill No 59 contained Nux Vomica yielding 1/14th grain of alkaloids, or say that less than 1/50th grain of strychnine per pill.

The other pills were similar to those in the case, such as pills of Opium, Conium etc., in non poisonous doses.

The box also contained a box of ordinary hypodermic injection tablets, and also a preparation of Corrosive sublimate for external use.

The single pill in paper weighed 2 grains or rather it is covering about 1 grain. Its exact composition could not be made out owing to lack of material but it was free from strychnine and other mineral poisons.

(Signed) THOS STEVENSON

Feb 11th 1892

To

Sir A. K. Stephenson KCB

www.ingramcontent.com/pod-product-compliance
Lightning Source LLC
LaVergne TN
LVHW081940020825
817741LV00004B/472